FIGHTING THE ENEMY

Fighting the Enemy is about men with the job of killing each other. Based on the wartime writings of hundreds of Australian front-line soldiers during World War II, this powerful and resonant book contains many moving descriptions of high emotion and drama. Soldiers' interactions with their enemies are central to war, and their attitudes to their adversaries are crucial to the way wars are fought. Yet few books look in detail at how enemies interpret each other. This book is an unprecedented and thorough examination of the way Australian combat soldiers interacted with troops from the four powers engaged in World War II: Germany, Italy, Vichy France and Japan. Each opponent has themes peculiar to it: the Italians were much ridiculed; the Germans were the most respected of enemies; the Vichy French were regarded with ambivalence; while the Japanese were the subject of much hostility, intensified by the real threat of occupation.

Mark Johnston is Head of History at Scotch College, Melbourne, and has tutored at the University of Melbourne. He is the author of a number of articles in *Journal of the Australian War Memorial* and *Wartime*. His previous book, *At the Front Line: Experiences of Australian Soldiers in World War II*, was published by Cambridge University Press in 1996.

FIGHTING THE ENEMY

Australian Soldiers and their Adversaries in World War II

MARK JOHNSTON

CAMBRIDGE
UNIVERSITY PRESS

CAMBRIDGE UNIVERSITY PRESS
Cambridge, New York, Melbourne, Madrid, Cape Town, Singapore, São Paulo, Delhi

Cambridge University Press
The Edinburgh Building, Cambridge CB2 8RU, UK

Published in the United States of America by Cambridge University Press, New York

www.cambridge.org
Information on this title: www.cambridge.org/9780521119955

First published 2000
This digitally printed version 2009

A catalogue record for this publication is available from the British Library

National Library of Australia Cataloguing in Publication data
Johnston, Mark, 1960– .
Fighting the enemy: Australian soldiers and their
adversaries in World War II.
Bibliography.
Includes index.
ISBN 0 521 78222 8.
1. World War, 1939–1945 – Personal narratives, Australian.
2. World War, 1939–1945 – Australia. 3. Soldiers –
Australia – Attitudes. 4. Combat – Psychological aspects.
I. Title.
940.541294

ISBN 978-0-521-78222-7 hardback
ISBN 978-0-521-11995-5 paperback

Contents

Acknowledgments

The number of veterans able to provide first-hand advice on topics such as attitudes towards enemies is falling rapidly. I owe an enduring debt of thanks to the veterans who have shared with me numerous conversations and their precious wartime writings. The generosity of people who donate material to institutions such as the La Trobe Library and, of course, the Australian War Memorial is also crucial to an endeavour such as this one.

My thanks to the staff of the Australian War Memorial, with its superb research facilities. My thanks also to the staff of the Scotch College Library, especially Des Gibbs, Brigitte Habel and Jan Tarver. Particularly useful extra information for this book was also provided by Alwyn Shilton, Douglas Lade, Pat Share, Joyce Boas, Joan Abraham, Joy Merritt, David Pearson and Peter Stanley. I gratefully acknowledge the assistance of the Australian Army, which through a Military History Research Grant allowed me to travel to London and discover valuable material in the Imperial War Museum.

Once again I am happy to acknowledge the assistance of Cambridge University Press staff in bringing this book to fruition. Sharon Mullins and Phillipa McGuinness were of great importance in the decision to publish. Paul Watt, Peter Debus and Adrienne de Kretser were the key figures in turning my manuscript into a book.

I was fortunate to have as readers of my manuscript two of Australia's leading military historians, Associate Professor Jeffrey Grey and Professor David Horner. I thank them for their constructive criticisms, for which the book is better than it would otherwise have been. Naturally, responsibility for any remaining deficiencies in the text is my own.

As in all things, my greatest supporter in this project was my wife, Deborah. To her go my deepest thanks.

Conventions and Abbreviations

The most detailed information about sources appears in the Bibliography.

The first time that each soldier-writer is referred to in a chapter, the reference is presented as follows in the Notes: the rank of the soldier at the time he wrote the relevant comment; his initial and surname; his unit at the time of writing; the written document (usually a letter or diary); and the date of writing. As the following typical note shows, most of this information is presented in abbreviated form:

Tpr B. Love, 2/7 Cav Regt, D23/12/42.

As explained in the key below, this example shows that the reference is to the diary entry written by Trooper B. Love of the 2/7th Cavalry Regiment on 23 December 1942.

More detailed information about B. Love and his writings can be found in the Bibliography, but subsequent references to him in the Notes will be less detailed. Unless the next reference to him concerns a comment made when his rank and/or unit was different from in the first reference, only his surname and/or details of the diary entry will appear, thus:

Love, D19/1/43.

If his rank and/or unit had changed that information would be included, in the order shown above, thus:

Sgt Love, 2/12 Bn, D20/12/43.

Any second or subsequent reference to a soldier will not include information about rank or unit unless at the time he wrote the pertinent comment these biographical details were different from in the preceding reference (not necessarily the first).

If I am in doubt about any of the biographical or bibliographical details – often the case with dates – a question mark appears next to the uncertain information.

Even with these abbreviations the Notes are lengthy, and so the subtitles of published works, which in unit histories tend to be very long, are generally cited only in the Bibliography.

Key to Abbreviations

Repositories

AAV	Australian Archives Victoria
AWM	Australian War Memorial
IWM	Imperial War Museum
ML	Mitchell Library
MS	La Trobe Library
PRG	Mortlock Library

Ranks

A/-	Acting/ (usually A/Cpl or A/Sgt)
Bdr	Bombardier
Brig	Brigadier
Capt	Captain
Cpl	Corporal
Dvr	Driver
Gnr	Gunner
L/-	Lance/ (usually L/Cpl or L/Sgt)
Lt	Lieutenant
Lt-Col	Lieutenant-Colonel
Maj	Major
Maj-Gen	Major-General
Pte	Private
S/-	Staff (usually S/Sgt)

Sgt	Sergeant
Sigmn	Signalman
Spr	Sapper
Tpr	Trooper
WOII	Warrant Officer, Class II

Unit Titles

AAMC	Australian Army Medical Corps
AASC	Australian Army Service Corps
AGH	Australian General Hospital
Amb	Ambulance
Amn	Ammunition
ATIS	Allied Translator and Interpreter Section
A-Tk	Anti-tank
Bde	Brigade
Bn	Battalion
Cav	Cavalry
Cdo	Commando
Con	Convalescent
Coy	Company
Div	Division
Fd	Field
Fd Coy	Field Company
Fd Regt	Field Regiment
Indep Coy	Independent Company
MG	Machine Gun
OCTU	Officer Cadet Training Unit
Pnr	Pioneer
Pro	Provost
Regt	Regiment
Reinft or Rft	Reinforcement
Rlwy Constr	Railway Construction
Sigs	Signals

Note: The type of unit most often referred to in the Notes is the battalion. Where 'Bn' is immediately preceded by a number, it always refers to an infantry battalion. Where that number has the prefix '2/', for example 2/24 Bn, it refers to an original 2nd AIF battalion; where it has a prefix higher than 2, or no prefix at all, it refers to an original CMF (Militia) battalion, for example 29/46 Bn, 24 Bn. The same system applies to most units other than battalions, although the brigades with numbers from 16 to 27 (without prefixes) and divisions numbered 6 to 9 (without prefixes) were original 2nd AIF formations.

Sources

D	Diary
DR	Diary with additional postwar comments or reconstruction
L	Letter
MS	Manuscript

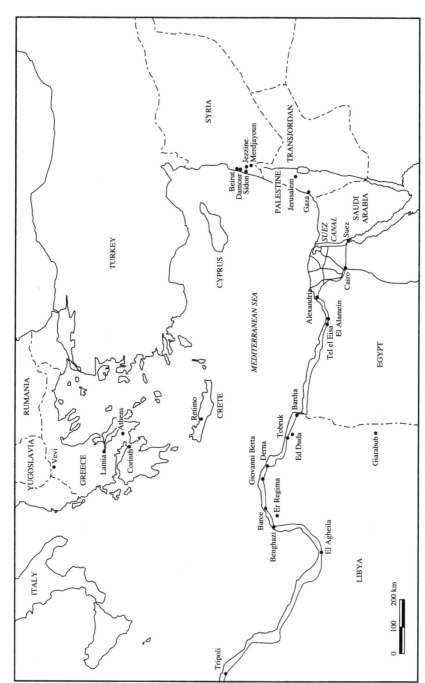

The Area of Australia's Campaigns in the Eastern Mediterranean

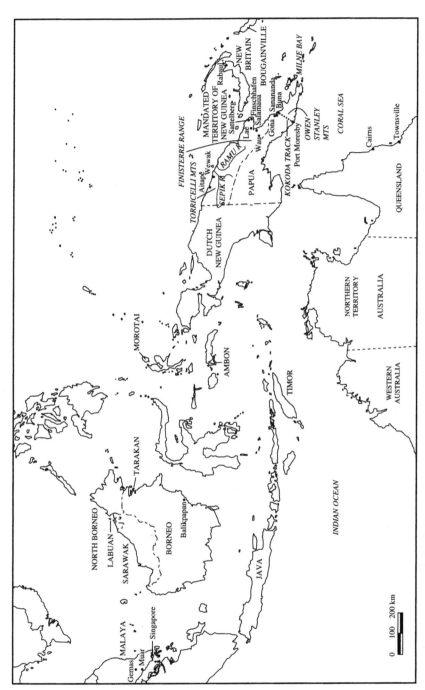

The Area of Australia's Campaigns Against Japan

INTRODUCTION

This book is about men with the job of killing each other. More particularly, it concerns the way Australian soldiers, as they engaged in the organised killing that is war, felt about the men they were ordered to kill. Their opponents served in the armies of four nations: Italy, Germany, Vichy France and Japan.[1] Each group aroused different emotions in the Australians who fought them. Some of these feelings, such as a sense of superiority over Japanese and Italians, owed much to prewar expectations that the soldiers took into the army. Other emotions derived from wartime events; for example, many civilians who joined after mid 1942 expected the Japanese to be virtually invincible jungle fighters. Other attitudes towards the enemy developed as soldiers campaigned: distrust or respect for an enemy arose according to Australians' experience of the Italians, Germans, French and Japanese as treacherous or decent, tough or weak, cunning or naive. Pre-battle expectations and battle experiences often interacted in a fascinating way. Thus, contempt for Japanese soldiers' military ability might give way to a belief that they were superhuman; ridicule of Italians might give way to compassion. In short, Australians had very diverse attitudes to their enemies, which owed much to their own preconceptions, much to their experiences on the battlefield, and something to the different ways their enemies behaved.

Readers may object that in modern warfare, front-line soldiers have precious little to do with their enemies. On the rare occasion that they saw the enemy, this argument might run, well-trained soldiers

1

would have thought of 'the enemy' simply as the objects of their military actions – nameless, faceless ciphers to kill or capture. There is some validity in this argument, as this book will show, for if soldiers are to operate effectively their training must dehumanise the enemy. This makes it possible to kill them. Yet when men actually kill, or when they see in prisoners the men they have been trying to kill, the enemy often ceases to be faceless; more complex observations enter soldiers' heads. Fortunately for our purposes, many Australians put those observations on paper, soon after the actual experience, or post-war. Where possible, this book is based on these observations, especially on wartime diaries and letters.

The idea that Australian troops, like all front-line soldiers, rarely saw their enemy, has an element of truth too. S.L.A. Marshall, the famous and controversial American military analyst of World War II, talked of the 'empty' battlefield.[2] Indeed, Australian soldiers in the Kokoda campaign often complained of being unable to see the enemy, not because the field was empty but because it was thickly vegetated.[3] In the desert, on the other hand, the uninhabited no man's land between Australians and enemy soldiers was often kilometres wide.

Many Australian front-line soldiers never spoke to an enemy, nor perhaps even saw one. In particular, troops in artillery, mortar and machine-gun units fought their opponents at a distance, and in an indirect way. Yet the status of men as 'front-line' troops depended on the enemy's presence within striking distance; the purpose of front-line soldiers was to confront their adversary. Moreover, the enemy's presence was very apparent to Australian soldiers. From Tobruk's Salient to the Owen Stanleys, the lines were often very close, but even where they were not, Australians knew something of their foe. The enemy was usually first encountered through aircraft: an unchivalrous, distant opponent, and a source of intense discomfort in the early campaigns. He was encountered in the vicarious form of other devices intended to kill or wound: mines, artillery shells, machine-gun bullets, sniper fire and booby-traps. Australians felt the enemy's presence in the wounds or deaths of their compatriots. They read it in his propaganda leaflets and broadcasts. They heard it in the noise of enemy weapons or voices. They saw it in the bodies they found as their forces advanced or went on patrol. Australians were well-known for their willingness to seek out the enemy on patrols, and a very large proportion of front-line troops observed or met the enemy by this means. Even in the jungle, where it was often hard to see friends, let alone foes, the enemy made a point of being noisy to frighten Australians; he was often so close that whispering or silence were necessary. Every Australian who served in the front line could have spoken about the enemy from experience.

Warfare as practised by Australia's front-line soldiers in 1939–45 was still the most direct confrontation any Australians had with the enemy. The riflemen who formed the bulk of Australia's front-line troops often confronted their adversaries face-to-face.

Front-line soldiers thus thought about their enemy differently from their friends and relatives at home. For the latter, 'the enemy' remained an abstraction, linked to 'Nazism' or 'the threat to Australia'. To combat soldiers, on the other hand, 'the enemy' became all too real, and in the life-and-death struggle with this opponent, abstractions usually became irrelevant. Even less could Australian troops afford the luxury, available to those safely distant in Australia, of smugly accepting propaganda that ridiculed the martial prowess of the enemy. Such complacency could kill. Even so, most had some ideas about the broader political issues, as well as preconceptions of their enemies that often remained fixed throughout campaigns. They shared a certainty that the enemy would be beaten.

Australians entered every campaign with some expectations of their enemy. Whether or not these impressions were confirmed depended on which enemy unit the Australians faced, and where and when the action took place. Thus, men of the 6th Division experienced only defeat against the Germans, whereas those of the 9th generally experienced victory. Men of the 8th Division suffered defeat at Japanese hands, while men in the other divisions experienced victory. Naturally, men in these formations developed different views of the Germans and Japanese.[4]

Inevitably, diverse experiences gave rise to diverse assessments of the effectiveness of the Japanese or Germans as soldiers. In human terms also, the armies faced by the Australians were extremely varied, so that for nearly every trait picked out by Australians as typical of their opponent, someone experienced the opposite. For example, there are many stories of treacherous actions from enemy prisoners, but there are also stories of docility.

Nevertheless, the Australians found distinctive traits in each of their enemies. These distinctions applied to the Australians' assessment of Italians, Germans, Vichy French and Japanese as soldiers and as human beings.

A recurring theme in Australians' assessment of their opponents as soldiers is that of quality. Australians used terms like 'good soldier' and 'soldier and a half' when referring to each other, and were concerned to see whether the same yardstick applied to their enemies.[5] They believed that they were better than any opponent, although this belief was difficult to defend in the light of the defeats suffered in 1941 and 1942. Australians considered themselves superior to their enemies, and assigned a hierarchy to the opponents they experienced.

When evaluating adversaries as soldiers and as human beings the great diversity within the Australian army was a major factor. For example, some felt hatred for all opponents, while others felt sympathy for any suffering person. However, it is possible to generalise the main trends of thought about the personal qualities of the enemy.

Related to these issues of measurement and empathy are the ways Australians treated their opponents. Reactions varied enormously, as one would expect in a huge group of men who were often under great strain and afraid of death. There was altruism, shown in the numerous cases where German wounded were tended by Australians. But there was also incomprehensible barbarism – some soldiers in the Middle East and the Pacific desecrated enemy corpses.

Another recurring theme is how it felt to kill the enemy. The need to kill was of course common to all Australians' dealings with the enemy, and to do this job properly Australians could not entirely dismiss the abstract view of 'the enemy' they held before they reached the front. Soldiers who thought too much of the enemy as individuals and fellow men might not be able to kill them.[6] In a recent work, American army officer Dave Grossman has argued that throughout history, whenever soldiers have been required to shoot at their fellow men in enemy uniform their civilian conditioning has prevented a sizeable proportion from doing so.[7] As evidence, he cites S.L.A. Marshall's famous but controversial contention that in any action not more than 25 per cent of the members of any infantry unit will fire their weapons unless compelled to do so by circumstance or constant urging.[8] Repeat this argument to Australians who fought in World War II and the usual response is laughter, incredulity and derision. Veterans do not accept that in action a large proportion of men do not fire; they consider

it ludicrous, and even an affront to suggest that they might not have
fired because of a psychological inability to shoot at, or kill, 'the
enemy'.[9]

Perhaps Joanna Bourke is closer to the truth than is Grossman, in
emphasising the pleasure that killing aroused in many Western soldiers
in twentieth-century wars. She included, in that category, Australian
soldiers in World War II. It is undeniable that there were Australians
who expressed pride, and even joy, on killing enemies during the war,
but even as Bourke conceded that some of the men she discussed did
not enjoy killing, neither did all Australians discussed in this book
enjoy it. Her implication – that most found killing pleasurable – is not
borne out by a wider reading of Australian World War II sources.
Attitudes towards inflicting death varied greatly between Australians,
and depended heavily on the identity of the enemy and the circumstances in which they were met.[10]

Much of *Fighting the Enemy* is about the practice of killing and
the feelings surrounding it. An apposite comment appears in the diary
of a militiaman on Bougainville. In April 1945, he noted that many
Japanese were being killed by his battalion, but said that 'even at 20–1
the price is too high'.[11] In other words, a human life on the enemy side
was not to be equated with an Australian life, or even twenty Australian
lives. There was, inevitably, a limit to the compassion soldiers could
exercise in an environment where the motto 'kill or be killed' was not
a cliché but a law. For armies to operate effectively, the lives of
individual components have to be regarded as expendable; in such an
environment, the lives of the enemy are of even less worth. Indeed this
is essential, for if men thought of enemy soldiers as identical to them in
rights and humanity, it would be hard or even impossible for soldiers to
operate – that is, to kill.[12] Adding to the factors which limited empathy
is the fact that killing in World War II was often done from a great
distance, by artillerymen, mortarmen and machine-gunners, or 'on the
blind', by firing in the general direction of heard or observed movement in the jungle. Clearly, there was much scope for dehumanisation
of the Australians' enemies.

For many combatants in World War II, 'the enemy' whom they
destroyed included civilians. Airmen in bombers, and soldiers who
fought house-to-house battles, often had to deal with the issue of killing
not only enemy soldiers, but also civilians who were only 'enemies' in
a very abstract sense. Perhaps the Australians' only compensation for

doing most of their fighting in the desert and jungle was that very few civilians came into their line of fire.[13]

When enemy soldiers were captured rather than killed, Australians' previous impressions of each enemy were put to the test, and they had a chance to vent their feelings. 'The enemy' ceased to be an abstract unity, and was seen to be a conglomeration of different types of men.[14] Australians' treatment of prisoners on the battlefield will be explored.

So too will the role of propaganda, politics and racism in soldiers' thoughts. In defining their enemies, Australian soldiers revealed much about themselves, their own psychology and their experience. Many wrote that the experience gave them a unique insight into war. It may also have given them more compassion for their opponents, whom they could visualise as real people and not as abstractions on a newsreel, in a newspaper or on a radio broadcast.

To some, however, the men they encountered were simply an embodiment of evil; they did not complicate the Australians' world view. And in some cases, the enemy's behaviour was worse in reality than the young men who enlisted in Australia could have imagined. Doubtless Italians, Germans, French and Japanese experienced the same feelings about Australians. How those enemies saw Australians is another theme to be discussed. We will find that the war against the Japanese involved extraordinary attitudes on both sides, that reflect no glory on those who held them. The comments made in this book on enemies' attitudes towards Australians make no claim to comprehensiveness, but in the absence of any previous systematic attempt to gather such impressions they should be a useful guide.

Fighting the Enemy is organised into two main parts. The first concerns the three enemies Australians encountered in the Middle East: the Italians, the Germans and the Vichy French.[15] The second part concerns the Japanese, to whom a very large proportion of the book is devoted. This is appropriate, given that this enemy fought the most Australians, killed the most Australians, suffered the most casualties at Australian hands and fought Australians over the longest period. An appendix explains the phenomenon of 'fifth columnists', which figured prominently in Australian writings about the enemy on both fronts. Appendix B lists, for each enemy, the major formations that fought Australians.

PART I

WAR IN THE MIDDLE EAST

CHAPTER ONE

THE ITALIANS

The first enemy soldiers who fought Australians in World War II were Italians. The average Italian soldier was poorly trained, poorly led, poorly fed and poorly armed.[1] The Italian conscript army was badly organised, and its tactical doctrine was unimaginative and inflexible.[2] Italians were less healthy than their European counterparts, let alone Australian volunteers.[3] The site of the first Australian–Italian contact was the Italian fortress of Bardia, in Libya. Men of the 6th Australian Division began joining the British forces surrounding the town on 19 December 1940. The first patrol clashes, on 28–30 December, resulted in casualties on both sides. Enemy aerial bombing had caused twenty deaths by Christmas Day. On 3 January 1941 the 6th Division, in conjunction with British armour and artillery, assaulted the fortress. By 5 January, Bardia had fallen. The Australians lost about 130 killed and 325 wounded.[4] The Italians had more than 40 000 men captured, together with approximately 400 artillery pieces, 130 tanks and 700 vehicles. Never had 'so much been surrendered by so many to so few', British Foreign Secretary Eden reported to Churchill.[5]

The 6th Division advanced westwards through Libya and, on 8 January, joined the British 7th Armoured Division outside the Italian fortress of Tobruk. After fifteen nights of patrolling, they launched an assault on 21 January. Again, the attack was very successful, culminating in the capture of the fortress, together with 25 000 of its defenders and 208 artillery pieces; the Australian losses were forty-nine dead and 306 wounded.

The Italians continued their westward retreat, occasionally offering resistance. By 7 February, the Australians were in Benghazi. The Allied advance was stopped and, in the course of the next month, the 6th Division was withdrawn for operations in Greece.[6]

In December 1940, a small Australian force was engaged in siege warfare against Italians at the Giarabub oasis, 230 kilometres south of Bardia. In hard fighting on 19–20 March 1941, an augmented battalion group from the 18th Brigade captured the fortress. Ninety-four Australians were killed or wounded (thirty-two of them by friendly fire); approximately 250 Italians were killed and 1300 captured.

Even after the arrival of German troops on the North African scene in March 1941, Italian forces continued to play an important role in operations against Australians. They generally comprised the majority of the force that besieged Australians of the 9th Division in Tobruk, after the successful Allied attack took it from the Italians, from April to December 1941.[7] The Italians were unable to recapture Tobruk and suffered heavy casualties from Australian patrols: on 16 April, for example, one Australian patrol captured ninety-seven Italians, another captured sixty-three.[8] When the 9th Division returned to the fighting in North Africa in July 1942, its first attack virtually destroyed an entire Italian division (the *Sabratha*) and caused heavy casualties in several others.[9] It continued to fight Italians – as well as Germans – until November, when it was relieved after the victorious conclusion of the Battle of El Alamein.

Australians went into action carrying not only weapons to defeat the Italians, but a set of attitudes that reflected a sense of superiority. Even before face-to-face hostilities began, the Italians were considered somewhat ludicrous. Two months before going into action at Bardia, an infantryman of the 6th Division concluded a letter to his father with a description of Italian bombing near his camp in Egypt: 'The Dagoes … lose no time in getting back to their spaghetti'.[10] About the same time, another infantryman wrote home that 'The "Wops" have been giving us a little nightly entertainment lately'.[11] The Italian predilection for pasta was a source of humour among Australians, who at times labelled Italians 'Signor Spaghetti', 'Spaghetti', 'Spag', 'Mr Macaroni' or 'Macaronis'.[12]

News of the 6th Division's successes reinforced the preconceptions of Australians in other units not yet committed to battle. In camp in Palestine, Private J.M. Butler of the 2/23rd Battalion wrote a diary entry which compared the siege of Bardia to a cricket match:

'LATEST SCORE: AUSSIE V. SKI [a slang term for Italians]:
At the drawing of stumps our score stands at 6000 with the loss of no wickets, play will be resumed at dawn tomorrow (Good old 6th Divvy)'.[13]

There was more open contempt in the note from a 9th Division infantry lieutenant who in February 1941 bemoaned the fact that the campaign against the Italians was going so well that he 'mightn't get the chance to dash about sticking bayonets through *greasers*' tummies'.[14]

At Bardia, Australians had 'met Mr Macaroni face to face, in the flesh', and there and in later campaigns the preconceptions that Italians were laughable, contemptible and dirty were put to the test. In the same letter that Sapper Cannam wrote home about meeting Mr Macaroni in the Libyan campaign, he contrived to use five other nicknames for Italians: 'Signor Spaghetti', 'Spaghetti', 'Dings', 'Iti' and 'Tony Wop'.[15] The multitude of nicknames (and we could add more from other writings: 'Dago', like 'Wop', a word of American derivation; 'Eyeties' or 'Ities'; 'Ski-ties', with its emphasis on the supposed conceit of the Italians; 'Ski'; 'Itos'; and 'Dages') could be regarded as suggesting a dehumanised, simplistic, contemptuous attitude to the enemy. Similarly, Australian soldiers wrote graffiti on Italian vehicles captured in Libya, using names such as 'Wop 73', 'Dago Dragon', 'Spaghetti Sue' and 'Benito's Bus'.[16] Cannam also ridiculed Benito Mussolini, writing scornfully of lines of prisoners from 'Il Duce's famed Desert Army'; this description was echoed by other writers who talked of 'Musso's braves' and 'Musso's minions'.[17] Just as the graffiti on vehicles was clearly meant to be funny, Cannam's phrases may have been intended to enhance the humour in an entertaining letter. However, other soldiers' writings leave no doubt that many Australians emerged from the experience of fighting the Italians with negative preconceptions reinforced.

For example, the idea of greasy, dirty Italians appears throughout soldiers' writings. An Australian writing home about occupying enemy entrenchments in an advance at Alamein said: 'These positions were *typically Italian* … it looked very much as if a cyclone had spent an hour or so in the trenches … we took cover and put up with the stench and rubbish'.[18]

Australians continued to find much to laugh at in the Italians. However, the experience of battle complicated matters. An infantryman writing home soon after fighting at Bardia noted: 'It has been most amusing in the last few days watching the huge streams of thousands of Italian prisoners being escorted down the road by one or two Australians. *The days before that were not so amusing*'.[19] The mortal terror of battle shattered many expectations. There emerged new, more informed ideas about war, including new thoughts about the enemy. Moreover, confronting real Italians enabled men to make a judgment based on evidence rather than on the second-hand and often propagandist reports on which they had previously relied. Thus, we read of a surprised Australian, wounded in the knee by a shell fragment at Bardia, calling out 'Blimey, these Dagoes are dinkum, all right!'[20] The picture of Italians that emerged in this new environment was a complex one.

Australians were preoccupied with proving their masculinity in battle, with upholding their sense of self-esteem and honour. This concern enabled them to keep their fear sufficiently in check to let them operate effectively as front-line soldiers. When assessing enemy soldiers, Australians' preoccupation with overcoming fear made them seek to determine whether the enemy was keeping his own fear in check: after all, this was a matter of more than academic interest, for it affected the Australians' chances of victory and an end to stress and danger.

Most experienced Australian troops considered the Italians ineffective soldiers. However, while some Italians offered little or no resistance, others fought hard.[21] This was the case at Bardia, where the men defending Post 11 fought very resolutely.[22] In the 6th Division's assault on Tobruk, the 2/8th Battalion suffered more than 100 casualties, and at the end of the first day's fighting a member of the unit wrote: '*Dago fought well* but nothing could stop the Boys'.[23] There were some courageous efforts by Italian units against Australians at Alamein, but these have gone largely unnoticed in Australian writings.[24] In wartime and published Australian accounts of Alamein actions, it is not always possible to determine whether 'the enemy' referred to was German or Italian. Perhaps this is partly because Italian and German forces were at times difficult to distinguish in that campaign, where the Germans were used as the whalebone in the Axis defensive girdle.[25] However, the lack of credit probably derives more from a desire to inflate Australian achievements, and an unwillingness to acknowledge reverses against Italians, rare though these may have been. Reticence is apparent in two of three accounts of an action on 17 July 1942, when the 2/32nd Battalion lost some men as prisoners in a generally successful operation. A private in the 2/32nd Battalion Intelligence Section wrote soon after the war that Italians were the enemy involved in the action, in which 109 Australians were captured. However, the official history mentions the capture of only twenty-two men and implies that they were captured by Germans; the battalion history states that 101 men were captured, by Germans. German records indicate that Italians of the Trento Division were responsible.[26]

An Australian account that does mention Italian bravery concerns the 2/43rd Battalion's attack on Trig 22 on the same day, 17 July 1942. It says that when the Australian advance persisted through heavy artillery fire, many Italians surrendered. However, 'A few made of sterner stuff, Italian artillery wallahs, had to be bayoneted'.[27] The Italian artillery was generally respected for fighting hard, especially at Bardia.[28] One sapper's descriptions of its efforts, written during the assault on Bardia, illustrate the difficulty of generalising about the Italian army: 'There is a battery of Blackshirt artillery still holding out + they have been keeping us down all day. The bastards are firing on their own men as we march them out. I have just helped some stretcher-bearers bring them in with their legs blown off'.[29] A widespread feeling was that Italians 'are poor fighters, the gunners being the only ones amongst them that are putting up any sort of a show at all'.[30] This disparagement of the main fighting soldiers – the infantry – to the profit of the gunners, reflects the majority Australian opinion towards Italians' fighting ability.

Other aspects of the Italian military effort did receive praise. Captured Italian equipment proved immensely useful to Australians in the desert campaigns, notably the drive across Libya and the defence of Tobruk.[31] Although some of the transport and medical equipment was considered to be good quality, its main value was as a substitute in the absence of Australian transport, machine guns, signals equipment and the like.[32] On the other hand, Australians also commented that most Italian equipment was vastly inferior to their own: men often had near-incredible escapes due to poor-quality Italian grenades and shells, like the lieutenant at Bardia who emerged virtually unscathed from the battle, despite being twice knocked over by shells landing within 10 metres of him, and having a grenade detonate almost between his legs.[33] Another Australian in the same battle reportedly lay flat under bombardment, only to have an Italian shell land beside him, pass under him close enough to cut his equipment and scratch his stomach, and emerge on the other side without detonating.[34]

Australians were often willing to praise the defences created by the Italians, notably at Bardia and Tobruk. A soldier of the 2/11th Battalion, which had gone into Bardia in the second day's fighting, noted: 'The place fairly bristled with guns and how the troops ever got through it is a mystery to us'.[35] Writing of the 2/8th Battalion's assault on Tobruk, an officer marvelled: 'We did the impossible. I've been over the ground again twice this week and ... there was even more there than I saw on the day'.[36] A private made a similar point in more earthy language, when he wrote from Tobruk in February 1941: 'The "Ities" ... certainly put in some work here and when the Aussies came and took it in one day, it must have knocked their arses in'.[37] Of course, these compliments were backhanded. They implied that the Australians were superior soldiers. Another implication was that the Italians defending these excellent positions had been inefficient. Some Australians stated this very directly. Cec Greenwood wrote as his battalion prepared to defend Tobruk in April 1941: 'We are now in our permanent defensive position south of Tobruk in an underground Itie fort. It is bonzer, if the Ities had of had any heart they could have held this place for years'.[38] Similarly, Private MacLeod wrote of the aftermath of the Bardia assault: 'In the fort, in which we camped, an open place with a stone wall encircling it, we procured hundreds of guns and ammunition, such that had any *real fighters* been there, no one would have taken it'.[39]

This notion that Italian soldiers were not 'real fighters' was very widespread among Australians. Near the end of the Libyan campaign, the 16th Brigade diarist, Corporal Hoffmann, expressed a common perception when he wrote to a friend:

> They can't take it. They can't take pain (I saw hundreds of their wounded ... all tears), they can't take shells (they flinch when one drops a hundred yards away), the sound of the British tanks

terrorised them and the sight of our bayonets was enough to make
them throw up their hands. Fascism ... pooh![40]

Hoffmann contrasted these qualities with the humour and courage of
Australians. Signalman Neeman, who won a Military Medal at Bardia,
reported that throughout the battle, 'once [the enemy] are out from
under the covering fire of their artillary [sic] they think "discretion
better part of Valour" '.[41] In February 1941, near the conclusion of the
chase across Libya, an artillery officer complained humorously in a
letter to his wife:

> the bloody Italian will not stand and fight. What the devil he has
> an army for passes comprehension ... The thing is definitely
> unsporting and one of these days we will catch up with him and
> might not be so willing to recognise the white flags his men so
> lavishly display.[42]

The 9th Division troops who relieved the 6th Division were
clearly given reason to expect a 'feeble' enemy; for example, Private
Butler reported that on entering Tobruk he was told that 'only eight
.303 bullets were fired in the taking of Tobruk'.[43] Like other 9th
Division men in Tobruk, he soon saw evidence that supported his
negative judgment. After his battalion's first action, supporting an
attack that captured an entire Italian battalion, he wrote: 'Tame affair.
Is no fight in them ... passed two who surrendered – both weeping –
hysterical'.[44] Later that month he went out as part of a ten-man fighting
patrol; it drove off a larger Italian patrol, which he estimated comprised
fifty men, and took two prisoners. He recalled in his diary a prewar
conversation in which 'I stated definitely that our race was distinctly
superior to others to the extent of 1 to 5 ... and today has proven it'.[45]
An officer in the same brigade made similar observations from his
personal experience in Tobruk: 'The Italians are not soldiers in the true
sense of the word ... are a race without a spine, without pride or
shame'. He argued that 'all Australians now know that 1 Aussie is still
equal to ... 50 Italians – almost, anyway'.[46] The following year a
wounded infantry officer, Gordon Combe, described from hospital an
Australian raid on Ruin Ridge, near Alamein: 'The troops [under his
command] moved on relentlessly digging *cowering Italians* out of their
holes and sending them back prisoners. It was nothing short of thrilling
to witness the magnificent courage of *our men*'.[47] These references

to the superiority of Australians suggest that Italians served a useful psychological function in boosting the self-esteem of Australian soldiers.

In the last days of Australian campaigning against Italians, a 9th Division infantryman wrote of prisoners he had seen during the battle of El Alamein: 'the Ities are the worst of the lot, underfed, miserable, and too bomb-happy to be any good'.[48] In each campaign, Australians commented about the underfed Italians, whose hunger perhaps partly explains their inefficiency.[49] However, Australians' usual wartime comments on stomachs were less in terms of hunger than in terms of guts or intestinal fortitude.

As much of the material quoted above suggests, Australian soldiers considered Italians cowardly. Jokes about Italian cowardice formed the staple of a newsletter published for the 2/23rd Battalion while it defended Tobruk. In August, for instance, the publication announced that the commanding officer of the unit had instituted a flea-catching competition. The article continued:

> The competition is not confined solely to fleas, but to vermin of all kinds, and a table of comparative values is given hereunder:
> One bug equals 3 fleas
> One rat equals 10 fleas
> Three lice equal 1 flea (easier to catch by far)
> One gazelle equals 300 fleas
> One I-ti prisoner equals 200 fleas (plus all 'catch' found on him).
> In criticising the above table which was laid down by the CO we think it an anomaly that 300 fleas are allowed for a gazelle and only 200 for an I-ti, whereas we all know the I-ti is much fleeter of foot than the gazelle, and is consequently harder to catch.[50]

A letter printed in the newsletter commented on the CO's equating one flea with 200 Italians: 'anyone who has spent a night in a dugout with 10 fleas will tell you ... 10 fleas can cause a lot more trouble than 200 I-tis. And you have to go looking for I-tis, while the fleas come looking for you'.[51] This genuine competition was won by B Company, who three weeks after the contest began had amassed 16 183 fleas – thanks to five Italian prisoners.[52]

Clearly this humour, like all joking about the fearful enemy, had a morale-boosting role. The Italians' cowardice, like the unhygienic conditions in which they were found to be living, frequently aroused

Australian contempt.[53] A particular source of disdain was Italians' supposed unwillingness to fight Australians face-to-face. They were said to be afraid to face the bayonet: no Australian would have been surprised by the story of the young Italian who fainted on seeing four Australians charging at him through the murk at Alamein. Even if they did put up a fight, Italians often enraged their opponents by firing at advancing Australians then trying to surrender at the last moment, when it was clear they could not halt the attack.[54] This occurred during the assaults on Bardia and Tobruk. At the end of the Australians' desert campaigns, an Australian NCO told his mother of the same practice at Alamein: 'on one occasion we attacked a position held by Ities and they fought like hell right up until we were 3 yds off them then they brought their hands up and called for mercy (they never got much)'.[55]

Australians were even more enraged by Italians who shot or threw grenades at them after surrendering. An example was reported by an Australian helping to transport the wounded from Bardia to Alexandria:

> chap with a head wound said that the Italians were very dirty fighters. firing untill [sic] our fellows were only a hundred yards off then coming out and surrendering. He said there were cases where some surrendered and then threw grenades at the Aussies and were taken unawares.[56]

The 2/8th Battalion history tells of an Italian who, after capture at Tobruk, threw a grenade at his captors and shot an Australian dead before meeting 'a spontaneous and savage reprisal'.[57] Such incidents seem to have been remarkably common: the official history alone records three.[58] Among some Australians, Italians developed a reputation as 'treacherous scum'.[59] One veteran asserted that, on the basis of the many incidents where surrendering Italians had killed their would-be captors, Australians did not trust Italians. He concluded that 'Musso's warriors might not be homeric; but they could not resist the temptation to be treacherous'.[60] These were damning words to apply to an opponent.

Not surprisingly, some Italian prisoners were accorded rough treatment. Ken Clift mentioned that an Australian soldier threw a grenade among Italian captives as repayment for the death of a mate.[61] A disgusted Private Butler recorded a conversation with a 6th Division signalman who had taken brutal steps in the advance to Benghazi:

'It appears that he was talking to a loquacious Italian or trying to talk, finally in desperation with a "that's enough from you" he drew his bayonet and thrust it through the Iti's body right up to the hilt'. Butler added, tellingly, that the 'brave Divvy sigs then told us to search prisoners under the armpits and round the knees for valuables'.[62] The Australians' greed for souvenirs undoubtedly made their treatment of some Italian prisoners rougher than it might otherwise have been. 'Souveniring' occurs in all armies. For example, Italian troops took the personal belongings of an Australian gunner captured at Bardia.[63] However, Australians seem to have been particularly eager. After Bardia, one private wrote home: 'Like all Aussies, we souveniered [sic] everything possible'.[64] The capture of Bardia and Tobruk gave Australian souvenir-hunters their biggest opportunity of the war. Vast quantities of Italian supplies and equipment were left on the battlefield, and there were more prisoners captured than in all the other Australian campaigns put together. The official history states that many, especially infantrymen, refrained from searching (or 'fanning') prisoners, but is surely understating the facts when it suggests that in taking pistols, watches and compasses, the infantrymen sought merely 'enough for their own needs'.[65] Certainly, the following extracts from front-line soldiers' letters suggest a different attitude:

> The souvenir-hunter was in his glory and buttons, badges, rings and such weighed down tunic pockets. S'Matter of fact, I scrawl this with an Iti pen – the best of six – and half a dozen rings have gone home.[66]

> Tobruch [sic] was a slightly smaller show than Bardia we only caught about 1200 all told, that is our Company did ... By the time we relieved them of watches, money, pistols, binoculars, rings or any other valuables we found that we were heavily loaded.[67]

There was certainly some rough treatment of prisoners during looting, but one battalion history suggests that when it occurred it was usually because Italian officers insisted, impractically, on not handing over pistols or swords to any but officers of equal or superior rank.[68] The official historian, Gavin Long, said that the 'bullying captor and the looter was seldom a front-line soldier with whom shots had been exchanged, but usually a man whose place in battle has been behind the lines'.[69] The official history is rather naive on the issue of the treatment of prisoners. Another example concerns the Australian engineers'

This humorous scene is based on reality. After the capture of Tobruk from the Italians in January 1941, some Italians did carry weapons for their fatigued captors. (Herald & Weekly Times Ltd)

Forlorn and embarrassed Italian prisoners with their triumphant Australian captors near Alamein. They and more than a thousand other Italians were captured in the Australians' first action in the Alamein campaign. (IWM E14388)

A common sight on desert battlefields. A dead Italian soldier lies at the end of an abandoned trench at El Alamein, October 1942. (AWM P1614.005)

In November 1942, these ten truckloads of Italians drove themselves into Australian captivity at El Alamein. (AWM 025253)

An Australian guards some of the first German prisoners taken in the North African campaign, on 17 April 1941. The Germans appear to be quite relaxed, despite the presence of Australian 'cold steel'. Australians sometimes described German prisoners as 'arrogant' or 'sullen'. (IWM E2479)

In May 1941, an Australian treats a wounded German prisoner in the desert. Australians and Germans were generally humane towards each other's wounded. In the background, other Australian soldiers take a good look at the Germans. (IWM E3098)

Australians often took photographs of each other examining destroyed German vehicles and guns. Here, Australians are looking over the most powerful type of tank they encountered in the war, a long-barrelled Panzerkampfwagen IV, in November 1942. (Donor: H.A. Hill)

illegal use of Italian prisoners to work on the anti-tank ditch at Bardia: Long talks of it as a brief, soon-remedied mistake, but is apparently unaware that Australians again forced Italian prisoners to work, at Tobruk a few weeks later.[70] However, Long was right to imply that in coming face-to-face with their Italian opponents, most Australians were not harsh, even if they had intended to be. He told an uplifting story of men from the 6th Division Cavalry Regiment who, in the advance across North Africa, caught up with and captured a group of Italians who had earlier fired on their medical aid post in an ambush. The Australians had 'sworn revenge, but having caught these dejected men the pursuers felt only pity for them'.[71] Time and again, when Australians saw the Italians face-to-face, they saw not treacherous men, but ones who had no fight in them at all. The following is typical of Bardia:

> They are surrendering everywhere ... The [sic] are nearly all kids, + all seem anxious to be friends ... a batch of nearly 3000 prisoners went out and their own artillery opened up on them, + they took shelter in the [anti-tank] trap with us I gave one sergeant the last of the biscuits, + the poor devil kissed me + wept + blurted gracias all over me.[72]

Their captors often felt that the Italians had no 'heart' for fighting.[73] Captain Laybourne Smith reported that at one position captured at Tobruk, 70 per cent of a group of 400 Italians had white flags ready in their pockets, and that dugouts everywhere contained white rags.[74] Barton Maughan spoke of white flags appearing to be 'standard battle equipment' for the Italian infantrymen who besieged Tobruk.[75]

As prisoners, Italians were generally very submissive. After capturing Tobruk, some fatigued Australians felt confident enough to allow their anti-tank rifles and other weapons to be carried by Italian prisoners.[76] One of the enduring images of Australia's war is long rows of prisoners escorted by small numbers of Australians. Private Ulrick said of Bardia: 'Were those prisoners docile. We were moving in the night when we met 6 Aussies with about 3000 Dagoes, looking for someone to give them to'.[77] Italian docility perhaps reached its peak at the battle of El Alamein, when some were permitted to drive vehicles to the Australian positions, or even to prison camps.[78]

It was often said that Italian prisoners were pleased to be getting out of the fighting. 'They are a greasy-looking mob but seem quite cheerful to be out of the scrap', wrote a 6th Division artillery officer of a group captured in Libya in February 1941.[79] The 9th Division, which soon assumed responsibility for the prisoners, saw their cheerfulness manifested in eagerness to help their new masters. For example, the 2/23rd Battalion historian reported that Italians pressed into service as personal valets to the unit during its stay at Derna were 'a happy lot [who] seemed well-contented to spend the rest of the war looking after their friends the Aussies'.[80] This seems a little too rosy to believe, although a soldier of the battalion wrote of the prisoners at the time: 'They are wonderfully willing workers and very cheerful. Of course our crowd start fraternising with them and spoiling them generally as they do everybody they meet'.[81] Lieutenant Gill was not quite so friendly when he wrote home during his battalion's journey to Libya, but his conclusion was significant: 'I had my hair cut and a shave by a Dago prisoner today, and ... he did quite a good job. They seem to be quite satisfied with the chain of events, and are so meek and harmless that one cannot be bothered even hating them'.[82] The Italians' meekness, diligence and cheerfulness worked against hate in Australians.[83]

Lieutenant Gill later condemned Italians for spinelessness, but others who saw the meekness and lack of commitment of Italian prisoners summoned up feelings other than contempt. The whole notion of their 'heart not being in it' left the possibility that Italians might have done better if their heart had been in it. Lance-Corporal Jones offered an explanation from Libya:

> I have seen thousands of Eyetie prisoners, and they certainly don't seem to worry about being out of the fight. Some of them have told me that they are Royalists who don't have a lot of time for Mussolini and that they did not want to fight. If their idea was to get Mussolini into trouble they certainly did a good job.[84]

However, such attempts to explain why Italians fought listlessly are almost entirely absent from Australians' writings. Usually, Australians' reaction to what they saw was emotional rather than reflective. Those not too contemptuous responded to prisoners with pity, sympathy and even kindness. Signalman Neeman wrote of his reaction to seeing huge numbers of Italians at Bardia coming forward and calling for water: 'I don't think I'm exactly cut out to be a soldier Barbara, gave the wounded our spare tin of water two gallons ... the tommeys are the boys knock hell out of the prisoners, don't spare the boot when it comes to moving'.[85] At an official level, too, the huge numbers of prisoners taken in the first Libyan campaign generally seem to have been treated sympathetically in the difficult conditions, although the selfish behaviour of some prisoners brought scorn.[86] As the 2/23rd soldier quoted above suggested, when given the chance Australians tended to fraternise.

Even in battle, Australians were said to have been rather squeamish about killing Italians at Bardia. To many Australians this battle was a hard introductory lesson in war, and a natural consequence was sympathy for the thousands of suffering Italians: 'we saw the first sight of intimate side of war, dugouts holding dead Italians and all over the place, personal stuff, such as letters, photos, etc., making us realise they are human allee [sic] same as us'.[87] This comment is a fine example of the way attitudes were complicated by seeing the enemy up close. Australians' tentativeness in killing Italians supposedly diminished during the capture of Tobruk, where men did not hesitate to throw grenades into positions if the defenders were slow to surrender. However, most Australians seem to have found it hard to hate the Italians, despite exhortations like that from the 6th Division commander to enter the attack on Tobruk 'angry and virile and hating'.[88] Usually, only treacherous behaviour in battle, witnessed or reported, aroused high emotion against Italians.[89]

Nevertheless, one can go too far in asserting the compassion and warmth of Australian soldiers towards Italians. The Australians who fought the Italians had volunteered to fight. Military prowess, the desire to be 'Homeric' warriors, was very important to them. The Italian conscript army ranked poorly on this scale. The Australians were determined to do their job well, and this involved defeating their enemy efficiently and impersonally. A good illustration of this attitude is a letter from an infantry captain concerning Bardia: 'During the advance one Italian took a shot at us from about 200 feet. John Hodge fired one shot – the Italian we found after – John rolled him over – "hit him where I aimed" was his remark'.[90] Only after Italians were defeated could they be pitied and even helped as fellow human beings – as long as they resisted the temptation to be treacherous. Until they surrendered, they were the enemy. That was their chief role, and as far as Australians were concerned they did not play it very well. Australians also firmly believed that the Italians played only a supporting role in the great drama in which Australians were participating. Italians were 'small fry' or 'satellites', as implied by a 6th Division private's report after the campaign against the Germans in Greece: 'We had just experienced our first taste of real warfare, the Libyan Campaign being in comparison a glorified bivouac'.[91] A 9th Division soldier wrote to a friend soon after his first battle in the desert: 'I told you we were in Action not with feeble Italians either we are up against the real enemy and are all confident of coming out on top'.[92] That 'real enemy' was, of course, German.

After the last battle in which they met Italians, Australian units checking the battlefield of El Alamein were methodical in collecting German artillery. Italian pieces were of much less interest. One veteran recalled that although Italian cases containing 'their cheesy shells' lay around, they were 'driven over regardless; they lay pressed into the roadways'. Recalling one gun with wooden wheels, dated 1907, the veteran concluded with a comment that captured the mixture of contempt and pity that was typically Australian: 'the tired-looking dead Italian reclining against the wheel with the flies buzzing into his open mouth looked as if he'd been made in that year too'.[93]

At about the same time, Australian soldiers were reported by those responsible for censoring their mail to be showing the 'usual contempt … for the cringing, filthy and unkempt Itis, driving themselves to the cages in their own trucks'.[94]

ITALIAN ATTITUDES TO AUSTRALIANS

An Italian lieutenant at Miteiriya Ridge, in the 'Alamein Line', noted in his diary in July 1942 that British forces had been interfering with his unit's communications, and broadcasting 'insults and enticements'.[95] These included a threat to attack them with two battalions of Australians. 'I suppose', he wrote, 'they think the word "Australians" will frighten us'.[96] Clearly these messages to the Italians were based on the perceived Italian fear of Australians. There is much evidence of that fear.

Italians themselves had been the first to describe Australians in a way which frightened Italian troops: Italian soldiers waiting for the assault on Bardia had reportedly been scared by Italian radio broadcasts about 'Australian barbarians'.[97] No wonder that an Australian captured at Bardia wrote later that the Italians had stared at him as if he were an exotic zoo animal.[98] Italian commanders had also, unwisely, told their men that Australians took no prisoners. Presumably, discovering the falsity of this story, which was still being told in 1942, was one reason for the cheerfulness of Italian POWs.[99]

There is no doubt that at Bardia the Italians were frightened and impressed by the courage with which Australians advanced steadily through heavy fire. Indeed, some believed that the leather jerkins worn by many Australians in the morning cold must be bulletproof.[100]

At Alamein, some Italian commanders offered a more plausible, but still inaccurate, explanation for Australian courage against them. They implied that it was really Dutch courage, based on drunkenness. A captured message from the commanding officer of the Brescia Division to his troops said in its opening paragraph: 'The enemy generally attacks with very well-trained troops ... These special units, generally Australians and New Zealanders, attack with decision and brutality generally rendered bestial and brutal by drunkenness'.[101] An Italian artillery captain only a few hundred metres from fighting involving Australians wrote in his diary at the height of the battle of El Alamein: 'Hand-to-hand fighting is going on. The Australians, *roaring drunk on whisky*, are like madmen ... The wounded, both German and Italian, have horrifying tales to tell'.[102] As descriptions of units, rather than of isolated individuals, these 'explanations' seem to have little foundation in fact. An Australian artilleryman reported the story that Australian infantry in the July battle had 'got on' the beer during the fighting, and terrified the Italians 'with their singing and yelling', until General Morshead had clamped down on the drinking.[103] There may well have been isolated cases of soldiers doing more than singing and yelling under the influence of alcohol, but there is very little direct evidence of it from the infantrymen themselves. Nor is there evidence that drink was a significant factor in Australian units' fighting performance. The Brescia description sounds like a ready-made excuse for failure, while the captain's account seems intended to explain the incomprehensible behaviour of Australians, whose enemies might call them 'madmen' and whose friends would dub them 'heroes'.[104] No doubt many Italians saw some very drunk Australians in the aftermath of the capture of Bardia and Tobruk, and even some who were drunk during the battles. However, these Italians were all prisoners or on the point of becoming so,[105] and drunkenness was a convenient explanation for an opponent's frightening behaviour. Similarly disingenuous were an Italian account of a unit being 'wiped out by drunken negroes with tanks', and the Italian official history's statement that Bardia was captured by masses of British armour. In fact the British used just twenty-three tanks in the operation and, important though they were, the Australian infantry did most of the fighting.[106]

In the static warfare of the siege of Tobruk and Alamein in the months before the great battle, Italians showed marked timidity towards Australian units, which invariably had a policy of aggressive patrolling.[107] This aggressiveness seems to have had an effect on Italian attitudes to Australians, and it almost certainly contributed to the theme of a piece of doggerel supposedly current among Italian soldiers at Tobruk:

> Take your last look,
> You're off to Tobruk.
> You're a goner.[108]

Similarly, during the static period at Alamein, a captured Italian document contained a regimental commander's warning to a subordinate that the Italians were faced by Australians, who were 'notable patrollers'.[109]

During the July fighting in the area, Australians on the receiving end of a rare Italian counterattack sent a message to a neighbouring South African unit which indicated surprise and supreme confidence: 'We are being attacked by Italians ... ain't it grand!'[110]

Italian attacks on Australians were seldom intimidating and, clearly, Italian aggression was cause for surprise, though rarely anxiety. The opposite was true of Australian advances, which were often frighteningly aggressive. An Italian account of the July fighting at Alamein spoke of Australians making a 'violent' attack on 10 July, 'a furious Australian advance' on 17 July and 'waves of Australian attackers' surrounding an Italian unit on the same date, and of Australians who, for three days in the great battle, 'came on regardless of their losses'.[111] The Italian author talked of the first of these actions as a 'shrewdly thought-out attack' and of the advance in the last three days of October as a 'steady methodical advance'.[112] However, the lasting impression is that Australians were considered a force that was terrifying, relentless and careless of life. Most Italians facing Australians in the front line seem to have had these impressions of their opponent. Enemies as careless of life also appear in Australian depictions of their foes, though not in their portrayal of Italians.

Soldiers careless of their own lives probably have little concern for their enemies' lives. According to one book on the desert war, Italians felt that Australians were merciless and they made a 'general claim' that Australians and New Zealanders 'often killed surrendering or wounded Axis troops'.[113] Given that tens of thousands of Italians successfully surrendered to Australians, it is very hard to believe that there was a widespread Italian conviction that Australians routinely butchered prisoners and wounded. The authors give only one rather tenuous example to back up their claim.[114] As we have seen, some Australians were indeed merciless against defenceless Italians, but ruthless behaviour toward surrendering or wounded men was exceptional and usually arose in the high passion of battle, especially where vengeance was desired.

CHAPTER TWO

THE GERMANS

THE REAL ENEMY

Australians who joined the Australian Imperial Force in 1939 and 1940 did so expecting to fight Germans. The Italians only entered the war in June 1940, by which time the formation of the 6th, 7th and 8th AIF Divisions was underway or complete. The Germans had been the main opponents of the 1st AIF, and the desire to emulate the deeds of that force was a motive for many who enlisted. Moreover, even though the Italians were very much part of the Australians' involvement in the Middle East, the Germans were regarded as the 'real enemy'.

The first meeting with German land forces was on 4 April 1941, when men of the 2/13th Battalion, part of the unblooded 9th Division, fought advancing German armoured and infantry forces at Er Regima. Its three lightly armed companies held off an estimated 3000 men until dark, when the battalion retreated towards Tobruk. The 9th Division had relieved the 6th Division in Libya and found itself in the path of the German-led Axis counterattack that began on 31 March. In the 'Benghazi Handicap' the Australian force came perilously close to being encircled, but most made it back to Tobruk.[1] The siege began there on 11 April, with German and Italian forces surrounding the 'fortress'. In May, German attacks broke through the fortress perimeter in the west, where a 'Salient' was formed, but the attacks did not capture the fortress. Australians confronted Germans on the Tobruk front line from April until the relief of most Australian battalions, in September–October. The last remaining Australian battalion, the

2/13th, suffered heavy casualties but won vital ground at Ed Duda, in the successful Allied attempt to open a corridor to and relieve the fortress in November–December 1941.

In April 1941, while the Tobruk siege was in progress, other Australian forces met another German offensive, in Greece. The Germans attacked in great strength, and within three weeks the Australian and other Commonwealth forces were evacuated to Crete or Egypt. About 6500 Australians were in Crete in May when the Germans sent paratroops and other forces to invade it. Despite some Australian successes, at Retimo and Heraklion, the Australians eventually surrendered or joined the retreat and evacuation of Commonwealth forces. More than 3000 Australian troops became prisoners of war.

In 1942, Australian forces re-entered the Western Desert, and near the coast and the railway stations at Tel el Eisa and El Alamein they confronted German forces in the bloody fighting of July–November that year. Australian forces suffered very heavy casualties in those actions; in the Battle of El Alamein they suffered 20 per cent of the 8th Army's casualties, despite representing a much smaller proportion of the army. In that battle they confronted the German elite of the Axis forces in North Africa and, though not entirely successful in all objectives, made a vital contribution to the Allied victory.

Australian attitudes towards the Germans were ambivalent, as hinted in the nicknames given to them. The World War I 'Hun', which then reflected German methods of fighting, was still widely used, but so were the neutral 'Jerry' and 'Fritz'.[2] The ambivalence was related to the fact that Germans were formidable enemies, who in two campaigns inflicted defeat on Australian forces. But even when victorious, Australian soldiers had different views or changed their minds in light of their experience. We have seen that military prowess was important to Australians, who frequently made comparisons with their enemies. They always considered Italians inferior soldiers: inferior not only to them but to the Germans. During the battle of El Alamein, Corporal Jack Craig found a logical explanation for the relatively high casualties of his unit, the 2/13th Battalion: 'The 2/15 + 17 Bn. met *Italians* in their attack, but the 2/13 Bn had ran [sic] into *the German* as they moved through them. That is why we had suffered more so than the other units'.[3] In mid 1941, when Private Alan Hackshaw wrote of his experiences in Libya, Greece and Crete, he commented on Bardia: 'We had very little trouble and very few casualties. The place was a real fortress. Had German troops been there we would not have taken it so easily'.[4] Later, the Japanese were also compared unfavourably to the Germans.[5] The belief that Germans were the 'real enemy' contained the idea that Germans were the standard by which Australians would measure themselves. They were the main foe in the sense of being the chief danger, but also being genuinely capable opponents.

Although the ability and character of the German troops varied considerably, Australians saw much evidence of German military prowess, not only in Greece and Crete, where the fighting was relatively brief, but also in North Africa.[6] They noted the Germans' ingenuity and efficient use of weapons. A corporal recently returned from Greece commented on Germany's 'amazingly brilliant engineers', who had overcome the obstacles of numerous bridges blown up as the Australians retreated.[7] With considerable aplomb, an Australian NCO reported the accuracy of German artillery at Tobruk:

> went up to the Blue Line [inner defensive line] yesterday and Fritz put five shells right in amongst us while the company was sitting down, we all dived into nearby holes and no one was hurt. Pretty good O Pipping [artillery observation work] though as the Hun O.P. [Observation Post] was at the Maidens Breasts about two and a half miles away and the first shell landed within two hundred yards and the last one about fifteen yards away.[8]

Even at the Battle of El Alamein, where the British artillery was overwhelming and invaluable, an Australian infantryman could feel: 'His Arty is better than ours – he knows how to use it'.[9]

To illustrate the accuracy of German snipers in the Salient, a lieutenant-colonel pointed out that his unit's only periscope had been hit immediately on being raised above the post.[10] Early in the siege of Tobruk, Private John Butler noted another German strength, the effective organisation of its arms:

> We can learn from the Germans. Their Bns. are a complete unit – with Anti-Tank guns, Tanks, Air-force and field workshops and Ack-ack defence and artillery – with us if we wanted support from the Air-force we must give 48 hours notice – a Gilbertian situation like writing a letter to the fire-brigade when one's home catches alight.[11]

The predominance and high quality of German airpower was constantly before the Australians' eyes in Tobruk, Greece and Crete, where the Germans had almost free rein. Captain Chrystal recalled for his family his first sight of German airpower in Greece:

> during the afternoon we had our first look at the great Jerry Luftwaffe. 190 bombers came over and bombed Servia and the Pass till there was not a thing left. They flew in close formation generally in flights of 30 to 40 and I can tell you we simply gasped in amazement and were absolutely spellbound to see such numbers but that was only a sample of what we were to see later unfortunately.[12]

Despite the stress caused by German airmen, their courage and skill were widely acknowledged. A diarist wrote at Tobruk: 'One cannot help but admire the Huns (germans) as they are game, one plane came down in Tobruk with an Iti pilot and a Hun observer aged about 15. The kid I believe kept the guns going until they crashed'.[13]

The courage of German ground forces was also recognised. Private Hackshaw acknowledged, after participating in heavy fighting against German paratroops on Crete, that they were 'very good soldiers. They were mostly small, but they made up for that in gameness'.[14] At Tobruk, Private Nowland concluded that Germans were 'born soldiers', and as evidence recounted the story of a wounded 'Nazi', who although shot in three places 'did not omit to keep in step and salute our officers'.[15] In the Tel el Eisa fighting of July 1942, a private of the 2/48th Battalion explained one of his unit's rare failures to achieve its objectives by saying that his side's 'leaders' had made the usual mistake of underestimating that 'good fighter the hun'.[16]

As the terrible Battle of El Alamein reached its climax in October, Private Paget recorded with some awe: 'Arty extra busy, the noise and concussion terrific, If Jerry is not bomb happy he is not human ... she sure is a willing war, but Jerry is putting up a great fight'.[17] Private Butler also recognised German valour: 'There are strong pockets of resistance and one must salute these brave germans [sic] who hold out'.[18] The Germans had not only defended at Alamein; they had counterattacked at every opportunity, and their aggressive doctrine was similar to that of the Australians.[19] Corporal Fairbrother described 1 November at Alamein as 'Black Sunday': his battalion was 'attacked by Panzer [armoured] div. many lives lost, most concentrated attack I have ever been in'.[20] German tanks were acknowledged as a fearsome weapon, and indeed whenever Australians surrendered in North Africa

enemy tanks were almost invariably present. One group of Australians
who would have testified to the tanks' effectiveness was a platoon of
the 2/24th Battalion who spent the night of 30 April/1 May 1941 trying
unsuccessfully to sneak past or knock out tanks which had surrounded
them at Tobruk. The lieutenant in charge said that when he and three
companions emerged from a tank-blasted pit to surrender, they were
'dumbfounded, incredulous and shocked'.[21]

The great ability of the German leader Rommel was well known
to Australians by 1942. As one Australian diarist's unit travelled in a
convoy towards its second campaign against Rommel, in 1942, he
recorded that its future was 'in the lap of the gods, at least the lap of
one god Mars, who has a worthy son in Rommel'.[22]

Of course many played down or qualified their admiration for
German soldiers: 'although we hate him and everything associated
with him, one can't help admiring his brilliant military achievements',
wrote a 9th Division infantry lieutenant. Similarly, a private recalled
in Papua in 1942 that his attitude to 'Fritz ... was tinged with
admiration'.[23]

However, there were also some very negative comments about
German military abilities, accentuating the poor quality or unfair
advantages supposedly enjoyed by German forces. They were said to
be poor fighters at night: 'Germans dread the dark', wrote an Australian
infantryman, with some self-satisfaction.[24] There was talk of Germans
attacking in 'hordes' and criticism of their lack of tactical imagination
or perception.[25] A tendency to bunch their infantry in attack, rather than
disperse it, came in for particular criticism. 'We place them in the same
class as Musso's dagoes as far as their Shock tactics are concerned',
wrote one triumphant Australian early in the siege of Tobruk.[26] Another
private wrote confidently at about the same time: 'They are good when
they out number the other side + have tanks in front of them but they
soon chuck it in when they met [sic] the opposition on equal terms of
tanks'.[27] The sort of numerical and material superiority referred to here
was used by Australians to explain the German victories in Greece and
Crete.[28] In his account of an incident during the retreat through Greece,
a survivor of the campaign implied another criticism of Germans as
soldiers:

> Talk about running a gauntlet of death! ... We had to dump most
> of our gear and run up the exposed side of a mountain about 50
> yards up the exposed side ... how they missed us I don't know.

> Then we would see the mountain gun with the machine guns belch
> out a long stream of flame and there would be a lovely explosion
> near us ... luckily they were pretty rotten shots.[29]

The perception of Germans as poor shots appeared occasionally in other accounts.[30]

Several components of the criticism levelled at Germans' soldiering abilities were apparent in an account of the Er Regima action by Private Armstrong of the 2/13th Battalion. He talked of 'hoards' of Germans attacking, forcing the 'heroic' Australians back but failing to take the opportunity to wipe them out, even though they were firing at point-blank range. His explanation: 'They must have been full of metho. or else they would have mowed us down'.[31] The suggestion about alcohol recalls the one raised by Italians about Australians. A notion of drugged Germans also appeared. Soldiers returning from Greece told stories of Germans with glassy eyes and pinpricks from needles, the supposed reason they would continue to advance despite appalling casualties.[32] The day after praising the Germans' courage during the battle of Alamein, Mick Paget noted 'Hun prisoners all are beleived [sic] to be doped'.[33] Was this someone's unfair explanation for German courage, a reference to the dazed look of utterly exhausted men, or a medical fact? Allan Jones was at Alamein, and in trying to explain motivation in battle said, 'We used to hear stories of how attacking Germans were drugged, but of course they were not'.[34] It does seem unlikely, although both Germans and British made some use of amphetamines.[35] Certainly the official histories make no mention of evidence of drugs. The motivation behind these claims seems like that of the Italians: to explain the enemy's success in terms other than courage. A similar logic lay behind comments such as the following, both concerning the Greek campaign: 'Given more air support and more men we will thrash the huns back to Berlin' and 'they would never have broken through if our infantry had had the support of fighter aircraft'.[36]

In Australians' attempts to assess the Germans, some felt that extraneous factors made it difficult to see how good the Germans really were. They complained that the playing field was not level. A perceptive and rather bemused German officer noted that a group of Australians surrendering on Crete spoke as if they had merely lost 'a sporting test match'.[37] Although in fact there was a considerable degree of 'sportsmanship' between the two sides, fair and balanced assessment of the other team was impossible for Australians. There were too many factors that clouded the issue.

Private Butler mentioned one of the obstacles, as he mused in Tobruk in June 1941:

> the German is a worthy opponent and in this campaign at least he is a clean and fair fighter – I have yet to see a German who is afraid: I have yet to see a German who resorts to low and mean subterfuge. [Butler changed his mind about this later.] What a pity they are so blindly fanatical in their political creed – what a pity they shun God and the Son of God – what a pity their courage, their talents, their thoroughness and ingenuity merely go towards building up a clay god of War.[38]

Few could have put it so well, but many Australians felt a similar ideological gap with Germans. At its most basic level, their feelings were those expressed by one of Butler's comrades to a prisoner at Alamein: 'Pity you didn't shoot Hitler instead of heiling him, we wouldn't have had all this trouble'.[39] Very few Australian soldiers described their participation in the war as part of a crusade against Nazism.[40] Indeed, Warrant Officer 'Cobber' Craig recounted an incident that illustrates beautifully how political questions were secondary to front-line soldiers. At Alamein, a German prisoner 'came up to two or three of us and produced his hand and on the little finger was a ring, rather a large one with the old swastika on it. He immediately pulled it off, looked at it and then threw it on the ground and said Nazi finish'. Rather than applaud the man: 'Well, everybody forgot about him and dived on this ring. There was a hell of a scramble; all of us on the ground, fighting for this ring and the "Jerry" standing there dumbfounded, couldn't make out why we were all wanting it'.[41]

Although Australians rarely spoke of the war's higher aims, they often felt, either through personal contact or through reading about Germany, that there was a psychological distance between them and the 'Huns'. A Tobruk diarist believed that he saw through a German prisoner's dull and lifeless eyes 'a mass produced mind', impervious to outsiders.[42]

Another private in Tobruk, G.T. Nowland, felt that 'Nazi courage is undeniable, proving that the German is potentially a superior racial type, *when moulded by a more humane culture*'.[43] The belief that Germans were 'a superior racial type' manifested itself in the arrogance often noted in Germans met face-to-face. Lieutenant Gill remarked that, unlike the Italian, 'the German holds himself up defiantly – the better type German that is, although *his face often registers sullenness and insolence*'.[44]

The issue of inhumanity mentioned by Private Nowland was taken up by another Australian soldier, who described a German attack at Tel el Eisa: 'you could not help but admire the waves of picked Jerry troops as they tried to get through the heavy artillery barrage, and as one wave was wiped out another seemed there to take its place. *What a callous disregard Jerry has for life*'.[45]

This callousness applied not only to their own men. Australians were angered by the destructiveness of 'Hun hate' against civilian targets in Greece.[46] They were flabbergasted by the sight of German forces bombarding or machine-gunning Italians who tried to surrender.[47] Most infuriating, and a major obstacle to impartial Australian assessment of the Germans, were the frequent examples of 'dirty', treacherous or callous actions against Australians. Such actions included attacking the defenceless: hospitals, ambulances and stretcher-bearers.[48] After the Cretan campaign, an ambulanceman wrote angrily: 'Never once did we know of the Itis firing on our ambulances or clearly marked stations, but my personal appearance [sic] is that 40% of Germans will delight in cleaning them up'.[49] The usual reaction of a footsoldier observing such incidents is well summed up by the comments of Private Derrick in the Salient at Tobruk: 'Seen a human side of the war yesterday arvo Red Cross partys [sic] burying dead & treating wounded one of our partys were fired on by enemy & *I will always remember it*'.[50]

In other cases Germans themselves pretended to be defenceless, then took advantage of the credulous Australians. Typically, Germans offering to give themselves up would draw weapons and fire on the men coming forward to capture them. This happened in Tobruk, on Crete and at Alamein.[51] A similar trick was for 'surrendering' Germans to draw Australians from cover, then open fire with concealed machine-guns.[52] An Australian in the Tobruk Salient was told that Germans there were using dead Australians as decoys, so that German snipers could shoot men who tried to recover the corpses. He concluded: 'Nice human enemy we are up against'.[53] At Alamein, booby-traps were allegedly left on dead enemy and Australian troops.[54] In the same campaign, Australians saw incontrovertible proof of German ambulances being used to carry weapons and troops into action.[55] Live prisoners were reportedly used as screens for German advances on occasion, in Greece and Crete.[56] 'It was a dirty trick, *typical of the Hun*' was the expression one Australian used to describe a ruse whereby a German, speaking English, had approached and killed an Australian, in the dark at Alamein.[57] Bitter recent experience also informed Private Butler's diary entry concerning a German propaganda broadcast during the Alamein fighting of July 1942:

> Lord Haw-Haw ... says in a broadcast 'The 9th Divvy is the world's second best fighter'. I suppose if we fired on ambulances, mowed down stretcher bearers, used the white flag illegally, use [sic] the anti-tank rifle on men and a lot of other despicable tricks, we would be the worlds best.[58]

The issue of who was best or second-best may have been complicated by the belief that Germans were a race apart, but Australians were still eager to make such comparisons. Perhaps the biggest obstacle to the conclusion that they wanted to draw was that Australians were prominent in the forces that the Germans had crushed in Greece and Crete. Australians involved in those campaigns were very aware that their defeat was a potential blot on the AIF's escutcheon, and they were keen to explain that they were not to blame.[59] The German army's numerical and material superiority made the outcome of the Greek campaign a foregone conclusion, and Australians did not fail to point that out. However, they also emphasised the effectiveness and eagerness of the Australians:

> they never had no dive bombing in the last war ... anyway although we were outnumbered by about 8 to 1, for every Aussie and N.Z. who made the sacrifice, they left behind 10 Germans ... we sure left the Anzac brand behind us.

> The only thing they couldn't destroy was the spirit of the boys and they were always only too willing to get to grips with him for a day or two when it was possible ... I've heard since that 75 000 Germans bit the dust. If we could have been on anything like equal terms with them that would have been made up to a million.[60]

Such claims were very exaggerated. In the entire Greek campaign, the Germans lost 1160 killed and 345 missing; there were 903 Commonwealth deaths, 320 of them Australian.[61] The inflated but eagerly accepted claims, which New Zealanders also circulated about their performance, were doubtless due partly to inaccurate news broadcasts to the troops.[62]

After Crete, Lieutenant-Colonel Cremor of the 2/2nd Field Regiment stated that the Australians had had no chance, and that with only a third of the airpower and manpower of the Germans the Australians could beat them.[63] A diarist wrote of hearing from 6th Division veterans from Crete that the Germans, whose 'loss of life had been appalling compared with our own', had been doped, and that with the co-operation of the RAF the Australians 'would have done alright'.[64] In fact, the Commonwealth force defending Crete outnumbered the invaders, whose 4000-odd fatal casualties were a little over twice those of the defenders (including 274 Australians).[65] Although their appreciation of the realities may have been flawed, Australians seem to have emerged from these defeats either confident or utterly determined about winning next time. A sergeant claimed: 'One thing has come out from the Greek campaign – we no longer believe in the superhuman prowess of the German fighting man ... in the infantry fighting they weren't a match for the Australians or New Zealanders'.[66]

Those who fought in Tobruk made similar claims. After the fierce battles in which the main German thrusts were halted and the Salient created, a driver in the fortress asserted: 'Jerry has had several tries to break through but the boys have given more than Jerry could take. This is the first time he has been stopped'.[67]

Such claims had considerable validity in relation to Tobruk, as there is evidence that the Germans were surprised at being defeated in their April assaults. A German account told of many Germans crying as they were taken into captivity after the 8th Machine-Gun Battalion's failed attempt to breach the Australian lines on 14 April.[68] German tank commanders returning to their own lines after being repulsed in the same battle 'jumped out of their Panzers sobbing hysterically'.[69] The Australians had allowed the attacking German tanks to pass through, into the fire of the supporting British artillery, while they dealt with the supporting Axis infantry.[70] Sergeant Symington worked in the 2/17th Battalion's Regimental Aid Post at Tobruk, and wrote a fascinating diary entry about the testimony of many wounded German prisoners:

> They seemed quite dazed and could not understand how they failed, whenever they had used Tanks before it was always a

success. One chap said 'Why in Poland they only had to march in behind the tanks and occupy the position and they were sure of this too, they even had their blankets with them'.[71]

The moral ascendancy won by Australians in these early stages was maintained throughout the siege and beyond. Their brilliance at night patrolling was unmatched by the Germans, and although Lieutenant Gill's comparison from 1942 has a *Boys' Own Annual* flavour, it is by no means greatly exaggerated. More importantly, it exemplifies the Australians' confidence in that field:

> On night patrols we put it all over the German. We go out in sandshoes or rubber desert boots, and silently put him and sometimes his tanks and guns out of action. The German often gets lost in the day time, and is pretty hopeless at night, while our chaps roam everywhere at night, guided by an occasional glance at the stars, or a sniff at the wind.[72]

The Germans very rarely sent out offensive patrols at Tobruk, and were unable to gain the ascendancy in no man's land at Alamein.[73] An Australian at Alamein wrote confidently of the Australians' superiority there: 'Sometimes we sight them – one night when I got near them they went for their lives back to their own lines I don't think they like meeting you man for man'.[74]

The belief that Australians were better 'man for man' persisted throughout the war.[75] With language typical of those who asserted Australian superiority, a young private at Tobruk claimed that when his unit had met the German, 'he has always come off second best'. He continued: 'he doesn't like our bayonet, and runs away nearly as fast as the "Eyeties" used to'.[76] This scoffing at the Germans' aversion to Australian cold steel had also occurred in the 1st AIF, which had a reputation for proficiency with the bayonet.[77] It was not merely a faint echo of an earlier reality, however; it was based on real events. On Crete, two Australian companies joined New Zealanders, who also had a reputation with the weapon, in a bayonet charge that forced their opponents back a couple of kilometres at high cost. A participant said of the enemy reaction: 'They were highly-trained Germans, but they got such a shock at our din and the way we ran that they forgot they were supermen and ran'.[78] Platoon bayonet charges, like the one which overran a battery of guns and took 106 prisoners (mostly German) at Tel el Eisa, were not uncommon.[79] Three of the four Australian soldiers who won Victoria Crosses for actions against Germans in World War II performed extraordinary feats with the bayonet: Private Gurney killed at least five Germans at Tel el Eisa; forty-year-old Private Gratwick killed all the occupants of an enemy post at Alamein with bayonet and grenade; Corporal Edmondson, though mortally wounded, killed five Germans at Tobruk.[80] Edmondson and six other Australians charged a group of about thirty heavily armed Germans who had penetrated the wire defences of Tobruk, on the night of 13/14 April 1941. One of the Australians, Private Ron Grant, described how they threw grenades at the enemy and then used the bayonet:

> with a blood curdling shout we tore into them. A machine gunner fired a burst at me + missed. Then he emptied a lugger [sic – Luger pistol] at me again missing. I got to him + fixed two more in my rush past ... The other boys got about 3 huns each + the rest of the 50 enemy that were estimated to be there fled, *some screaming*, + *the others in tears*.[81]

A few days later, Sergeant Symington heard evidence of other German responses to Australian use of the bayonet at Tobruk: '[The wounded German prisoners] can't understand how our Infantry stood against their Tanks and one officer, prisoner, said he was going to complain about the Aussies using bayonets, he said it was inhumane. Didn't we laugh'.[82] We can picture the amusement caused by the German officer's complaint. We can also imagine the boost that German failure to cope with bayonet charges gave to Australian morale, which depended on being the best.

After a patrol action in which a man had bayoneted three Germans, Private Nowland offered a tongue-in-cheek explanation of the Australian supremacy with the bayonet in terms of civilisation versus barbarism: 'Fortunately our fortitude seems more than a match for Nazi science. The civilized Nazi, like the Italian, shows a marked distaste for the bayonet, which the barbarous Aussie does not hesitate to employ as a last resort'.[83]

A former officer on Rommel's staff wrote that Australian troops 'won a grim reputation among our men for their terrible work with the bayonet'.[84] That 'terrible work' involved brutal killing. How did Australians feel about killing Germans?

In World War I, Australians had a reputation, probably deserved, for being among those most ready to kill.[85] Clearly, men who killed with bayonets had to be able to banish sensitivity and moral scruple. Yet the man whom Nowland mentioned for bayoneting three men was 'tormented by the recollection' later that night.[86] A British history of the war in the North African desert described Australians as 'an implacable foe', and illustrated it with a story of an Australian at Tobruk fol-lowing his mates' instructions to kill a wounded German with the bayonet.[87] That was not typical, but in action there were certainly some men who had no qualms about killing Germans. The 2/23rd Battalion's newsletter at Tobruk told of a soldier who during a raid 'managed to work up quite a hate for Jerry'. He had shot a fleeing German from a considerable distance, then stopped and used a pocket-knife to cut a nick in his rifle-butt; he was keeping count of the Germans he killed.[88] One famous patrol leader won the appellation 'Tex' for adding notches to his submachine-gun.[89]

Another soldier wrote with pride and only a little apparent discomfort of a souvenir he was sending home: 'Am posting you some photos of Hun gunners we had to –. Some might strike you as being very young but a young viper has plenty of sting'.[90]

Some soldiers depicted the killing of Germans as a pleasure, like sport. An infantryman wrote of his experiences on Crete: 'Never will I forget the glorious sight of those paratroops coming down. Have you ever done any duck-shooting? Especially when they're in big thick mobs'. The same man found grim humour in killing: 'One of the boys took a flying leap over the vines and landed bayonet first on a Fritz – did that square-head scream?'[91]

Men in artillery units often took a more detached view of killing. An artilleryman described an action in Greece thus: 'I ... had a good view of one troop shelling Jerry and through my glasses there were dead everywhere, the old 2/2nd sure did a couple of good days work that hectic two days'.[92] Such attitudes had less to do with hatred of Germans than with professional pride and the callousness imposed by war.

Another artilleryman recalled that as the opening barrage rained down on the Germans at Alamein, he and his comrades said 'Serves the bastard right!' Retribution was what they wanted.[93] Other Australians nursed a desire for revenge, like the soldier who wrote home that on Crete the men had been 'out to get square' for the Greek campaign.[94] After Tobruk and Ed Duda, a veteran reflected: 'I came through it O.K. ... others of our mates were not so fortunate but they can rest assured we squared up for them against the Huns'.[95] More often the urge to kill Germans hit men suddenly, for instance in a bayonet charge.[96] Vengeance could be a tremendous motivating force, as described in this instance at Tobruk: 'Lt. Jess, I am sorry to say was killed in this action and the four men who saw him fall were so mad with rage they charged the German who had shot him and each one bayoneted him at the same time'.[97] Or in this incident at El Alamein: 'When our Sergeant, Harold L– was killed, George B– went off his head + charged the German post single handed, killing them right + left'.[98] Not surprisingly, instances of treacherous behaviour from surrendering Germans brought swift death. The 2/1st Battalion history records that when one of three surrendering Germans on Crete shot and wounded an officer, all three were shot dead in 'the heat of the moment'.[99] The 2/43rd history tells of two Germans at Tobruk meeting an identical fate after one shot an Australian in the stomach.[100] In another incident there, a wider group of German prisoners suffered the revenge: 'One Jerry walking up too [sic] surrender pulled a firearm and shot one of our men. Our lads then turned a machine gun on a no. of the prisoners killing many'.[101]

Sometimes the killing of surrendering Germans was attributable not to rage or the heat of battle, but to the cold calculation of higher authorities who deemed it militarily necessary to take no prisoners. After the Cretan campaign, two Australians from the 2/11th Battalion wrote that they had been ordered to take no prisoners on the first day of the German landings – an order that, they imply, was obeyed.[102] German participants in this campaign had certainly been told by their superiors that Australians took no prisoners, or at least no wounded ones.[103] Sergeant Lovegrove recorded that the instructions to a fighting patrol at the commencement of the Alamein battle were 'to kill and destroy all we can – then withdraw bringing our wounded and THREE ONLY enemy prisoners, required for interrogation'.[104]

Another soldier spoke of authorities taking a different approach, reprimanding an NCO on hearing that his platoon was not taking prisoners. The platoon had earlier watched as several of its wounded men were killed when trying to surrender to Germans, who had beckoned them in then laughed at their deaths. After this incident, on 22 July at Tel el Eisa, the platoon resolved to take no prisoners for a month. Those they took in the period that followed were bayoneted or shot through the shoulder.[105]

Crawford told of an incident during the battle of El Alamein when, as he tried to help a badly wounded and truculent German, a passing signaller told him to 'finish the bastard off', and offered to do it himself. Crawford's reply was: 'What if you were wounded. Wouldn't you expect to be looked after?' The signaller, claiming to 'know the German bastards', asserted that Germans didn't look after Australian wounded [a claim contradicted by much evidence], and warned that Crawford would be stabbed if he turned his back to his prisoner. The tale ended with the German reaching for a pistol, only to be overpowered by Crawford. Crawford chose not to shoot his captive, but sometimes men like the signaller did so.[106] Other German prisoners were shot while trying to escape or for no apparent reason, but the shooting of Germans who wanted to surrender was unusual.[107]

More common was rough handling of prisoners. This could be very menacing, as in the instance of a sniper captured at Tobruk: 'the boy that brought him [in] used to kick his behind every few yards to make him hurry. He will no doubt get his *just deserts* later'.[108]

The haughty behaviour of some German prisoners occasionally attracted physical violence. Jack Craig reported the story of a German officer who told his escort, a wounded Australian, at Tel el Eisa: 'Rommell [sic] has something up his sleeve for you Aussies', to which the reply was '+ I've got something up my sleeve for you "Hun bastard"' – followed by a flooring punch.[109] When a German officer spat at the feet of an Australian who gestured for him to pick up a stretcher during the fighting at Alamein, he received a bayonet prod in the backside.[110] Lieutenant-Colonel Burrows of the 2/13th Battalion was so enraged by the insolence of a captured German tank officer at Er Regima that Burrows 'spun him around like a top and fetched him an almighty kick in his rear'.[111] Early in the siege of Tobruk, an Australian captain whose men had just repulsed a German attack met the captured enemy leader. The 'arrogance' of this German led the infuriated captain to exclaim 'You killed one of my men' and to punch the German. Remorseful, the captain then apologised.[112]

Physical abuse of captured Germans was uncommon, and most Australians clearly thought it wrong. Nowland recorded that when a fighting patrol at Tobruk captured twenty Germans, and for some unknown reason one of the Australians machine-gunned the group, 'the rest of the patrol condemned the action of the gunner as *treacherous and brutal*'.[113] Treachery and brutality were qualities ascribed to Germans at their worst, and were ones Australians prided themselves on not having. Australian treatment of German prisoners of war was generally humane.

CHAPTER THREE

THE GERMANS

MUTUAL RESPECT

German souvenirs were very highly prized by Australians: indeed, a British author in the Middle East weekly publication *Parade* asserted in August 1942 that 'Were the Aussie to define his war aims, he probably would reply in terms of Zeiss Field-glasses and Leica cameras, with a Luger thrown in'.[1] The article featured the illustrious 2/48th Battalion, which that same month came under considerable pressure from senior officers to return a watch taken from a German officer. A poem published in the battalion's newsletter angrily criticised the way the authorities overemphasised such a trivial incident. Presumably some Australians treated German prisoners roughly and unfairly in the search for treasures, but this does not feature in soldiers' writings.[2]

A 2/17th Battalion veteran, Charles Lemaire, told of an incident at El Alamein, where a member of his platoon souvenired a cap from a captured German soldier. According to Lemaire, 'the cap was the symbol of a proud corps which had waged war meticulously observing the rules of the Geneva Convention', and one of his mates, a lance-corporal, 'abruptly and with a bit of asperity' demanded that his compatriot return the cap. The Australian sheepishly complied.[3] The Australians treated German POWs fairly not only because of high-mindedness, but also because Australians believed that they themselves would be treated humanely if captured by Germans. One ex-soldier recalling his capture in Libya said 'We were well treated, exactly as I would have treated a prisoner of war'.[4] News of such treatment got

41

back to the troops: Private Butler recorded in Tobruk that all prisoners who had been captured and escaped said that they had been treated very well by the Germans.[5]

This mutual respect and good treatment extended to other areas. Both sides were impressed by the others' concern for enemy dead. The soldier quoted in Chapter 2, regarding the humorous and enjoyable aspects of killing German paratroops on Crete, also wrote of giving many of the paratroops 'a burial of an honourable soldier killed in action (which they were)'.[6] He remarked that the German prisoners were very complimentary about this practice.[7] An Australian private at Tel el Eisa wrote home about searching for two missing men of his battalion, and finding that the Germans had buried them, with everything they had taken into the attack still on them – including watches and money. In contrast, the Germans buried a nearby Italian merely by throwing a few handfuls of dirt over him.[8] An Australian captain killed at Ruin Ridge is known to have been buried by the Germans, who inscribed on a rough cross 'A gallant Australian officer'.[9] Immediately after the battle of El Alamein, Corporal Douglas Lade was in a group from the 9th Divisional Cavalry Regiment given the task of excavating and reburying Australian bodies buried by Germans during the battle. They were most impressed by the fact that the Germans placed his personal belongings on the chest of each corpse.[10] However, there were exceptions to this chivalrous treatment of enemy dead. For example, Lieutenant Crawford recalled seeing an Australian at Alamein lift a dead German machine-gunner by the ankles and kick him in the behind, saying 'many's the time you've scared the tripe out of me'. This was unusual, however.[11]

The wounded were also well treated by both sides. Sergeant Symington recorded that when ten wounded Germans were brought into his post at Tobruk, 'We treated them like our own and gave them water, Bovril and cigarettes and best of attention'.[12] Private Cyril Martin of the 2/24th Battalion both gave and received such treatment on 22–23 July 1942, at Tel el Eisa. He had captured a teenage German early in the action, then was himself wounded in the leg. The German helped him and another Australian to cover, and was then wounded in the arm. As bullets flew overhead, Martin and the German bandaged each other's wounds. After a bombardment, Martin gave the German a drink and told him to leave. Shortly afterwards, German soldiers approached and captured Martin. They took him to a German aid post, where the young German was being treated. A German doctor spoke to the boy, who said that Martin had behaved well.[13]

Australian wounded could generally expect the Germans to treat them as humanely as they treated the Germans. At Retimo and at El Alamein, captured German doctors could be found helping the wounded.[14] Private Butler reported an incident during bitter fighting at Tobruk:

> One [enemy] post was approached, just in the act of drawing the pin [on a grenade] when a voice was heard from Sangar 'Stay Aussie – we have two wounded Diggers here'. [Two Australians were found with their wounds dressed by a German] … the Aussies said the Germans had shot them and then went out at great personal risk, brought them in and dressed their wounds, gave them hot coffee and then sent for their medical assistance. Thank God there is chivalry.[15]

Germans clearly felt similar emotions, as shown in an incident recalled by an Australian stretcher-bearer who met one at Alamein: 'A German officer I raked out of a trench from among some bodies, and patched up, also seemed grateful. Shook hands! That would have made Adolf smile'.[16] After the battle, an Australian brigade reported that throughout the operations the Red Cross appeared to be 'scrupulously respected' by the enemy wherever it was recognised.[17] In all campaigns, Germans rarely fired on Australian stretcher-bearers, or vehicles and buildings clearly displaying the Red Cross, though as we have seen there were exceptions that horrified the Australians.[18] As the official historian said, the Geneva Convention 'was seldom dishonoured in the desert war' and gave a good example in one part of the El Alamein fighting, where 'there were several notable instances of chivalrous consideration given by the Germans in withholding fire from men helping or carrying wounded'.[19] On the same day at El Alamein, an Australian corporal recorded some Australian goodwill: 'the Germans brought in an Ambulance close to our lines to take away their dead and wounded. We granted them a truce'.[20]

There were other truces to allow removal of dead and wounded from the battlefield. The most famous of these occurred in the Tobruk Salient on 3 August 1941, when both sides sent vehicles out into no man's land to recover men killed and wounded in the 2/43rd Battalion's costly counterattack of the previous night.[21] The Germans brought

drinks and medical help, and even made part of one minefield safe so
that a wounded Australian could be removed.[22] A participant wrote that
while the medical work was going on:

> men of both armies stood up under an astonished sun. The
> absolute stillness almost tinkled with tension ... It was the more
> incredible in contrast with the fury of the night ... The truce was
> as if two armoured combatants had paused and raised their
> visors, and for a moment one had glimpsed the human faces
> behind the steel.[23]

The concept of the knight raises the question of whether the term
'chivalry' might be applied to the war between Australians and
Germans in the North African desert. Soldiers contemplated the issue
during the conflict. A German tank officer outside Tobruk wrote in his
diary in April that the desert fighting was different from the fighting in
Europe. He concluded: 'If the struggle were not so brutal, so entirely
without rules, one would be inclined to think of the romantic idea of a
knight's tourney'.[24] The Australians in Tobruk knew of this description
and in their writings appear to feel the same qualification about a term
that, on the face of it, seems appropriate.[25] In one book, a veteran
pointed out that 'there was *an element* of chivalry on both sides';
another said 'there was *some* chivalry in the Desert War'.[26] The truces
that provide evidence of chivalry were very fragile; for example, after
the truce expired around noon on 3 August, twelve incendiary bombs
and more than 140 artillery shells fell on the 2/43rd Battalion during
the afternoon.[27] The 2/28th Battalion, which had also suffered heavy
casualties in an attack on the night of 3 August, was not even granted
a truce.[28]

Other tacit agreements existed where Germans faced Australians,
but the motive was less one of humanity than of mutual convenience.
Fearnside claimed that on one occasion in the Tobruk Salient, his
reconnaissance patrol did not fire on an enemy working party because
that was outside the patrol's prescribed role and would have precipi-
tated a firefight all over the Salient.[29] This was probably not a common
practice. In the Salient there certainly were unofficial truces, which
lasted for several hours after sunset and permitted ration parties to
bring forward rations by an otherwise-perilous route.[30] Similar 'gentle-
men's agreements' existed in the Alamein area in the months before the
great battle, as Private Jack Craig's diary entry explained: 'A few shells

over every now + again to let us know Jerry is still awake, but early breakfast + just on dusk for tea both sides call a truce + let each other have their hot meal in peace, but after it's over all start up again'.[31]

Such truces could be easily violated – the day after Craig wrote that, shells landed near him and his assembled mates near the dugout kitchen at breakfast-time.[32] The truce was not literally 'called' and contact in such agreements was very indirect, largely by the presence or absence of shells; inevitable, in a campaign where the front lines were so far apart. Between August and mid October 1942, the forward Axis and Australian lines were rarely less than a kilometre apart, and sometimes they were more than 4 kilometres apart. Men in these lines had a sense of what the enemy was doing and how similar their activities were to their own, as shown in these two comments:

> Occasionally a M[ortar] shell whines overhead but neither I nor my opp no in the Jerry post bother to fire and so we just watch and wait and read eat and smoke.[33]

> Things are very quiet, and all we do all day is sit on a ridge and look at Jerry and he sits on another ridge a couple of thousand yards away and looks at us. Very occasionally he may send over a shell or a mortar or two, but they never go near anything, and then our blokes send a double issue back, and … it keeps him quiet.[34]

However, in other places the lines were much closer (generally 140–550 metres in the Salient, for example), and the sides occasionally made more individual contact.

Any evidence of contact is invaluable for our examination of Australian attitudes to the Germans. However, that evidence is very rare, because there was great danger in making one's presence, and thus location, known to the enemy during operations. Visual communication with Germans in the desert front lines usually took the form of humorous bravado accompanying the exchange of bullets. Private Nowland recorded a mischievous form of assessment used by Australians who were regularly fired on by an artillery piece in Tobruk:

> Doesn't this take the prize for impudence? – no wonder the Jerry gunner is vindictive; some of our chaps this morning were marking his shots in the conventional range system; giving him magpies, washouts etc. for wide shots; as far as I know he did not score a bull.[35]

Three months later, an Australian in Tobruk was overheard saying: 'I had a shot at Jerry but the bastards waved me a washout'.[36] Private Clothier saw two Germans simply waving to him from 500 yards away at Tobruk.[37] A German recalled that on one occasion during the siege, a machine gun had opened fire on an Australian-occupied trench just forward of him when, to the astonishment of the German troops, 'one Australian coolly seated himself on the parapet and waved his broad-brimmed hat at us as a stream of machine-gun bullets splashed by'. Such foolhardiness was not unique, but it was unusual.[38] Fearnside stated that a policy of brashly and provocatively walking about in daylight in the Salient was soon discontinued.[39] He also recorded a rare occasion where soldiers called out so as to be heard by the enemy. He recalled Germans in the Salient singing provocatively 'We're Going to Hang our Washing on the Siegfried Line' and then 'erupting into bouts of ironic cheering and shouted abuse'.[40] Private Rudder of the 2/15th reported contact that turned menacing in Tobruk. Germans singing this song, as well as 'Silent Night' and 'Tipperary', managed thereby to entice Australians to sit up on the parapet, then opened fire with machine guns on the unsuspecting listeners.[41] During a two-hour armistice after a failed German attack on Tobruk, both sides climbed out of their trenches to stretch their legs. An Australian participant wrote: 'we were sitting upon the parapet, waving and singing out to them. There were shouts of "Heil Hitler." "How would a pint of beer go, mate?" "Have another go to-night," and many other remarks not so complimentary'.[42]

These scenes, which are rather reminiscent of incidents in World War I, suggest that there was little chance to know much about the enemy from the front line. Meeting enemy prisoners, or becoming a prisoner, was the best way to do that. Crawford recorded a conversation he had with a wounded German as they stood on the Alamein battlefield. The German asserted that 'All men are brothers', and that instead of trying to kill each other Australians and Germans should meet in each other's countries and fish together. 'You started it all – you invaded Poland', said Crawford. The conversation continued:

'Yes, and England invaded Iran and Iraq.'
'Only to defend ourselves.'
'We took Poland only to defend ourselves too.'

'You bombed England', said the now-angry Australian, to which the German had no answer beyond a doubtful murmur that German pilots bombed only military objectives. Crawford told the German that if he were sent as a prisoner to Australia there was much that he would like, and that many German settlers there had made 'good, hard-working citizens'. As the German boarded an ambulance, he wished the Australian good luck.[43] The atmosphere was one of mutual respect of soldiering abilities, a fellow-feeling of being men, and mistrust of the other as an enemy.

A fleeting but frightening exchange is described in the reminiscences of Edgar Randolph, a private in the 2/7th Field Ambulance on Crete.[44] Soon after the first paratroops landed near Retimo, on 20 May, a group of about thirty Germans captured the medical post where Randolph was working. The paratroops' officer ordered all Australians who could walk, except the doctors, to line up. He explained that all the men in the line would be shot, as the Germans could not look after prisoners while they fought their way through to their comrades. The senior Australian officer, Major Bert Palandri, asserted that all the Australians in the line were needed to look after those already wounded, and any German wounded who came in. At this 'The German went berserk and, cocking his Luger, shoved it under the Major's chin and screamed that they had already been told by their Intelligence that Australians tortured and killed all German wounded they captured'.[45] Palandri said loudly that German wounded were already arriving, but that he would allow them to die if his men were harmed. Palandri's death seemed imminent when shots over the horizon heralded the arrival of an Australian stretcher-party with a wounded German. The German officer discovered that the casualty had been well treated, apologised to Palandri and allowed the Australians to live. The incident gives an inkling of the ruthlessness demonstrated by Germans on the Russian front and in northwest Europe, where of course they did not meet Australians. This meeting with a desperate group of Germans, all of whom were reportedly killed fighting Australian infantry soon afterward, was atypical. More common was the mood described by another Australian when he and his comrades surrendered at Retimo: 'The atmosphere was reminiscent of the end of a hard-fought football match, when the opposing sides are friendly, but not too friendly'.

In World War I, Australians had also used sporting metaphors to describe war, but there had been nothing 'friendly' about their attitude to their opponents. Indeed they had nurtured a great hatred for Germans.[46] Was that the case in World War II? Butler met a batman in

Tobruk whose solution to the world's problems was 'to machine gun all the kids in Germany', as 'they're the ... who grow up and in twenty years become soldiers'.[47] Butler did not agree, and most Australians did not seem to concern themselves with such issues. However, when Private Nowland told his companions in Tobruk that he felt sorry for the Germans, given what their previous generation had suffered, he found himself in an argument, particularly with a Jew. He concluded that both Germans and Australians were 'ignorant, superstitious, docile sheep', thus suggesting that political issues were not very important to most Australians of his acquaintance.[48]

Some Australians developed hatred, particularly those who suffered defeat in Greece and Crete. An infantry corporal recently evacuated from Greece wrote home: 'we developed a real hate for the Hun which has done some of us a lot of good'.[49] Another veteran of the campaign said 'What I saw these German pilots do to these Greek villages has made me hate all Germans'.[50] Ironically, the division that went to those campaigns did not fight the Germans again. News of incidents such as bombing of hospitals created rage, as did the killing of comrades and the realisation among the 9th Division that the German advance in the desert in mid 1942 would prevent the division from returning to Australia that year.[51] However, such anger generally did not last, and was not constantly near the surface. Australian hatred, where it existed, was nothing compared to that of other nations.

This surely owed something to the fact that the Germans were not threatening Australian territory and civilians in the way they did the land and people of Australia's allies.[52] When Polish troops came to Tobruk, the depth of their hatred of Germans surprised Australians.[53] Lieutenant Gill, who wrote that he hated the Germans despite their brilliance, later modified his attitude as he focused his anger on Japan after it entered the war. He wrote home: 'I've always felt a sort of sportsmanlike enmity towards Jerry and the Iti, but this is different. *Now I know how the English hate the Germans*'.[54] The Japanese were to him what the Germans were to the English. At Ruweisat Ridge in July 1942, a group of Australian infantrymen observed an English officer in a truck halt and call out to a nearby German prisoner: 'How do you like being captured, Hun?' When the German replied 'How did you like Dunkirk?', the Australians' response was not anger but laughter. One of them simply advised: 'Better be quiet, Jerry'.[55]

Australians found it hard to work up hatred for the Germans; it came best through anger that rose in combat. A regimental historian noted perceptively that, against Germans and Italians, Australian hatred was 'so dependent on the heat of battle that it was not hatred at all'.[56] Another veteran reflected that although Australians had a preconception that the only good German was a dead one, they found it hard to maintain any feeling of enmity. He asserted that many of the best men in the AIF had German names and were from German stock, and that this 'makes us wonder'.[57] As shown above, some Australians were callous where the enemy was concerned, especially when they had vengeance on their mind. A Tobruk veteran recalled that when a platoon section leader was shot dead by Germans pretending to be Indians, 'hate ... sprang into every man's heart' and a few minutes later the platoon gunned down two Germans approaching with their hands raised.[58] Even when vengeful, however, Australians were often restrained by their humanity. Fearnside recounted a poignant story on this point. Immediately after the successful attack on the German positions at Ed Duda he was told that his brother, a fellow member of the 2/13th, had died of wounds. On learning soon after that there was a wounded German 50 metres behind the Australian position, Fearnside went to kill him with a souvenired pistol:

> An eye for an eye, a tooth for a tooth. He was wounded and alone and he would die in a strange and unfamiliar place ... He lay in a fold of the rocky slope of the ridge. He couldn't have been more than 18 years of age and even in the poor light I could see that his hair was red, the same as the bandages wrapped around his legs ... His face was pale, devoid of blood, which seemed to be draining out of his legs, and he looked frightened. He moved before I did, raising his hand in a half salute. '*Wasser, bitte, kamerad!*' he whispered. I hesitated, impulsively looking around to see if there were any witness to my guilt. Then I gave him a drink of water and went back up the ridge, angry and confused, the unused Biretta cold in my hand.[59]

In the aftermath of battle, Australians often expressed pity for their enemy. As prisoners arrived towards the end of the Alamein battle, a private admitted in his diary: 'You find yourself at times with a little sympathy for the enemy that is surrendering a lot of them just kids you might say, some of them a fine type of soldier, that is the German, but nevertheless famished and frightened'.[60] After leading his platoon in a raid on German positions at Alamein, Gordon Combe wrote that he had 'thanked God for our delivery and prayed for the enemy'.[61] Another committed Christian, Sergeant Longhurst, showed compassion when, in the aftermath of fighting for which he was decorated, he bandaged one of the Germans he had wounded.[62] There was also pity for those who did not survive. Allan Jones recounted that as he and his comrades toured the battlefield after Alamein, they were so moved by the pathetic sight of some of the German dead that they buried them. Jones was particularly embarrassed for one poor man, 'swollen indecently in death', who lay with his trousers around his ankles.[63] A more complex set of feelings emerged in a comment by Lieutenant Hirst, an anti-tank gunner, at the end of the Alamein battle. He wrote to his wife of seeing lines of captured Germans:

> Lots of the prisoners are boys of sixteen and seventeen years and it is tragic to realise that they have been trained from birth to such a grisly role. Two days ago they were shelling us mercilessly with the most vicious guns in the world, one in particular, his 88 m.m. almost got me three times in one day. Today they are marching back into our lines, beaten. One Jerry Major complained that our artillery barrages were inhuman – I'll say no more.[64]

Hirst obviously felt sorry for the German boys in that they were products and in a sense victims of an aggressive system but, like so many Australians who had been on the receiving end of German technology, he had limited sympathy for German complaints about Allied artillery.

Australians sometimes empathised with Germans about artillery bombardments, particularly at Alamein.[65] One veteran wrote that even when German troops advanced on his position at Tel el Eisa, the sickening sight of the courageous attackers' bodies being thrown into the air by artillery fire aroused sympathy in the hardened viewers.[66] Men who professed joy at killing them could still write of the 'poor bloody huns'.[67] Sergeant Symington 'couldn't help but think the position could just as easily be reversed', as he tended wounded Germans in Tobruk.[68] In such cases, Germans were regarded as fellow humans.

That this was not always so was not necessarily due to callousness or stupidity. Germans were largely an abstraction, rarely met even by soldiers who were in the front line against them for a long time. Moreover, they were 'Huns', a name that denied its bearers human

With the possible exception of tanks, the most feared German weapon faced by Australians was the 88 mm dual-purpose gun. They took many photographs of destroyed or captured examples of this weapon. (Donor: David Pearson)

This photograph, taken near Tel el Eisa in July or August 1942, was simply captioned 'Dead Jerry'. The man who took it later felt some remorse at doing so. (Donor: H.A. Hill)

At Tel el Eisa in July 1942, a captured German officer talks to an Australian officer of the 9th Division. The German had become separated from his men during an artillery barrage, and surrendered when his pistol jammed. Mutual respect was generally shown during such discussions. (AWM 041951)

In July 1942, Australian and German wounded lie in a tent at the 2/11th Australian Field Ambulance near El Alamein. The original caption said that 'the man sitting up in the foreground is a Nazi' but in circumstances such as this, political differences tend to be forgotten. (AWM 024620)

An Australian soldier bringing in wounded Vichy French prisoners from the front line, in July 1941. (IWM E4120)

Vichy French prisoners carry the wounded Lieutenant A.R. Cutler towards safety and treatment in Syria. Shells can be seen exploding in the background. (AWM 128440)

attributes. One wonders whether the term had any meaning, when men wrote diary entries such as this: 'One hun badly dazed walked over and gave himself up. He asked for medical aid. Hun ambulance very busy this morning'.[69]

Grappling with Germans was largely about grappling with war. In the Tel el Eisa area on 14 July 1942, Private Tom Derrick (who later won the DCM and VC) was in no man's land when he:

> saw my most horrible sight, a German, one of a Tank crew had crawled some 20x [yards] from the tank, badly wounded about the body, and one leg blown completely away from just below the knee, he apparently had a ton of courage, as attempts had been made to place a tornquay [sic] above the knee. – One wonders if there is a rightful solution to all this horridness, + can get no intelligent answer.[70]

Yet the following day, after courageously blowing up an enemy vehicle with a 'sticky' grenade, he recorded '[I] was blown to the ground, but had the satisfaction of hearing a dozen or more Huns screaming'.[71] The explanation of this apparent contradiction does not lie simply in Derrick's exceptional nature as a fighter. Butler was also aware of a paradox, when he noted the 'shout of joy' that greeted the destruction of a German mortar position:

> How strange that men jump for joy at such a scene, but weighing it all up it is not the fall of men we rejoice in, but the excellent marksmanship; not death for death's sake but so many less to oppose us, so many less to give us trouble as we remain cooped up and down to earth in our foul hole.[72]

The 'joy' came from celebrating prowess and the fact that the chance of survival had increased, but it required that the men being blown up be considered only as abstractions. Attitudes changed when Australians could see flesh and blood – dead or alive – right before them. An Australian recalled that in the battle of Alamein he helped to carry his wounded CO to the 'Blockhouse', where Australian and captured German doctors worked together to save lives. Afterwards, he and his mates shared their food with some German prisoners. 'Though we could not converse', he said, 'all had a happy time and I remember considering how damned silly it was to be fighting coves just like ourselves'.[73] Of course, in many ways Germans were not 'just like' Australians, but they did share many attributes and Germans were the enemy with whom Australians felt the greatest affinity. They were also the enemy to whom Australians showed the greatest respect. Australian attitudes to Germans were complex, but an appealing and uplifting Australian interpretation of the Germans' place in their war, and indeed of war in general, is Combe's reflection on an incident at the height of the Alamein raid on 7–8 July 1942:

> a young German soldier cowered before me on his knees and clutched at my leg with both hands, pleading 'Camarade, camarade'. Minutes before we were unseen strangers striving to kill one another, now we met, man to man, in the glow of the explosions and the eerie light of the parachute flares and there was no way then that we could have harmed one another. I disarmed him and he was taken back as a prisoner. At this moment, one came face to face with the paradox of a war, at one and the same time both righteous and inhuman.[74]

Of course, not all Australians would have been so compassionate or philosophical in such circumstances. But many elements of this description – strangers becoming identifiable men, potential killers becoming 'camarades', the Australian triumphant in the man-to-man meeting, war against the Germans as wrong but also right – apply to many other scenes between Germans and Australians.

GERMAN ATTITUDES TO AUSTRALIANS

The way in which Australians hoped the Germans regarded them was confidently stated as fact by a dashing young infantry lieutenant, Tas Gill, in July 1942, just over a week before he was killed in action: 'When the German meets Aussies he seems to go half crazy with fear – he shouts with a high pitched, hoarse, almost hysterical voice, while our lads are perhaps brewing a cup of tea, + joking + laughing'.[75] Although this picture seems rather exaggerated, especially in its depiction of the nonchalant Australians, there does appear to be some truth in it as a description of Gill's experience. He was a member of the 2/48th Battalion, which was Australia's most decorated battalion in World War II. When Gill's company commander wrote a letter of condolence to Gill's family, he mentioned that Gill had, just before writing his last letter, been involved in an attack which had taken a hundred prisoners. Gill had led his platoon in driving off enemy tank and infantry attacks at Tel el Eisa, thus 'routing the Hun, who was in a panic'.[76] An Australian in another battalion reported that a German prisoner he met in July 1942 claimed that the Australians had gone home, but that English troops were continuing to *dress up as Australians to frighten us*.[77]

Of course, Germans were not always 'half crazy with fear' when they met Australians. They had some successes against Australians in the desert and routed them in Greece and Crete. Even in Crete, however, Australians won accolades from the Germans they faced. A corporal who escaped German captivity on the island reported that the officer commanding the German paratroop guards had told Lieutenant-Colonel Walker that Walker's battalion, the 2/7th, were the best troops that his men had so far encountered.[78] A private in another Australian battalion on Crete talked at length to the German paratroopers his unit had taken prisoner. He painted a picture of men very impressed by their captors' martial prowess. The prisoners reportedly stated that whereas the enemy had fled previous German landings, the Australians stayed to fight.[79] Those were not the only Germans who suffered their first defeat at Australian hands. As we have seen, German infantry–tank attacks at Tobruk were foiled, with Australian infantry playing the key role.[80]

One of the most thoughtful historians of the Afrika Korps argued that the Australian 9th Division was 'the first good enemy the Germans had fought at length since the invasion of Poland', and that fighting such a capable opponent at Tobruk did much to create *esprit de corps* in the Germans there.[81] Whether or not this is true, the Australians facing the Afrika Korps certainly won a great reputation among the Germans. Early in the siege, the German commander, Rommel, described Australians as 'fighting magnificently' and showing 'remarkable tenacity'.[82] In a well-known passage he described a group of fifty or sixty Australian prisoners as 'immensely big and powerful men, who without question represented an élite formation of the British Empire, a fact that was also evident in battle'. It is interesting to note that in the same passage Rommel spoke of 'British' troops involved in counter-attacks in early May as having low morale. Those men were almost certainly Australians.[83] One of Rommel's British biographers said that while the 'Desert Fox' rated Australians highly as individual fighters, he considered them 'inclined to get out of hand'.[84] One wonders on what Rommel based that observation. Perhaps stories about Australian treatment of prisoners led him to say that Australians were rough, especially in their treatment of Italians. However, he defined that roughness as amusing, and not reflecting a 'bad heart'.[85] The Desert Fox reportedly said that although he would have liked a division of Australians under him, they would be no easy command. He supposedly rated New Zealanders as his finest opponents.[86]

A German infantry major described the Australians at Tobruk as 'extraordinarily tough fighters', superior to the Germans in their use of camouflage and individual weapons, particularly as snipers.[87] German accounts of the desert campaigns describe the Australians at Tobruk as 'crack shots', delivering 'incredibly accurate' fire.[88] A mortally wounded German infantryman brought into Private Butler's post in the fortress in May said, as he smoked a cigarette, 'Thank you, you very good fighters'.[89] Another German captured at Tobruk in vicious hand-to-hand fighting during the first German attacks on the 2/17th Battalion, told one of his wounded captors, 'Australian soldiers are very brave', to which an Australian in the party replied 'My bloody oath'.[90]

The Tobruk experience won Australians a reputation with the Germans. Heinz Werner Schmidt recalled that as a young German officer wounded by enemy fire at Sidi Rezegh in November 1941, he 'could not help thinking of Australian bayonets'.[91] When Australians returned to the desert in 1942, their arrival was noted. In first mentioning their role in the 1942 campaign, Rommel wrote of knowing them 'only too well' from Tobruk.[92] General von Mellenthin, a senior officer in the Afrika Korps, wrote that in the Tel el Eisa fighting the Australians 'showed that they were the same redoubtable opponents we had met in the first siege of Tobruk'.[93] By the time of the October fighting at Alamein, the Australian reputation was firmly established. On being told that his captors were Australian, a young German lying on a stretcher at the aid post of the 2/17th Battalion reportedly smiled and said 'Ah, good. Australian, Tobruk, Tel el Eisa'. The man's smile briefly turned to terror when an Australian with a bayonet reached forward into his coat, but changed again when he saw that the Australian had given him a packet of cigarettes.[94]

British historian Ronald Lewin said of the Australians and Germans at Tobruk that no two forces could have been more different: the Australians with their 'independent, self-sufficient, iconoclastic' outlook, and the Germans with their 'inbred sense of order, discipline and hierarchical values'.[95] While it is easy to overemphasise the independence and self-sufficiency of Australian troops, who were after all part of a highly sophisticated twentieth-century army, Lewin's contrast has much merit. A good example of that contrast lies in two accounts of Australian and German officers' comments to their prisoners in Tobruk. On 14 April, a group of shocked and bloodied German troops were ordered by their senior officer to lay down their arms, and according to a German account an Australian major stepped forward to accept their surrender. He offered a cigarette to the German officer and said nonchalantly, 'Good fight'.[96] This informality is in sharp contrast to the spirit behind a comment reportedly shouted two weeks later by a German major at a captured Australian lieutenant: 'Take that cigarette out of your mouth while you are talking to a German officer'.[97]

Another example of the contrast between formality and informality appeared in Private Hackshaw's account of a conversation with German prisoners on Crete. He told of a German captain, supposedly only eighteen years old, who asked the identity of an Australian whose shooting had disrupted a German attack and led to his capture. When the Australian came forward, the German supposedly said '"my word that was good shooting, it was 600 yds. and you were inflicting casualties". Onions [the Australian] looked at his rifle and said "yes, 600 is what I've got her on"'.[98] That contrast – of technical knowledge and professionalism on the German side, and gifted amateurishness on the Australian – is surely what Lewin described. Crawford told of a similarly illuminating incident in the Alamein line, where one of a group of German prisoners marching to the rear pointed to a Bren carrier and drew a laugh from his compatriots by saying: 'Panzer, Australian big tank'. The gunner of the carrier rose and replied, 'A bit too good for you, though, Jerry'.[99]

An Australian captured at Tobruk in August 1941 recalled how interested the German troops were in seeing the 'mad Aussies' up close, and one Australian source suggested that Rommel told his officers before Alamein that 'all Anzacs are animals'.[100] In his description of the conversation with German prisoners on Crete, Hackshaw also mentioned the Germans' surprise that Australians were not 'savages', but instead had much in common with their opponents.[101] It appears that at least some Germans had believed propaganda about Australians.

Hackshaw noted another recurrent theme of German conversations with Australians: the men in his captivity 'could not understand
why we volunteered to fight for these bastard English'.[102] This theme
also emerged when the roles of captor and captive were reversed: the
German officer quoted above as forbidding smoking was said to have
pointed to the 'Australia' titles on the shoulder of another prisoner and
shouted: 'you are an Australian and you come all the way over here to
fight for the filthy, bloody English!'[103]

German propaganda portrayed the Australians and their pre-
dominantly English comrades in Tobruk as 'rats', but the men there
took it as a badge of pride.[104] When German propaganda later tried
to exploit a point of tension between Australians and British by dub-
bing the 9th Division the '20 000 thieves', the intended slur was also
upended and taken as a compliment.[105]

German soldiers in the field tended to treat their enemy with more
respect. An Australian private at Tel el Eisa described a German soldier
who came forward in a vain attempt to negotiate an Australian surrender as 'a storm trooper, one of Germany's crack regt Hitler always
uses where Aust tps are'.[106] The writer may have been trying to boost
his own image here, but he was also expressing a belief that the
Germans considered the Australians the best and felt they needed to
oppose Australians with their best.

In the desert this was close to the truth. Early in October 1942, a
German intelligence summary concluded that the Australians were, in
attack, the best British troops on the Alamein front.[107] At about the
same time, General Stumme, the acting commander of the German–
Italian *Panzerarmee*, told a conference of commanders that Australians
were the enemy's 'best troops'.[108] Similarly, in 1983 a German writer
claimed that the General Staff of *Panzerarmee Afrika* had considered
Australian soldiers 'the best we found in Africa'.[109] Another comment
which validated the Australian belief that Germans regarded them as
their best opponent came from the same Alamein front. Many members
of the 9th Division had gone into the campaign believing that it had
thwarted their return to Australia, in the wake of the 7th and 6th
Divisions:

> One of the boys was going crook at a hun prisoner. he said to him
> – you b– we w[oul]d have been home now only for you and the
> hun s[ai]d 'yes and we w[oul]d have been in Alexandria only for
> you b–' so it cut both ways.[110]

This story sounds apocryphal, like many about conversations between enemies. Yet there can be no doubt that conflicts between Australians and Germans 'cut both ways': each side lost heavily at the other's hands. Despite some distrust and exceptions to the rule, Australians and Germans also generally respected each other as among their toughest opponents.

CHAPTER FOUR

THE VICHY FRENCH

The Vichy French were unusual opponents. In World War I, France had been the location of battles crucial to the birth of the Australian military tradition, and French and Australian troops had fought side by side. They did so again in World War II: the Free French fought with the Australians in Syria. However, in Syria, the French (the Vichy French) were also the Australians' main opponents, and although they fought the Australians for little more than a month the 'Frogs' or 'Froggies' inflicted about 1600 casualties on them.

Australians of the 7th Division joined a force sent into Syria in June 1941 to remove the threat of its use as a German base. The force had to subjugate the sizeable Vichy French forces then occupying Syria. The Australian 7th Division included its 21st and 25th Brigades, as well as a mixture of divisional troops such as 2/3rd and 2/5th Battalions and the 6th and 9th Division Cavalry.[1] The only other sizeable contingents were two understrength brigades of Free French, and an Indian brigade.[2] The Australians were the single largest national contingent in the initial invasion force. Opposing them were the equivalent of two and a half strong divisions of Vichy French.[3] The French forces consisted of 35 000 regulars, 8000 of them French and the remainder Senegalese, Algerian, Tunisian and Moroccan.[4]

The preliminaries to the campaign were in many ways farcical. Senior Allied commanders, such as de Gaulle, expected a walkover. He suggested that while the invaders advanced they should shout to the

58

Vichy French occupiers to get out of the way so that the attackers could get at the Germans![5] However, although senior officers of the Vichy French army in Syria may have disliked the Germans they were also no friends of the British, whom they believed to have deserted France in 1940 and whose motives in the Levant they distrusted.[6]

In line with de Gaulle's suggestion, the Australians were informed that French-speaking officers and Free French officers would be attached to their units on a scale of one per battalion: these men would use white flags and megaphones to approach the 'enemy' and persuade them to surrender and join de Gaulle and the Free French. This proposal met the scorn of Australian commanders. They doubted the efficacy of such ruses, even though they had very little hard information about their opponents. As late as eleven days before the invasion began the Australians had only a few copies of an intelligence handbook on the enemy force and the ground it was defending. Indeed, the only maps of the rugged country ahead were not the desirable 1:25000 or 1:50000 scales, but an almost-useless 1:200000. The defenders, on the other hand, knew the ground well and apparently also knew that an attack was imminent. In the weeks before the invasion they reinforced Syria's frontier posts and created new defences behind the lines.[7]

When the invasion began on 8 June there was at least one incident in which the notion of 'persuasion before force' was vindicated. On the morning of 8 June, men of the 2/14th Battalion fired on a group of Spahis. When the Spahis surrendered, their sergeant-major asked why they had been forced, rather than invited, to surrender. It emerged that he was a member of a French rugby team that had played the AIF at Beirut in 1940, and he expected that some friendly feeling had been created.[8] Further north, an Australian battery commander was present when the forces negotiated rather than fought for much of the first day. He described the day as reminiscent of Gilbert and Sullivan, considering 'the parleys, the envoys, and the flags of truce going to and fro'.[9]

However, there was nothing comical about the reception afforded to most Australians who encountered the Vichy French forces that day. The 2/31st Battalion, for example, did not find the French defence to be the brittle shell expected. When a Free French officer accompanying the battalion went into the town of Khirbe a few kilometres from the border, the Frenchman in command there refused to surrender; indeed, his troops shot and wounded the envoy as he marched back towards the Australians.[10] The latter, by then edging forward across open fields, were also hit by artillery, mortars and machine guns fired from Khirbe, where the defenders had held their fire until it was likely to do most damage.[11] The attackers' safety was not helped by the fact that they had been ordered to wear their slouch hats, rather than helmets.[12]

Troops of the 2/16th Battalion had also been ordered to go into the battle wearing hats instead of helmets, in the mistaken belief that the Vichy French would not fire on them. Although some enemies they encountered on the first day offered little resistance, others inflicted casualties on the battalion, and after the first day the 2/16th wore their helmets.[13]

In the campaign that followed, culminating in a ceasefire on 12 July, Australians generally had to fight the Vichy French troops in their path. The invasion force advanced in three columns, two of which were composed of Australians. One column, the 21st Brigade, moved along the narrow coastal plain towards Beirut. A central column, the 25th Brigade, marched along mountain roads towards the Beirut–Damascus road. Beirut was the goal of the third (Indian and Free French) column. The Australians on the coast encountered strong resistance from the outset, but within a week took the city of Sidon, some 65 kilometres from the frontier. By that time, the central column had been unable to advance beyond Merdjayoun, just a few kilometres from the border, though a large detachment had reached Jezzine, due east of Sidon. On 15 June the Vichy French launched a counterattack. Using infantry, tanks and artillery, they recaptured Merdjayoun. The counterattack lost impetus within a few days, but disrupted Allied plans. Australian troops helped the Free French to capture Damascus on 21 June, then advanced along the Damascus–Beirut road. Other units of the 7th Division worked with British reinforcements to recapture Merdjayoun.

On 26 June, the 7th Division's effort was concentrated on capturing Beirut, the centre of Vichy French government. It involved four days of heavy fighting to cross the Damour River to the south, and combat in mountainous country to the east. Weary and threatened from two directions, the Vichy French sought an armistice. They had suffered some 2350 wounded and missing, and about 1000 killed. The Australians lost 416 killed and 1136 wounded.[14]

The realisation that the enemy was serious about making war struck Private Wright of the 2/16th during the battalion's advance on

Sidon on 13 June. In a letter home, he described the heavy enemy fire: 'they were dropping shells + mortors [sic] amongst us I was always wondering when one was going to lob under me the cobber would say when one lobbed rather close, "By Jesus the bastards are dinkum" '.[15]

To many of the Australian infantry, the enemy's determination to fight may not have been a great surprise. The historian of the 2/33rd, William Crooks, was surely right to note that to most of the men whose Syrian campaign was their first, the finer points of the potentially friendly status of the Vichy French were insignificant. The Vichy French were simply 'the enemy' to men going into their first battle, as nearly all men of the 21st and 25th Brigades were.[16] Crooks said that the soldiers of the 2/33rd went into the action with a spirit of adventure and excitement that was never recaptured in later campaigns.[17] An enemy was vital to adventure, and men were not very interested in any grey area.

Crooks argued, however, that 'deep down' most Australian soldiers felt distaste for French who were on the same side as the Germans.[18] This was almost certainly true. At the very least, most would have agreed with Signalman Neeman's description of them as 'misguided Frenchmen'.[19] The official historian recorded an instance where an Australian and a French officer discussed the moral and political issues of the campaign. Captain Murchison, of the 2/3rd Battalion, came upon a French artillery officer on Jebel Mazar on 27 June. As Murchison pointed his pistol, the Frenchman said 'Ha! There are no Germans here'. When the Australian replied 'What of it?', the Frenchman asked 'Then why are you fighting?' Murchison rather glibly and perhaps automatically replied with 'Because I've been told to', then hesitated and added 'Because you are collaborating with the Huns'. The official historian reported that there followed a 'brisk argument on the rights and wrongs of the campaign'.[20]

A former Australian infantryman said in his reminiscences that, in hindsight, the situation of the Vichy French, particularly their relationship to the Free French, was more complicated than Australians had realised. He conceded that Australians had perhaps often been 'too harsh in our criticism and too unbending in our outlook' towards the Vichy French.[21]

At the time, however, the harsh criticism was directed not only at the abstract beliefs of those French but also at their behaviour on the battlefield. As with their other enemies, Australians branded Vichy

French fighting methods 'treacherous'. One veteran of the campaign admitted that perhaps soldiers in all armies resort to treachery 'when things get tough'.[22] Perhaps, too, soldiers are very willing to ascribe treachery to the enemy; deep distrust, with racial overtones, was certainly a feature of Australians' attitudes to their opponents. On the other hand, the belief that Vichy French troops used underhand methods was not entirely unfounded. One example occurred during an attack near Ibeles Saki by the 2/33rd Battalion on 23 June. An Australian private was reportedly shepherding a group of Algerian prisoners into a trench when one lowered his arms, grabbed a rifle and shot the Australian dead. An infuriated Australian officer clubbed the Algerian to death with his pistol.[23] On an earlier occasion, another officer of that battalion, and some of his men, were convinced that Vichy French troops disguised in peasant clothes had fired on them from behind.[24] On 24 June, the battalion found further evidence to deepen their hostility, when they discovered the bodies of civilians executed by the Vichy French before 15 June.[25]

Other battalions saw behaviour that was likely to anger any soldier. On 6 July, as the 2/27th Battalion advanced near El Boum, a strong Vichy French post manned by Senegalese and French Foreign Legionnaires inflicted casualties on the Australians. After the Australians fired mortars on the Vichy French positions, a white flag was raised. The Australians moved towards it, only to suffer casualties when a machine gun recommenced firing. Although the machine-gunners later said that a French officer had threatened them with death if they did not fire, it probably did little to temper the victors' annoyance.[26] Two days later, the 2/27th had further reason to curse their opponents. On the night of 7–8 July Australians managed to get within 165 metres of Vichy French positions on a feature called Hill 560. They expected that, with daylight, the Vichy French would realise that their position was hopeless, and surrender. This expectation seemed to be confirmed when a Vichy French officer came forward to parley but, as one diarist said, 'it was a ruse enabling the enemy to crawl to a ledge overlooking our men and launch a dastardly attack with grenades, the officer disappearing behind a rock'.[27]

There are other such stories about Vichy French officers. One concerned an officer who was among a group of thirty French prisoners taken by Australian carrier-borne troops on 10 June. He allegedly shot and wounded one of his captors, and was machine-gunned by an

Australian lieutenant.[28] A 2/5th Battalion veteran told of another Vichy French officer who, near the end of the campaign, was 'stitched to the wall' after surrendering and then reaching for his pistol; he also recalled a colonel who, on being captured at En Naame, 'called on the Geneva Convention + anything else he could think of to evade capture'. The officer's arrogant behaviour was met with very colourful Australian slang and an insistence that he raise his hands immediately.[29] The arrogance of the Vichy French also struck H.D. Steward, who said that a German member of the French Foreign Legion captured by the 2/16th Battalion 'was so arrogant that we longed to kick him in the pants'.[30] Indeed, he went so far as to assert that the man was lucky the Geneva Convention protected prisoners.

On other occasions, though, Australians showed compassion towards Vichy French opponents. On 16 June a company of the 2/31st Battalion finished the day exhausted, hungry and cold on the slopes of Hill 1277, near Jezzine – yet their stretcher-bearers went forward to collect enemy wounded who had been hit in an attack against the hill. And although the Australians were very short of water, they shared what they had with Vichy French casualties.[31]

On the same day, at Jezzine, an Australian in a field ambulance described a chivalrous gesture by the Vichy French. Private Hughes noted in his diary that as the advanced dressing station in which he was working withdrew from the battle area, Vichy French held their fire until the medical men were clear.[32] Vichy forces respected the Red Cross flag.[33] Similarly, when parties of men from the 2/14th Battalion scoured wheatfields near Jezzine for dead and wounded comrades on 24–25 June, Vichy French permitted one stretcher-party to go within 30 metres of a machine-gun muzzle without opening fire. They later fired on them, at long range.[34]

French chivalry also features in the story of perhaps the most famous Australian soldier in Syria, Lieutenant Cutler, VC. After a series of heroic actions, Cutler was severely wounded in the leg and, unknown to his compatriots, lay in an isolated position for some hours. He was found by a group of Vichy French prisoners whom he had captured earlier that day. On their own initiative, these men carried him to a position where he could be treated. According to Cutler's regiment's history, the men were motivated by the fact that Cutler had earlier spared their lives: if so, this story illustrates the capacity of both sides for compassionate action.[35] Perhaps the most touching story of

Vichy French chivalry concerns an incident on 6 July. A Vichy French doctor and two stretcher-bearers were captured during intense fighting, but continued to risk their lives collecting wounded of both sides under fire. Indeed, one of the bearers was killed trying to rescue a wounded Australian.[36]

In a reported conversation between wounded men from the three AIF divisions in the Middle East in November 1941, each boasted about the achievements of his division. When the 7th Division man mentioned his formation's successes in Syria, the others replied 'You've only met French civvies and wogs, you don't know what fighting is yet'.[37] We have no record of the 7th Division man's reply, but can imagine that he may well have disputed that assertion. Certainly, some Australians who fought in Syria stated that the Vichy French – at least some of them – were 'dinkum' soldiers. The French artillery was recognised as efficient.[38] It was so accurate in the early stages of the advance that espionage was suspected.[39] A more likely reason for the impressiveness of French gunnery was that many targets had been carefully ranged before the attacking force arrived.[40] Given that the Australians lacked effective anti-tank weapons, French armoured units probably also impressed Australians on the uncomfortable occasions when they met.[41]

In *Active Service*, the 'Christmas' book published by the Australian War Memorial in 1941, an account of the Syrian campaign gave considerable praise to the Vichy French, who were said to have fought in a manner suited to a professional army. In terms that were surely never used for Australians' other wartime opponents, the account said of the Vichy French that, contrary to the expectation that they had no heart for a fight, their 'professional honour and the tradition of their service summoned up an instinctive effort'.[42] The report specified that the comment applied to officers and 'white men'.[43] Official praise for the Vichy French effort continued after the war. The Australian official history of the conflict described the Vichy French as 'not a half-hearted enemy', but 'resolute and skilful troops'.[44] The campaign had received virtually no publicity when it was on, or even soon afterwards, and one wonders whether the official praise of a beaten enemy was intended to make the Australian victors of a little-known campaign look more impressive.

We can perhaps see such thinking in the official wartime report on the Syrian campaign, written by the senior Australian intelligence officer in the Middle East, Lieutenant-Colonel Rogers. He described the Vichy French as 'a skilful, brave and stubborn enemy who knew every inch of the country, made excellent use of his arms, and boldly counter-attacked whenever the situation warranted it'. He drew the conclusion that 'It is remarkable that we, with the weaker force and lacking tanks and other modern weapons should have reduced the enemy to the point of surrender' in just five weeks.[45]

A similar point arises in an anecdote published much later, in the 2/33rd Battalion history. On 11 June, a lone Spahi (probably an Algerian cavalryman) had his horse shot from under him in an Australian ambush. He rose from the ground, and advanced with his hands up. When an Australian prodded him and motioned him towards the rear, the Spahi grabbed his rifle and a mad wrestle ensued. A second Australian pushed off the Spahi, who 'bravely' got up and grabbed at the second man's rifle, only to be shot dead.[46] The 2/33rd historian concluded that this 'foolish but brave enemy soldier … was a sample of the type of enemy we fought'.[47] If the word 'sample' is supposed to mean 'typical example', it is not really accurate. Most French soldiers did not fight to the death. Grim scenarios such as this were far more likely among other opponents.

Indeed, in describing their Vichy French opponents, Australians were in a dilemma. They wanted to show that the Vichy French were worthy opponents, but they also wished to demonstrate that the 'Froggies' were inferior to Australians. Also, as with all opponents, there was great diversity of ability and willingness within the Vichy French army, and this is reflected in Australian accounts. The odd circumstances of the Syrian campaign also made for a slightly comical element in many comments.

A story recounted by Cam Bennett is enlightening. He told of the 2/5th Battalion CO, Lieutenant-Colonel King, sitting on a high ridge with his RMO and adjutant, to observe a forthcoming attack by one of his companies. King began describing the work of a platoon on the plain below:

> 'See them spread out. Good control, very nice. A very nice set-up, Doc. By God, that platoon's well trained … a grand bit of work'. When the doctor credited the good work to Captain Rowell, of the 2/5th, King replied: 'Christ, I'm not talking about Rowell. I'm talking about the bloody French. Call that attack off, Jim, or some one will get killed. We're up against professionals here, Doc, real bloody professionals'.[48]

Although this story acknowledged the skill of the French, it did so in humorous terms: such a story would never be told of the Germans or Japanese, whose most efficient soldiers were truly worrying. Stories like this were a backhanded compliment.

There was also a double-edged aspect to the commonest praise of the Vichy French, their good use of terrain. The Syrian campaign was one of the most physically demanding campaigns of the war for Australians. Many of the battlefields were in what one soldier called 'terrible country', and the mountainous terrain was sometimes said to be worse than at Gallipoli.[49] The Vichy French made good use of this terrain in important battles at Merdjayoun, Jezzine and Damour. They also sited forts in tactically important positions. Five months after the campaign, an experienced 6th Division officer wrote of one such position: 'On viewing the Vichy defenses on Khiam, it beats me how our fellows took the Fort'.[50] A 9th Division infantryman who looked over positions near the border early in 1942 said 'It's marvellous they ever drove the Froggies out of the pill boxes they have stuck in among the hills'.[51] Even when the Vichy French defences were not grand, they could be impressive. A private of the 2/2nd Pioneers wrote of the fighting for the approaches to Damour: 'Rather astounding to me how our boys succeeded in hunting the froggies out of dense banna [banana] groves as after we succeeded in dislodging them we were amazed at the preparations they had made against us'.[52]

Of course, to Australians the logical inference was that the Vichy French had been good enough to make and site their defences, but not good enough to hold them. The private did not mention an earlier 2/2nd Pioneer attack against strong French defences, at Merdjayoun, which had been repulsed with heavy losses.[53]

After overcoming the Litani River defences near the border, Australians of the 2/16th Battalion were more direct in their criticism of the enemy, saying that if the Vichy French had been attacking Australians who held those positions, they would never have broken through.[54] In another account of the fight for the Litani defences, a private in the 2/16th said of the Vichy French that 'They wouldn't face the bayonet' – a standard criticism of Australia's enemies.[55] With some justification, a veteran of the 2/5th stated that the Vichy French were good at using artillery and mortars to defend positions, but 'once our troops got to the eyeball to eyeball stage, they rather lost interest, either moving back quickly or surrendering'.[56] Some Australians also felt that the Vichy French, especially the West Africans, were not enthusiastic or able night-fighters.[57]

An account by a participant in several events involving C Company of the 2/14th Battalion on 28 June illustrated several features of Australian attitudes to the Vichy French. Private Matt Power was one of three men sent on a patrol to Mount Kharat, a dominating feature near Jezzine. On a fog-bound terrace below the summit, the bayonet-wielding patrol captured four terrified Senegalese in a listening post. After handing them to a following platoon, the three Australians continued towards the peak. A few metres from the summit, they emerged from the fog to see seven Frenchmen, silhouetted against the sky with their hands raised. The Vichy French section commander had a sudden change of heart, and was shot dead as he sought to cock a machine gun. The three Australians had captured a significant piece of ground yet, soon afterwards, another member of the company was shot dead on the terrace below. For five hours, the lone Vichy French corporal who had killed him held at bay all Australians, defending the terrace and a large sweep of the mountain. Eventually he was killed by machine-gun and mortar fire.

What conclusions did Power and his comrades draw from these events? Power's description makes it clear that most of the Vichy French encountered were interested in 'their own survival, rather than the honour of the French Colonial Army'. There were two exceptions: the section commander, whose actions were marked by 'treachery'; and the corporal, who had all the attributes of a good Australian: 'a disciplined and determined soldier, using his skill and the natural features of a forbidding landscape'. He, however, like the Spahi, was 'a lone brave Frenchman'. His more numerous comrades had not only been cowardly, but had 'astonished' the patrol by failing to use their tactically superior position to wipe out the Australians.[58]

This one small sequence of events displayed the different features of the Vichy French to Australian eyes: sometimes treacherous, sometimes brave, generally not as good as Australians. Contrary to official accounts, most Vichy French were probably perceived as not having their heart in the fight, or at least not as much as the Germans or Japanese.

On 17 June, two platoons of the 2/31st Battalion launched a surprise attack against a body of Vichy French troops estimated at a battalion in size. According to one account of preliminaries to the action, the Australians' officer, Captain Robson, said 'there are thirty of us, each of us is as good as ten of them, so the odds are even'.[59] Although the ten-to-one comment was obviously intended to improve morale immediately prior to battle, it was a typical Australian estimate of their enemies. Bennett compared the Vichy French unfavourably to another enemy, the Japanese. He was essentially dismissive of the Vichy French, commenting that 'the French were not hated and we did not worry too much about them. When confronted at one stage by some of the Foreign Legion, we considered them about average and cleaned them up smoothly and efficiently'.[60] This comment typified the laconic self-confidence – one could say arrogance – of Australian troops towards the Vichy French, and towards their enemies generally.

During the major Vichy French counterattack, Signalman Tom Neeman witnessed a bloody battle in which determined French attackers were 'mown down' by Australian small arms and heavy machine-gun fire. He commented that the Australian mortars were 'blasting them to blazes, poor cows, but just serves them right, teach them a lesson'.[61] Australians could see the humanity of their opponents and pity their fate, but ultimately the Vichy French were enemies trying to kill Australians for a dubious cause: if they died, it 'served them right'.

The official history implied that any animosity towards the Vichy French was forgotten after the campaign. Indeed, Long went so far as to say that the Australians 'had a warm fellow feeling for the Vichyites'.[62] As evidence, he cited the fact that at the armistice General Lavarack, an Australian, noted the 'very gallant defence' put up by the Vichy French, who deserved 'all possible courtesy and consideration'.[63] However, there is other evidence that soldiers of less exalted rank were not as respectful of the Vichy French. The 2/33rd Battalion history cited a story about a member who was captured during the campaign. In accordance with the terms of the armistice, he was returned to his unit and 'spoke long and splenetically of the cruel and vicious treatment' given to prisoners. It is difficult to imagine the existence of 'warm fellow feeling' among his acquaintances in the 2/33rd Battalion.[64] It is also difficult to imagine Australians maintaining warm feelings towards the 85 per cent of the Vichy French army who chose to be repatriated to France in August and September rather than join the Free French and thus align themselves with the Allied cause.[65]

VICHY FRENCH ATTITUDES TO AUSTRALIANS

The Australian official history holds that Vichy French commanders stated after the Syrian campaign that Australian troops were more rugged than their own. Long quoted a report in which a French colonel supposedly said of Australians: 'Until I saw your infantry crossing the Damour River and fighting in the mountains, I believed the Foreign Legion were the toughest troops in the world'.[66] The 2/14th Battalion history stated that a Foreign Legion colonel was alleged to have said: 'I thought the Foreign Legion were the best soldiers in the world till I saw the Australians coming over the hills at Damour'.[67] Although the Foreign Legionnaires on the Vichy side of the campaign did most of their fighting against Australians, this story has an apocryphal ring about it.[68] More credible is the reported description, by a French prisoner taken near Khirbe, of Australians as 'mad but brave'.[69]

We can also believe a story concerning a group of Vichy French troops who, with mortars and machine guns sited in a large house, held up part of the Australian advance across the Litani River early in the campaign. After six 25-pounders of the 2/4th Field Regiment sent several direct hits through the roof of the house, forty Vichy French surrendered; they reportedly expressed 'great fear and respect for the Australian guns'.[70] There were numerous other occasions where the Vichy French praised the accuracy of Australian artillery.[71] Doubtless Vichy French defenders in many other places were also impressed by the ability of Australian attackers, although several Vichy French comments were less than respectful of Australian infantry. One Vichy French soldier who wrote of the effectiveness of the Australian guns, said also: 'The infantry do not worry us much'.[72] Vichy French reports early in the campaign criticised Australians for a supposed unwillingness to exploit successful attacks, and a tendency to retreat in disorder if attacks failed. The reports were unspecific: there were some such cases, but Australian failures were far less common than their successes in Syria.[73]

Perhaps the best published testimony to Vichy French respect for Australian opponents was a statement made twenty-five years after the campaign. In December 1966, Gerry O'Day, the Australian Defence Attaché in Laos, was making a farewell visit to the head of the French Military Mission, General Jacques Leport. It emerged that they had been on opposite sides in the fighting on Feature 1284, near Jezzine, on

23–24 June 1941. O'Day had been a lieutenant in the 2/14th Battalion, Leport a company commander in the Foreign Legion. Leport recalled that an Australian *'bon soldat'* had been wounded in front of the Vichy French defences; after dying in the aid post he had been buried with legionnaires. Leport opined that in his long career, for 'courage and endurance the Australian infantrymen of 23rd/24th June 41 were incomparable'.[74] Leport was doubtless too diplomatic to say whether he and his Vichy compatriots had thought the Australian presence in Syria justified, but his tribute to the Australians' fighting prowess was clearly genuine.

PART II

WAR IN THE PACIFIC

CHAPTER FIVE

THE JAPANESE

MOST ENCOUNTERED, MOST HATED

Australian soldiers had more nick-names for the Japanese than for any other opponent: 'Nips' and 'Japs' were both very common terms, but there were also 'Nippon' or 'the Nippon', 'Sons of Nippon', 'Merv', 'Claude', 'the angry man' or 'the angry Jap', 'Tojo', 'Hap the Jap', 'Hashi tashi', 'pongs', 'pongo', 'slant-eyes', 'shinto', 'Japan man' and names with references to the word 'honourable', such as 'Hon Jap'. This plethora of names reflected the fact that the Japanese were the main opponent of the Australian army in World War II. They killed more than twice as many Australians in battle as the other enemies combined.[1] More than three times as many Australians were captured by the Japanese than by the other enemies, and thirty times more Australians died as prisoners of war of the Japanese than as prisoners of European opponents.[2] Far more Australians fought the Japanese than fought European enemies, and Japanese were the only antagonist faced by men in the CMF and in the 8th Division. Of the other three AIF divisions, all but the 9th spent far more time campaigning against the Japanese than against any other opponent.

The first of the campaigns was in Malaya where, in their initial contact on 14 January 1942, Australians of the 27th Brigade inflicted great casualties in an ambush at Gemas. Six Japanese tanks were knocked out in another action the following day, but enemy pressure forced the Australians to withdraw. This was the story of the Australian campaign in Malaya: local successes, in which heavy casualties were

73

often inflicted on the Japanese, followed by a withdrawal forced by Japanese strength or outflanking manoeuvres. There was particularly heavy fighting at Bakri, in western Malaya. On 18 January 1942 eight Japanese tanks were knocked out there by Australian anti-tank gunners, but by the end of the month surviving Australian forces had retreated to Singapore Island.

Japanese aerial superiority was pronounced, and bombardment from aircraft and artillery preceded the Japanese invasion of Singapore, on 8 February. The main thrust of their attack was against the Australian 22nd Brigade, defending a very long stretch of the island in the narrowest part of the straits. Though the Australians resisted, they were unable to prevent the Japanese landings. The following night, Japanese overcame the 27th Brigade defenders in the causeway sector. Over succeeding days the defenders' perimeter narrowed, and on 15 February they surrendered. About 15 000 Australians were among the 133 000 Allied troops who were captured.[3] In the Malayan campaign, 1789 Australians were killed and 1306 wounded.[4]

The Japanese also inflicted heavy defeats on Australians elsewhere early in 1942. On 23 January they landed on New Britain, and overwhelmed the small garrison in a day. On 30 January another Japanese force landed on Ambon, and by 3 February all the Australian defenders of the island had surrendered or been killed in fighting or massacres, or were trying to escape. On 20 February, the day after a major air raid on Darwin, Japanese amphibious units and paratroops invaded Dutch Timor. The main Australian force surrendered on 23 February, though for another year some survivors, and the 2/2nd Independent Company, harassed the Japanese from bases in Portuguese Timor. On 28 February, Japanese forces landed in Java. By 8 March the defending forces, including two experienced battalions from the Middle East, had surrendered unconditionally.

In July 1942, New Guinea became the setting for struggles between Japanese and Australians. After landing at Buna and Gona, on the Papuan north coast, Japanese forces set out to cross the Owen Stanley mountains and capture Port Moresby. They had initial successes, but were halted by Australian forces at Ioribaiwa Ridge in September. Led by 7th and 6th Division troops, the Australians forced the Japanese back along the Kokoda Track.

The Japanese strategy for the conquest of Papua included the capture of Milne Bay, a natural harbour and airbase on the island's eastern tip. In August 1942, a Japanese Special Naval Landing Force came ashore there, but in several days of vicious fighting with the 7th (militia) Brigade and the 18th (AIF) Brigade it was defeated and forced to withdraw by sea. It was the first defeat the Japanese had suffered on land. The Australians were joined by Americans in the campaign to force the Japanese out of Papua, by shifting them from formidable defences on the north coast at Buna, Gona and Sanananda. Organised Japanese resistance to the Australians and Americans in Papua ended on 23 January 1943. Unprecedented numbers of Australians participated in the Kokoda and Buna–Gona–Sanananda fighting: the 7th Division, one brigade of the 6th, and six CMF (militia) battalions. The campaign was an extraordinarily demanding one, partly because of the appalling conditions but also because of the skill and tenacity of the Japanese, who never again fought the Australians with the same determination. In the Papuan operations, 2165 Australians were killed and 3533 wounded. The Japanese lost approximately 13 000 men.[5]

After February 1943, when the 9th Division returned to Australia from the Middle East, all Australian land forces were engaged exclusively in the South-West Pacific Area.

The Japanese still had major bases in New Guinea at Lae and Salamaua, and at the end of January 1943 they sent an overland expedition to capture the airfield at Wau. The force was blocked and defeated by the 17th Brigade. Wau soon became the headquarters of the Australian 3rd Division, which oversaw operations by AIF and CMF units to recapture Salamaua. After months of fighting in mountainous terrain, Salamaua fell to the Australians on 11 September.

Five days later Australian troops reconquered Lae, following an airborne transfer of the 7th Division to Nadzab, north-west of the town, and a major amphibious landing by the 9th Division to the east. That operation was relatively easy, but the Japanese fought harder against another amphibious landing by the 9th Division, at 'Scarlet Beach'. Nevertheless, they were unable to prevent Finschhafen falling to the 9th Division on 2 October 1943. A major Japanese counterattack towards the beachhead was halted, notably at Jivevaneng. By November the Japanese had been cleared from Sattelberg and Wareo. CMF troops took over as the Japanese went into full retreat.

The 7th Division had gone inland after the fall of Lae. They captured the airfield at Dumpu and cleared the Japanese from the Finisterre Range, before being relieved by CMF units of the 11th and

5th Divisions. These captured the port of Madang in April 1944 and reached the mouth of the Sepik River in July.

In October and November 1944, Australian soldiers relieved the American garrisons on Bougainville, at Aitape in New Guinea and on New Britain. The Japanese garrisons in these areas were virtually isolated from outside help, and their American opponents had been content to maintain a tacit truce. However, the Australian senior commanders were determined that their troops would take a more aggressive role towards the enemy.

On Bougainville, Australian CMF units had gained full control of the centre of the island by the end of the war, and separate offensives in the north and south had brought the Japanese close to defeat in those areas also.

The 6th Division had responsibility for the Aitape region. An offensive along the coast culminated in the capture of the main Japanese base, Wewak, on 11 May 1945. Inland, although a drive over the Torricelli Mountains took Maprik, the Japanese in the area were still resisting strongly when the war ended.

On New Britain, the Japanese forces far outnumbered the Australian 5th Division, but it advanced east along the north and south coasts to the neck of the Gazelle Peninsula, where from February 1945 it confined the Japanese.

The final Australian campaign of the war was fought on Borneo, which was attacked by the 7th and 9th Divisions. The first phase of the operation was an amphibious landing on the island of Tarakan, off the east coast, on 1 May 1945. The 26th Brigade conquered the island, but only after nearly two months of vicious fighting. The remainder of the 9th Division landed in North Borneo on 10 June, and overcame the rather dispirited defenders. On 1 July, the 7th Division landed in the Balikpapan region, on the island's east coast, and by 22 July had achieved all its objectives, despite determined Japanese resistance. The war ended on 15 August 1945, though at least one soldier records that his unit was fighting Japanese after that official date.[6]

A KNOWN ENEMY

So many Australians fought the Japanese that one might expect numerous soldiers to have been well-acquainted with Japanese fighting troops, and to have much more complex feelings toward them than the attitudes generally held by civilians. Yet soldiers quite often commented on how little they actually saw this enemy. An artilleryman whose regiment engaged in considerable action in Malaya and Singapore wrote in his diary after the surrender: 'Do you know that I never fired a hostile round all thru the campaign + never saw a Jap. I wasn't the only chap either'.[7] In jungle fighting on New Guinea, many soldiers did not see a live Japanese. On the Kokoda Track, Acting Sergeant Clive Edwards lamented 'one can't see a thing and certainly never claps eyes on a Jap'.[8] Three weeks into their involvement in the Owen Stanley campaign, many 25th Brigade soldiers are said to have rushed out for their first look at a live Japanese when they heard that one had been captured.[9] George Johnston argued that 75 per cent of the soldiers who had been constantly in action in that campaign had never seen the enemy, and Osmar White recorded that he had heard hundreds of men say 'You can't *see* the little bastards'.[10] Similar comments were made about other places where thick jungle and effective Japanese camouflage made it hard to see enemy forces.[11]

However, often there 'was no question of *not* seeing the enemy', as White said of conditions during the battle at Wau.[12] Battle was usually at close range in the jungle. American casualty figures in the South-West Pacific graphically illustrate this: small arms claimed nearly twice as many American lives as artillery (32 to 17 per cent); generally, across all fronts the respective rates were 19.7 and 57.5 per cent.[13] Very similar figures would apply to Australian forces. Thus, even where Australians saw no live Japanese in combat, they observed many significant traces: Japanese gunfire, dead, war debris and the operation of small-unit tactics.

The jungle that enabled soldiers to kill in close proximity also enabled them to live close together. At Gona in December 1942, a temporary stalemate left troops just 30 metres apart. General Vasey reported that the foremost Australians at Sanananda were entrenched 20–75 metres from the enemy positions. For some time in mid 1943, opposing trenches near Salamaua were close enough to permit grenade duels, and later that year periscopes – reminiscent of Gallipoli – were used to scan the 75–90 metres or less between the foremost posts in the Kankiryo Saddle–Shaggy Ridge area.[14] The outnumbered side usually withdrew before the relationship developed a semblance of permanence, and between combat both sides generally tried to avoid contact. We read of Australians whispering at Gona, and having much of their hot food thrown to them in the foremost pits at Sanananda.[15]

Australians got an impression of the Japanese from the noise they made during these lulls, and indeed on many other occasions. At Gona, Lance-Corporal Spindler wrote in his diary: 'we learn that enemy are only 35 yd forward of us, in fact we can here [sic] him talking + working on his positions. needless to say we don't sleep on guard all night'.[16] Occasionally, the two sides called to each other. Captain Ben Buckler reported that at one point during the Kokoda fighting Japanese forces had called out 'Gas, Gas', as they fired smoke. Buckler's men yelled 'suitable Australian epithets' to the Japanese, who replied 'Where are you Digger?'[17] Another veteran recalled that a feature of his first day in action, as a reinforcement to the 2/6th Battalion in 1945, was hearing each side shout obscenities at the other. Many of the Australians, mostly 'new hands', were laughing, but the 'laughter ceased abruptly and gave way to shouts of rage when 14 Platoon suffered its first casualty – one of its Middle East veterans being killed'.[18] As this example suggests, the experience of front-line contact with the Japanese enemy gave rise to a unique perspective, and in many respects an informed perspective. The 'rage' felt by those reinforcements is a key part of that image.

A HATEFUL ENEMY

Captain Gordon Combe, whose humane observations on his capture of a German at Alamein were quoted in Chapter 3, wrote home during the Finschhafen campaign that when an earth tremor shook their positions, 'everybody hoped that the earthquake would split Japan asunder'.[19] Australian soldiers commonly felt hatred for the Japanese but compassion – or at least respect – for European enemies, and they were aware of that contrast both during and after the war.[20] Whereas in the European conflict the concept of the 'good German' was ambivalent, and could mean one who fought chivalrously, the term 'good Jap' was used only in the sense applied by an infantryman in a letter from Sanananda: 'I souveneered [sic] a fountain pen from a good Jap *i.e. a dead one*'.[21] The good Japanese was equivalent to the 'good Indian' in American frontier days.[22]

Two writers have argued since 1945 that their CMF units, the 3rd and 58/59th Battalions, did not really hate the Japanese: that the enemy was regarded in 'a somewhat impersonal light'.[23] Although others probably shared that attitude, there is no doubt that the Japanese were the most hated enemy. This was obvious in Australians' greater enthusiasm for killing Japanese. 'If an Italian or German were running away, one might let him go,' wrote Gullett, 'but never a Japanese'.[24] Soldiers from other Allied armies felt the same.[25] Another perceptive 6th Division veteran argued that the Japanese brought out an instinct which was not characteristically Australian and which Australian commanders had previously been unable to awaken fully, 'the killing instinct'.[26]

In June 1943, at Lababia a company of 2/6th Battalion soldiers was surrounded by Japanese, who exerted much pressure through attacks and through eerie shouting. The Australians received assistance in the form of mortar support, and its arrival caused what one of the defenders called 'the most glorious sound of the whole fight – moans from hundreds of Japanese throats ... Cries of "Take that, you bastards" and "How do you like that?" rang out from the Australian lines'.[27] Similar pleasure in the enemy's pain sometimes occurred in descriptions of European enemies, but was unusual. Corporal Jack Craig wrote of meeting soldiers during the Lae–Finschhafen campaign who did not want to be relieved, they were so enjoying wiping out the tactically inept Japanese.[28] Again, it is just possible to imagine this happening against the Germans, but another passage in Craig's diary introduced an entirely different spirit. Below is part of his description of an action at Blucher Point in 1943:

> Japs are running out of the jungle everywhere and we start some very good shooting. Got on to one with the Bren gun trying to crawl away in the grass ... Saw one with his pack on his back walking up the track and soon everyone was stuck into him. He soon hit terra firma. Later in the day we saw his body and pushed it over the cliff into the sea.[29]

A wartime Department of Information brochure stated that at Wau 50 Japanese were 'hunted down and exterminated'.[30] The concepts of 'hunting' and 'exterminating' capture the mood of the time, which was not one of trying to bring an essentially like-minded foe to accept defeat by the rules of war, but one of seeking to annihilate an alien foe.[31] An American soldier claimed in a letter to the magazine *Yank* that 'The motto in the Southwest Pacific is "Kill the bastards"', and this rings true of Australian attitudes in that theatre.[32]

Australians often killed defenceless Japanese. Men found sleeping were shot.[33] Near Limbang, Corporal O'Brien recorded: '7 Pln. trap and do about 20 while they are eating'.[34] Another diarist wrote that a Japanese infiltrator on Tarakan had bumped into a noted boxer, who 'bashed him up. – then they shot him'.[35]

This probably seemed amusing at the time; certainly other killings struck Australians as humorous. Private Wallin was involved in the frustrating fighting in northern New Guinea in June 1945 when he noted:

> The latest joke. Last night the nips who are dug in only a few yards from Don company sang out. Come out and fight you yellow B – ds This morning Don Company did go out killing six and knocked them off two hilltops without suffering any casualties themselves.[36]

A tank commander reported cheerfully in January 1944:

> At LAKONA 'A' Sqn employed five tanks in line against a coconut plantation where they succedeed [sic] in driving 40 Japs over a cliff into the sea when the infantry did the rest by play-fully tossing hand grenades as if on a fishing expedition with dynamite.[37]

A battalion magazine praised one of its number on Tarakan as being a popular comedian with the Japanese, 'for whenever he takes his Owen [submachine gun] to a party, Nips chatter with delight, and many are heard to say "Boy, you're killing me"'.[38]

During the Finschhafen campaign, a grim joke concerned 'the wounded Jap who said to the Aussie, in a sarcastic tone, "You think you're going to be home for Christmas", to which the digger replied, "And you think you're going to hospital!"'[39] As this anecdote implied, sick or wounded Japanese were often killed on the spot.[40] Watching an attack on a nearby hill in 1945, one soldier recorded: 'I should say they are killing off any Jap wounded and making sure none are hiding in the holes'.[41] Official war artist Ivor Hele produced a drawing, dated 30 July 1943 and entitled 'Shooting Wounded Japanese, Timbered Knoll'.[42]

The killing of unarmed Japanese was common, and pressure was put on troops to take prisoners, who often proved surprisingly garrulous.[43] It is important to note that the Australian and American armies sought to persuade Japanese to surrender: there was no official policy of extermination.[44] When Japanese prisoners were dealt with according to regulations, their treatment was infinitely better than that given to Australian POWs. However, Australian footsoldiers, like their American counterparts, had little desire to take prisoners, and it often proved difficult to prevent them from killing captured Japanese before they could be interrogated. At Wau, Captain J.J. May was given the responsibility of ensuring that a prisoner was taken safely to Port Moresby. His description of the man at the airfield is evidence of widespread homicidal attitudes to the Japanese:

> prisoner is leaning against the galvanized iron front, grinning from ear to ear. He has a King Billy notice hanging from string around his neck it is cardboard and roughly printed on it is 'I am not a Jap P.O.W. I am a Korean a prisoner of the Japanese and made to be a carrier for them. I have given valuable information' signed Motan Brig [Brigadier Moten].[45]

Another officer, of the 2/3rd Battalion, recalled having a Japanese prisoner tied to him for two days to prevent the prisoner being shot by Australian troops. After being escorted back to divisional headquarters under great security the prisoner was shot dead by 'an angry cook'.[46] The infamous excuse 'shot while trying to escape' was heard from Australian soldiers who killed their charges.[47]

According to Charles Lindbergh, Australians often threw prisoners out of aircraft then said that the Japanese had committed suicide.[48] Some Japanese soldiers were almost certainly deterred from surrendering to Australians because they knew of Australian mercilessness. A similar attitude among Americans discouraged Japanese surrender to them.[49] Other reasons also dissuaded Japanese from surrendering to Australians, including warnings from Japanese headquarters that they would be tortured or even eaten if captured.[50] Corporal Jack Craig reported that at Sattelberg a Japanese prisoner 'said the forces there would have willingly surrendered in a body if they thought they would be treated as P.O.W. and not killed off hand'.[51] The idea of a large group surrender seems most unlikely, but that some individuals were frightened off is probable.

Japanese dead were not considered in the same light as German or Italian dead. Frank Legg, who was a member of the 2/48th Battalion at Alamein and became a war correspondent in the Pacific, noted while first reporting 9th Division fighting against the Japanese that the Australian attitude towards dead opponents was very different from in the desert. Whereas the common practice in North Africa had been to bury each other's dead, in the Pacific Legg soon noticed a 'strange callousness', usually expressed in jokes or contempt.[52] For example, a Japanese who lay dead on the track to Jivevaneng had a bullethole between his eyes and a note pinned to him which read: 'Don't bury this bastard, it's the best shot you'll ever see'.[53]

The disdain for enemy dead was at times expressed more actively. The commanding officer of a militia battalion on Bougainville noted in his diary after a day of action: 'Heard today in the battle "This won't hurt you" as the soldier knocked out the gold tooth of a dead Jap'.[54] Three months later, a field censorship report on Australian soldiers' mail in January 1945 complained that an 'alarmingly high number' of soldiers in the Aitape area had broken censorship instructions by discussing 'desecration of enemy dead', and gave two examples. In one letter, a writer made the comment 'Gee I had to laugh yesterday', then explained that one of his mates had produced about a dozen gold teeth extracted from Japanese corpses.[55] Another quotation in the report said: 'A couple of hard cases of the patrol kicked two gold teeth out of one skull and brought them back. Another is making a tobacco jar out of another skull'.[56] The vast majority of Australians clearly found such behaviour abhorrent,[57] but one lieutenant reported that when in November 1942 his battalion headquarters had demanded an end to the practice of extracting teeth, 'two of the nicest chaps I had freely admitted they had done it and could see no harm in it as the Japanese were dead'.[58] This suggests that the men who did that were not all 'hard cases'. There is at least one recorded instance of an Australian taking a gold tooth from a German corpse in the more 'chivalrous' atmosphere of North Africa, but the practice was obviously more common in the South-West Pacific. One could argue that greed rather than hatred was the motive, but utter contempt for the enemy was also present.[59]

Moreover, making souvenirs of skulls is malevolent and spiteful, and Australians apparently did it only to Japanese. Americans did it so commonly that passengers returning home from the Pacific were routinely asked in Hawaii whether they had any bones in their baggage.[60] Souveniring bones was a crime in both the American and Australian armies,[61] but the hatred behind such behaviour was far from being considered criminal and was not atypical. Indeed, at times it affected behaviour at higher levels. In June 1945, after the fighting

Australians and Vichy French soldiers exchange cigarettes on the outskirts of Beirut, soon after the Vichy surrender. Many of the Vichy French troops who confronted the Australians were African. (AWM 020030)

Two Australian lance-corporals with a Japanese soldier captured in the Ramu Valley, December 1943. Australians were not always so cheerful in these circumstances. (AWM 016310)

In April 1945, an emaciated Japanese is escorted to a jeep by a 6th Divison soldier near Wewak. A second soldier remains alert, with an Owen gun. (AWM 018549)

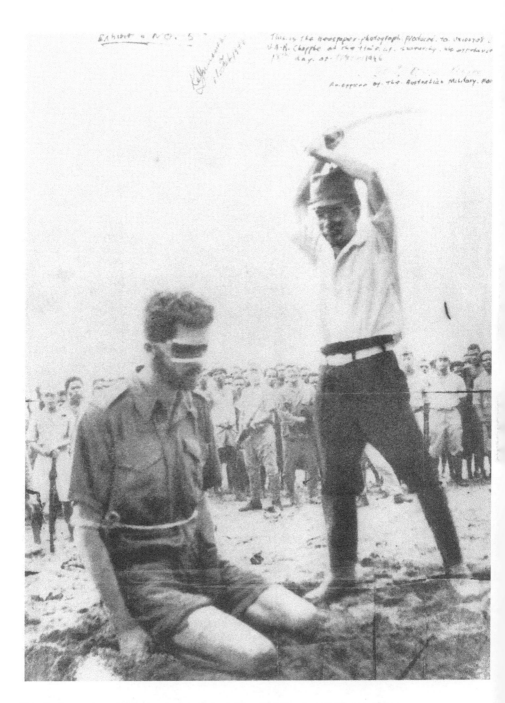

This famous photograph shows Sergeant Leonard Siffleet of 'M' Special Unit about to be beheaded by a Japanese at Aitape in October 1943. The chilling picture was discovered on the body of a dead Japanese. (AWM 101099)

**As the war proceeded, Australians marching along any New Guinea track were
increasingly likely to see dead Japanese. Here a soldier passes one of many dead
or dying Japanese left behind in the retreat from the Sanga River area, January
1944. (AWM 016448)**

had ended on Tarakan, Brigadier Whitehead ordered that a Japanese shrine built to honour Japanese who had died on the island since 1942 be burnt down to make way for an Australian war cemetery. Only prodding from corps headquarters made Australians follow the requirements of the Geneva Convention at Tarakan and build a war cemetery for Japanese dead.[62] The various reasons for Australian hatred of the Japanese are discussed in the next chapter.

CHAPTER SIX

THE JAPANESE

SOURCES OF HATE

THE YELLOW PERIL

Japan's entry into World War II made the conflict much more personal for Australian troops. Three weeks after the Japanese invasion, Private Jack Sewell wrote home from Malaya: 'the only place I am at all concerned about is Australia + everything must be done to keep these Yellow bastards well away from the place'.[1] Sewell was killed in the fighting, and the tragedy that engulfed him and thousands of other Australians in Malaya and Singapore made the threat he worried about even more terrible to Australian soldiers elsewhere. Even as the fighting raged, in mid January 1942, a signaller in the Middle East wrote home of his concern about the 'yellow horde', saying 'my thoughts are full of smashing them, before they reach what they desire'.[2] In March 1942, after news of further catastrophes in the Far East, Private John Butler noted the sombre feelings of his 9th Division comrades in Syria: 'Our thoughts are always with those boys and nurses left behind in the Malayan battles – wattle blossom, the kookaburra, and kangaroo, the tall timbers and desert places, the mountains and plains, yes this war means more to us all now'.[3]

Tied to awareness of the threat the war posed to their homeland was hatred for those who menaced it. An Australian private wrote from Papua in December 1942 that the 'vindictive hatred' Australians felt for the Japanese was largely because of fear of their 'policy of conquest brought so near to Australia'.[4] Early the following year, General

Blamey, commander of Australian forces in the South-West Pacific, tried to stir up hatred of the Japanese among veterans of the recent campaign by emphasising that the Australians were fighting to prevent the deaths of their families and the end of civilisation.[5] Three years after the war, the Japanese forces which advanced along the Kokoda Track were described by the historian and former second-in-command of the 2/14th Battalion as 'cocksure hordes' seeking for the first time in the war 'to glut their lust and savagery in the blood of a conquered white nation'.[6] The language indicates that fear of invasion gave rise to hatred. Such a fear was not new: Australians had perceived a Japanese threat to their country since at least the beginning of the century. As talk of threats to 'civilisation' and to a 'white nation' suggest, Australian soldiers' hatred of their Japanese foe was racial, or racist.[7]

RACISM

The Australians who fought the Japanese in World War II had grown up in an era when assertions of racial superiority were far more acceptable than they are today.[8] When Japan attempted, in 1919, to have a statement against racial discrimination included in the covenant of the new League of Nations, the proposal was stridently and success-fully opposed by William Morris Hughes, Prime Minister of Australia.[9] In 1941, Prime Minister John Curtin justified Australia's entry into the war against Japan in terms of the nation's commitment to maintaining the 'principle of a White Australia'.[10] Racism was written into the Defence Act which governed the composition of Australia's forces – it specifically excluded 'full-blooded' Aborigines from enlistment. Some Aborigines did join, however, and the general Australian attitude towards non-Caucasian ethnic groups was made clear in a comment about an Aboriginal soldier who played a heroic role in the Kokoda campaign: he was described by a war correspondent as establishing a reputation as 'a white man through and through'.[11]

Like Aborigines, Japanese were occasionally classified as 'black' by Australians.[12] However, far more common was the adjective 'yellow', usually as part of expressions of hatred and contempt: 'little yellow stinkers', 'dirty yellow bastards', 'bloody little yellow swine' and 'the ugly yellow "??"'.[13] The contemptuous term 'little' was also common: 'Little Dead Sons of Nippon' was the title Eric Lambert thought appropriate on a drawing of dead Japanese.[14] Added often was the term 'dirty', which was also used to describe the reality of captured Japanese positions.[15] Indeed, an Australian at Lae used it to criticise the entire nation, asserting that 'If the Jap population are as dirty as their soldiers they must be the filthiest people in the world'.[16]

In Australian eyes, the small, filthy, yellow men were racially inferior. The commander of the 7th Infantry Brigade at Milne Bay reported after the historic Australian victory there that destroying the enemy was 'a most effective way of demonstrating the superiority of the white race'.[17]

As this implies, the notions of white superiority had been challenged in earlier campaigns. The racist explanations of Australians who had scoffed at the Japanese in 1941 had to be refined after defeats in Malaya, Singapore, Java, Timor, Ambon and New Britain. The surprise they received is well summarised in the POW diary of a gunner, who said of the decision to surrender on Singapore that when 'our chaps heard this order they were like myself sick at heart *to think that we were beaten by the Nipponese*'.[18]

Singapore and other Japanese successes in early 1942 added a hysterical edge to racial hatred against them. An image of Japanese as 'supermen' or 'super-soldiers' grew up.[19] This concept was fairly widespread, but soon received a knock in battle, and indeed the feeble physical condition of many Japanese encountered in campaigns after 1942 heightened racial contempt for them. An infantryman in New Guinea wrote home dispassionately and disdainfully in February 1944: 'what Japs are left in New Guinea and New Britain will never get home to their own land. They will be wiped out. The specimens I have seen aren't much. They live in filth + those not killed will die of sickness'.[20]

A far more common image than that of supermen was that of creatures less than a man. 'Jo' Gullett concluded from his experience in the 2/6th Battalion: 'They were like clever animals with certain human characteristics, but by no means the full range, and that is how we thought of them – as animals'.[21] Australian soldiers, like Americans, often compared Japanese to animals, especially rats or vermin.[22] Officials encouraged that attitude. General Blamey told Australian troops at Port Moresby in 1942 that a Japanese was 'a subhuman beast', and at the beginning of the following year he informed soldiers that the Japanese were 'a curious race – a cross between the human being and the ape'.[23] Ninth Division soldiers preparing for the 1943 campaign were told in lectures, by officers who had campaigned in New Guinea, that a Japanese was 'merely an educated animal'.[24]

This idea helped Australians account for Japanese success in early campaigns, as it explained Japanese adaptability to primitive conditions.[25] It also excused the Australians' murderous treatment of Japanese. A normally very humane veteran of the North African desert, Private John Butler, wrote of his first brush with the Japanese: 'Out foraging this morning I came across the head of a good Jap – for he was dead – like a damned baboon he was; this is not murder killing such repulsive looking animals'.[26] He used the same epithet two months later, after a day carrying wounded Australians: 'Healthy, intelligent fellows bowled over by a vastly, inferior being, a semi-educated baboon'.[27] Descriptions of the Japanese as baboons, apes and monkeys ('hon. monkey-man' was one soldier's expression) recall white descriptions of Aborigines as 'monkeys' in the early days of Australian settlement.[28] These stereotypes emphasised white superiority, but it is interesting that the Chinese also called Japanese 'monkey people'.[29]

Expressions of physical repulsion by Australian soldiers were, however, based on experience as well as prejudice: many soldiers talked of dead or dying Japanese 'squealing' like animals, rather than screaming – or keeping quiet – like men.[30] There was also belief based on evidence in a wartime account by a medical officer in an infantry battalion. The Regimental Medical Officer wrote thoughtfully of the first Japanese he saw, casualties in the Papuan fighting around Christmas 1942:

> I do not want to sound as if I am exaggerating, writing propaganda, or trying to appeal to public taste, but I can honestly say that I have never seen anything more repulsively ugly than these cringing, shabby, ill-looking men. 'They look like animals', said the padre. Others likened them to loathsome insects or vermin.[31]

Another soldier wrote home about a Japanese captured on the Kokoda Track: 'there, between two sturdy, muddy guards, stood a greasy servile Jap prisoner, for all the world like a wizened, undergrown monkey'.[32]

In today's climate of racial sensitivity, such descriptions of 'sturdy', 'healthy', 'intelligent' Australians and 'wizened, undergrown', 'semi-educated baboons' are disturbingly reminiscent of Nazi race propaganda, although in most respects Nazism was repugnant to Australian soldiers. However, the same racist disdain appears in American writings of the time, and there is no doubt that on this issue many otherwise compassionate western soldiers held attitudes which today seem insupportable.[33] It must be remembered, however, that this was a racist age: the Japanese also harboured racist attitudes, towards whites. An English priest trying to surrender to invading Japanese forces near Gona in August 1942 was told by a Japanese officer: 'I have no time for whites'.[34]

We must not exaggerate the importance of racism in wartime Australian hatred for the Japanese. When the Australian government launched an intense hate campaign in March–April 1942, the *Sydney Morning Herald* argued that Australians needed no stimulus to fight the Japanese aggressor, and certainly not 'a torrent of cheap abuse and futile efforts in emulation of … Goebbels'.[35] The campaign was opposed by 54 per cent of Australians surveyed in a Gallup Poll.[36] Neither should we assume that Australian soldiers swallowed the propaganda fed by commanders such as Blamey: most troops did not regard him as an oracle of wisdom.

Some expressions which appeared to degrade Japanese were also used about fellow Australians who angered, frustrated or disgusted their compatriots. A diarist who wrote that in the fighting at Buna one had to be wily to compete with these 'bloody mongrels' was using a phrase that might have been used about white Australians at home in civilian life.[37] Not only Japanese, but also white Australians, could be called 'dirty rats' or 'slinking curs'.[38]

The peculiar circumstances in which Australian front-line soldiers served gave them reasons to temper their racism, or at least to suppress it on occasion. An overblown sense of martial superiority was liable to explode, with fatal consequences, in the face of a complacent individual. Realism was important: Australian training staff did not want their soldiers to feel inferior to the Japanese – a real danger in the early years – but they did want them to be level-headed about Japanese strengths. Propagandist notions were dangerous when formulating tactics. On the battlefield, being realistic about the enemy's capacities was a matter of life and death.[39]

Although the life-and-death realities that Australian soldiers faced in their confrontation with the Japanese ameliorated racism towards them in action, they also largely determined the character and intensity of Australian hatred for the Japanese. Among soldiers, the racist language of the prewar era was a convenient means of expressing feelings that owed most to the unique circumstances of the front line. The special character of Australian soldiers' hatred of the Japanese derived from the reality of the fighting rather than from the prejudices of civilian life.

LACK OF UNDERSTANDING

One might expect that contact with Japanese would bring greater comprehension of their approach to life. In fact, as Gullett said, 'there was no point of sympathy, no communication between us at all'.[40] Of course the language barrier was a factor: Japanese was an utterly alien language to Australians. Ironically, Japanese often called out in English to confuse the Australians.[41] However, Japanese actions rather than words bewildered Australians most, and in doing so intensified their racial hatred. Australian comments about the differences tended to be understated and laconic, even humorous, but they also included a sense of incomprehension.

Much of Japanese soldiers' incomprehensible behaviour could be summarised under the heading 'fanaticism', a word often used about the Japanese. As the appalling fighting at Sanananda drew to a close, Trooper Ben Love put common thoughts into written words: 'What a peculiar manner these fanatical Jap soldiers display in their utter disregard of lives – their own as well as others. They say all Jap positions are now smashed, it is just a matter of mopping up. This mopping up costs lives against these mad-men'.[42] 'Disregard of life' is to some degree necessary in all effective soldiers, especially officers who order men to take risks. Australian officers gave their share of orders to fight 'to the last man' or hold 'at all costs', but such orders are surely rarely executed by any army.[43] The Japanese army, however, approximated that ideal, and made it clear what was expected: its written code told soldiers to 'Bear in mind that duty is weightier than a mountain, while death is lighter than a feather'.[44]

It has been argued that Australian and other Allied commanders were hypocrites in praising the self-sacrifice of their own men who died for their countries, while belittling the Japanese who showed similar patriotism.[45] However, what seemed exceptional and bewildering to Australian troops was not so much the practice of self-sacrifice as the alacrity with which the Japanese embraced death. Such enthusiasm appeared bizarre and foolish to men who constantly fought their own fear of death in battle, and who knew their other enemies felt the same emotions. There was no such empathy with the Japanese. Occasionally Australian troops noted fear in their enemies: Captain Buckler commented that 'dying ones did not have a contented look and would have liked to delay their entry to heaven'.[46] However, in every campaign Australians noted the apparent willingness of Japanese to die. As early as 1933, the Director of Military Operations and Intelligence, Lieutenant-Colonel Sturdee, described Japanese as 'fanatics who like dying in battle'.[47] Although that observation was probably unknown to most Australian soldiers, they came to similar conclusions on the basis of experience.

Japanese were prepared or even willing to die in defence, to the last man. One of the features that made the Gona–Buna–Sanananda fighting so appalling was what the official historian described as 'the fixity of purpose of the Japanese for most of whom death could be the only ending'.[48] The matter-of-fact way in which they faced death is exemplified by their use at Gona of comrades' corpses as protection on the parapets, as firesteps in the slime and as a storage surface for food and ammunition.[49] Fearnside said that in the last months of the war, Japanese still defended with 'fanatical zeal' in northern New Guinea, and recalled an occasion where a lone Japanese soldier near Wewak tried to ambush a party of thirty Australians. Rather than surrender or run, he threw grenades until killed.[50] A battalion history spoke of an incident in the same campaign, where an Australian patrol attacked a defended ridge. All defenders were killed except one, who was wounded. He continued to fire at the patrol from behind a rock until a grenade 'flushed' him out: 'He then charged with a fixed bayonet and was gunned down, mortally wounded and finally killed when he was pinned to the ground with his own bayonet and rifle'.[51]

Japanese showed a willingness to die in suicidal attacks. Corporal Hackshaw witnessed this in a night raid at Brunei Bay in 1945:

> About 2 hrs. before dawn this morning all hell broke loose. A fair size party of Jap. suiciders broke through into our area … For quite a while it was pretty hot, but as it got lighter the Japs. had no chance. Quite a few completed their own destruction. I had a look at a row of them. They had all sat in the gutter and held grenades to their stomachs.[52]

The Japanese penchant for suicide was even more outlandish to Australians than their reckless attacks and 'fanatical' defence, which at least had some military rationale. There was no apparent logic to some of the suicides Australians witnessed. During the advance towards Sio, for example, Private Fred Camarsh noted an incident in which a shot had been fired and a grenade had exploded just before dawn within Australian positions. Two young Japanese were found dead:

> They had sheltered the night in [a] bunker in the heart of our perimeter with the intention of escaping in the darkness but had been foiled by the alertness of 11 Platoon's sentry. They had then stood together, face to face, placed the grenade to their chests and pulled the pin ... We wondered why they had not waited, used their grenade to better effect and then gone for a break.[53]

There are numerous similar stories of armed Japanese killing themselves for no obvious reason in the vicinity of Australian troops.[54] On Balikpapan, near the end of the war, two Japanese advanced openly towards the 2/33rd Battalion's lines: one was shot and the other committed suicide with a knife 'there and then'.[55] Many such incidents may have flowed from an official order that soldiers save a last grenade to kill themselves, but the motivation certainly remained mysterious to the Australians who witnessed the bloody outcomes.[56]

Stories of Japanese suicide in such circumstances were corroborated by other evidence, such as a captured Japanese report on the Ito Battalion's fighting near Wewak, which stated that on the night of 24 March 1945, 'everyone except the Bn Comdr and 3 committed suicide'.[57] Even Japanese commanders became concerned, as the war proceeded, that many of their men were disloyally killing themselves to escape appalling conditions or as a glorious end, rather than dying in the attempt to destroy the enemy.[58]

Suicide was often used as a means of avoiding capture, a preference which was generally alien to Australians.[59] The difficulty of capturing Japanese is illustrated by the fact that even in the very one-sided final campaigns, when Australians were more willing to take prisoners and when more Japanese surrendered than previously, the numbers of POWs were very small. In the Wewak campaign, 9000 Japanese were killed and 269 captured. On Tarakan the figures were 1540 and 252, at Balikpapan about 2000 and sixty-three, and in British Borneo 1375 and 130.[60]

On 7 October 1943, two patrols of the 2/33rd Battalion had experiences in New Guinea which showed the reality behind the low figures of Japanese prisoners. On one patrol, three men saw a Japanese soldier trying to cross a stream; they called on him to raise his hands. Instead, the Japanese unslung his rifle and made to shoot. He was killed. The other patrol, at platoon strength, found a Japanese asleep on a small knoll about 50 metres away. They crept towards him with the intention of capturing him, only to see him suddenly sit up and reach for his rifle – he was shot dead. The battalion historian who recorded these incidents concluded: 'Such was the Japanese soldier. Both of these could have been taken prisoner and the chance was offered them … Japanese [were] incapable of surrender. Harsh campaigns for all involved against the Japanese Imperial Army were inevitable'.[61]

Japanese soldiers were instructed not to allow themselves to be captured, and the primary reason for their refusal to surrender was the dishonour attached to it, not fear of Australian treatment of POWs.[62] A bemused Major Harry Dunkley illustrated the unwillingness of men who were captured:

> One cove tried to bite his tongue out when he was captured so he couldn't be questioned. Didnt quite succeed and retained quite a lump of it. Then tried poking his own eyes out but was tied up until he calmed down. Will probably recover his sight. They dont want to be prisoners – much![63]

The bitter resistance offered by some prisoners cost them their lives. Near Gona, an officer recorded the capture of three Japanese: 'They had no arms but one when trying to evade capture was kicking + scratching + bit one of our men on the chin taking a piece out. The boys had no mercy on them then + shot the lot'.[64] Similarly, at Sattelberg, a private wrote of a patrol which 'captured a Jap, bound and gagged him and tried to get him back to our lines, he proved to [sic] stubborn so they just shot him'.[65]

Other Japanese unable to avoid capture pleaded for execution, pointing to their foreheads or chests to beg for a bullet.[66] One prisoner is said to have 'wept with frustration and humiliation' when his Australian captors did not shoot the chest he bared to them. Instead the Australians made what the storyteller called 'characteristic' replies: 'Wake up to yourself you stupid bastard, you don't know when you're well off!'[67] To the Australians, only a 'stupid bastard' would want death; to be alive was to be 'well off'. The Japanese attitude was incomprehensible. Official historian Dudley McCarthy described the Japanese as 'superb in their acceptance of death *as a soldier's obligation*', but the typical Australian opponent would not have put it that way. He did not consider the Japanese as an enemy fighting the same internal struggles as Australians or Americans or Germans, but as someone with an alien world-view.[68]

Sick or badly wounded Japanese showed an amazing preference for death, as illustrated in a story about a patrol of the 22nd Battalion near Finschhafen. After killing a Japanese on a nearby track, they searched a large Japanese pillbox:

> [On] a bed in one corner ... was a heap of filthy bed-clothes, under which there was very obviously a body. These feet were very large, very white, very dirty and very still – still that is, until a big toe moved. With no further delay Lieutenant Haynes flung back the blankets to reveal a sick but angry-looking Jap.
>
> To the concern of all in the pill-box ... it was seen that the Jap was clutching a hand-grenade to his breast. All minds had but a single thought and in the flash of a second, Brens, Owens and rifles let go. In the confusion that followed and as the grenade exploded [one Australian] was wounded.
>
> Whether or not this Jap intended to use the grenade on himself or on the patrol was not known but it was apparent that neither he nor his colleague on the track had any intention of being taken prisoner.[69]

Sick or wounded Japanese often opened fire on approaching troops rather than surrender.[70] After an action at Sanananda, a battalion commander reported:

> As in many other cases enemy wounded engaged our troops and had to be shot. This may give rise in future to Jap propaganda but they are doing it so consistently that our troops cannot take any chances.[71]

The Japanese attitude to surrender partly accounts for the Australian willingness to kill vulnerable Japanese. It also helps to explain what happened when the tables were turned and the Japanese could choose whether their potential Australian captives should live or die. The cruelty towards Australians who surrendered en masse in the early campaigns, and the practice of taking virtually no prisoners in the

South-West Pacific campaigns, doubtless owed much to the Japanese idea that surrender was dishonourable.[72]

When Japanese did surrender, their subsequent behaviour seemed odd to Australians, whose military tradition involved surrendering when all was lost, but maintaining a strict silence on all but name, number and unit.[73] Japanese prisoners did not follow that international convention; instead, they frequently gave valuable information, as reported by Corporal Craig:

> Another Jap caught has dropped his 'guts' in a big way. He has informed HQ where all their troops are, who they are, Generals names + everything. He said he knows his mates will be killed after giving this information but war was war + the Australians have been very kind to me [sic] ... This information was found to be correct.

Given that Australians were committed to the idea of loyalty toward mates, it is not surprising that Craig concluded the description with the comment: 'I think they are crazy'.[74]

In 1943, Lieutenant Crawford wrote home from New Guinea of his bewilderment about the Japanese: 'I have not worked out yet whether the Nip is fanatically brave or idiotically stupid – he has very little regard for life'.[75] That disregard for life was dubbed a 'cult of death' by American historian Eric Bergerud.[76] It is a useful description, as it captures the quasi-religious quality of the Japanese attitude to death. Like a religious cult, the Japanese approach was incomprehensible to those not involved in it. Thus, Crawford and other Australians scratched their heads and wondered whether the Japanese were fanatical or stupid. Neither quality made for empathy.

Whether they considered Japanese to be idiots or fanatics, Australians agreed that they were inhumane. The inhumanity was also a source of perplexed anger. The normally restrained official history noted that the Japanese committed 'deeds of barbarism and wanton cruelty of a kind quite beyond our own understanding'.[77] In some ways inhumanity could be understood – it was an underhand means of obtaining an advantage on the battlefield – but the Japanese behaviour was at a level new even to veteran Australian soldiers. The hatred they and other Australian troops felt towards the Japanese owed more to their supposedly inhumane behaviour than to any other factor.

PERSONAL DETESTATION AND FEAR OF JAPANESE METHODS

Observation and experience heightened the hatred that Australian front-line soldiers felt for the Japanese. Racist prejudgments, an inability to understand the suicidal attitudes of Japanese and even the threat to Australia did not goad Australian soldiers in the same way as personal experience, or personal expectation based on reports from other front-line soldiers. Many Australians who campaigned against the Japanese considered their opponents evil, detestable, underhanded and frightening in their methods. Although these methods were comprehensible, aimed at winning the war, they horrified and enraged the victims' comrades.

A lieutenant recently involved in his first action against the Japanese wrote home that 'the Nip ... uses many tricks to lure our boys into his web'.[78] At Australia's jungle training school at Canungra, recruits were told that the Japanese were 'cunning little rats' who were 'full of little ruses and tricks'.[79] Some of the ruses employed by 'the wily Jap' seemed treacherous or unchivalrous to many Australians, and helped to make them such a hated enemy.[80] One example was the practice of 'playing dead' then leaping up to take Australian soldiers unaware. During the Milne Bay battle, Brigadier Field noted in his diary that enemy troops lay among their own dead, waiting until Australian soldiers passed nearby then rising and shooting at them. In response, infantrymen were ordered to 'ensure that all Japs in a recumbent position were dead': an approach likely to save Australian lives, but one which also helps explain the lack of Japanese captured.[81]

Australians were unwilling to take Japanese prisoners largely because of distrust born from bad experiences of Japanese offering to surrender then acting as human bombs by detonating concealed explosives.[82] The thousands of Australian soldiers who passed through the Australian jungle warfare school at Canungra were advised to shoot Japanese surrendering with their hands closed.[83] Frank Rolleston recalled that an apparently defenceless Japanese carrying a white cloth at Milne Bay was shot, on the grounds that 'we were not prepared to take the slightest risk with an enemy that had proved to be the limit in deception and treachery'.[84] On at least two occasions deception extended to wearing Australian uniforms or helmets.[85] Japanese also booby-trapped their own and Australian dead.[86] The Japanese proclivity for using explosive or 'dum-dum' bullets, in violation of the

Hague Convention, was also considered unchivalrous.[87] An Australian infantryman on Bougainville wrote of finding a comrade dead: 'It was not pleasant seeing one of your mates like that. The dirty yellow bastards are using dumb-dumbs now'.[88] The fact that Australian wounded, and the stretcher-bearers who carried them, could not expect immunity from enemy fire was another source of criticism, as was Japanese bombing of medical facilities.[89] A medical officer wrote about a tent 'ward' attacked by enemy aircraft in Papua:

> It had come into the direct line of a burst of machine gun fire from one of the strafing planes. When the smoke cleared the twelve lads [patients] were still in the tents, but each one was dead – killed by the deliberate sub-human fury of Tojo's men.[90]

Japanese callousness and brutality towards helpless men caused real animosity in Australians. Although unchivalrous and callous behaviour occurred among the Germans, the Japanese lifted brutality to a higher level and brutal acts were committed more often by Japanese than by any other enemy. The historian of a battalion which fought in the brief Malayan and Singapore campaigns wrote apologetically that in order to minimise repetition and keep the history to an acceptable length, 'many reported incidents of the brutality shown by Japanese troops to the wounded have been deleted'.[91] Although the Germans committed massacres of groups of Allied troops, there are no records of them massacring Australians. In the Middle East there certainly were no incidents like the one reported by a sergeant who, during the battle for Singapore, was among a group of Australian infantrymen in a depression, surrounded by Japanese:

> The Japs were standing around, deciding whether they would take them prisoner or massacre them. Some of the men were endeavouring to make a deal with the Japs and had indicated they had families at home. Suddenly the Japs opened fire and mowed them down.[92]

In a scene reminiscent of the inhumanities of the war in Russia, four Australians captured on Timor in February 1942 were pushed into a ditch beside the road, their hands tied behind their backs. They were shot and, when one moved, all four were bayoneted.[93] Approximately 150 Australian prisoners were bayoneted and shot at Tol on New Britain in February 1942.[94] The Japanese also executed 150 men at the 2/13th Australian General Hospital during the fighting on Singapore.[95]

Four mass executions at Laha on Ambon during February 1942 involved the bayoneting and beheading of 229 Australians.[96] At Parit Sulong in Malaya, 110 Australian wounded who were unable to escape following the battle at Muar were sadistically beaten, then tied together, shot, doused with petrol and burnt.[97]

As these stories suggest, not only were large numbers of Australians killed in a merciless fashion, but the brutality they suffered was frequently more horrific than in the conflict against European powers. One cannot easily imagine Germans or Italians doing what one survivor saw three Japanese doing to wounded at Singapore, namely, hacking them with swords.[98]

It is likely that details of atrocities against Australians in the Singapore and other early 1942 campaigns rarely came to the notice of Australian soldiers fighting the Japanese in New Guinea, and thus did not inform their hatred as much as they might have. The Australian wartime government, like the British and American, was unwilling to publicise material about atrocities, for fear of worsening the conditions of POWs.[99] One anti-aircraft gunner wrote home from Port Moresby in May 1942 that he had met men who had escaped from the Japanese in New Britain: he had 'seen their wounds and heard their stories and my advice to you is – if you see anything around Sydney that looks like a Jap, push him under a tram on principle'.[100] Stories about New Britain became widespread, and well-informed Australians knew of Japanese excesses against the Chinese.[101]

The immediate relevance of the issue of brutality was brought home to Australians in New Guinea by stories of Japanese atrocities at Milne Bay, a battle that involved many more Australian troops than New Britain. Most of these troops were, unlike the men in the early 1942 campaigns, neither captured nor killed, and so were able to pass on their tales to a wide audience of soldiers.[102]

They had appalling tales to tell. Private Ron Berry recorded in his diary that a member of his battalion was trapped behind Japanese lines, and on managing to rejoin his unit said that: 'he had come across some Australian bodies that had been tied to Palm trees + heads or arms + legs chopped off. Also saw native men + womens bodies hanging to trees. The woman had their breasts cut off. Some had been set fire too [sic]'.[103]

After the war numerous Australian eyewitnesses, of varied ranks, gave sworn affidavits to an inquiry into Japanese atrocities at Milne

Bay. They testified to: natives tied to trees and bayoneted, apparently for practice; natives with bayonet wounds in the rectum; a native woman spread-eagled on the ground, her hands and legs tethered, then being raped, mutilated and killed; another dead native woman tied by her arms and legs to a verandah, with seventy or more condoms lying around her; Australians with their hands tied behind their backs and their heads caved in, or long slashing wounds, or simply lying dead with no obvious wounds; six bayoneted Australians who had had their arms smashed with bullets at close range; Australians tied to trees, with bayonet wounds to the stomach, some apparently used for bayonet practice, and in one case with dried blood all around the fork of his trousers; three Australians hanging from tree branches by groundsheets which were tied around their necks – their chests were bare and covered with blood from bayonet wounds; two men in a hut, suspended from the rafters by wire or rope around their thumbs and mutilated around the head; at least two Australians who had been disembowelled; an Australian 'with his thumbs tied to his ankles behind his back, his head severed, and a bayonet pushed to the hilt in the anus'; a soldier with his head burnt off, apparently by a flamethrower; a man found with his head nearly severed, apparently from a sword stroke, and with stab wounds criss-crossing his back; a soldier with the tops of his ears cut off, his eyes removed, his hands tied in front of him, his trousers pulled down and tied to his boots by the belt, his body subjected to about twenty stab wounds, and his buttocks and genitals 'frightfully mutilated'.[104]

Michael O'Brien, a veteran of Tobruk, joined the fighting at Milne Bay having heard stories of Japanese maltreatment of wounded Australians and of natives, but believed them only after he saw evidence himself. He said that, whereas Germans and Italians would not ill-treat wounded or prisoners, 'the cursed Japs are not human'.[105]

As the war proceeded, soldiers were probably more willing to accept hearsay about Japanese atrocities: soldiers entering the Kokoda fighting a week after the Milne Bay battle knew that they could expect no mercy if wounded and caught by the Japanese.[106] The atrocities continued throughout the war. On the Kokoda Track, men of the 3rd Battalion found two bodies left by the retreating Japanese: one had been tied to a tree, the other was decapitated.[107] Campaigning near Sattelberg in November 1943, Private Murphy recorded angrily: 'The singing out [we heard yesterday] was coming from one of our chaps who was wounded, he had been laying out all night. the Japs kicked him, slashed his face with a knife and left him for dead'.[108] In March 1945, a signalman on Bougainville reported that Australian provosts caught in a jeep by Japanese had been tied to their vehicle and set alight.[109] During the Aitape–Wewak campaign, the corpse of a member of the 2/3rd Machine Gun Battalion was found 'badly mutilated, disemboweled, the left leg was missing from the hip, as well as portions of the right leg, and the hips had all flesh removed'.[110] This was an atrocity of a type that horrified Australians – cannibalism.[111] It also occurred in the Papuan campaign.

Written confirmation of this practice came in a Japanese diary captured in November 1942. The acting commander of No. 2 MG Company of the Japanese 144th Regiment was found to have written in his diary, somewhere near Eora on 19 October: 'Because of the food shortage, some companies have begun eating human flesh (Australian soldiers). The taste is said to be good'.[112] The editor of the Allied Translator and Interpreter Section, responsible for translating this document and disseminating its contents, added a note at this point: 'Because of the *incredible implications* of this statement (the translation of which is concurred in by 3 independent translators) it is transcribed herewith'.[113] The Japanese characters followed. Clearly this discovery staggered even Allied translators, who knew more of the Japanese than other Australians. For the men in the field, Japanese cannibalism made the foe seem even more repulsive and alien.

Similarly, a lieutenant of the 2/1st Battalion recalled that during their advance on the Kokoda Track, the sight of a dead young Australian soldier with one of his thighs stripped of flesh 'incensed all our party and feeling against the enemy was explosive'.[114] However, Ken Clift concluded that, on seeing Australians who had been partly eaten, on the Kokoda Track, he and his comrades 'certainly did not condemn them on this cannibalism', which they considered sprang from determination to fight on rather than from sadism.[115] Such an unusual rationalisation ('forgiving' cannibalism as due to extreme hunger) could not be applied to other Japanese acts of mutilation, and the atrocities outlined above created intense anger in most soldiers. For example, Michael O'Brien recalled that, at the sight of men who had been bayoneted to a slow death at Milne Bay, 'my hatred rose to boiling point and I cursed those cruel, cowardly yellow curs of hell'.[116] An astute regimental historian said that not propaganda stories but the physical evidence of Japanese atrocities was crucial in making Australians hate Japanese in a way they had not hated Italians and Germans.[117] This is a valid, and indeed vital, point in understanding Australian attitudes towards the Japanese.

Jo Gullett, a veteran of the fighting at Wau–Salamaua in 1943, explained Australian soldiers' animosity towards their Japanese opponents: 'Because of the things they did to our dead and wounded we hated them'.[118] The hatred did not diminish in the last, strategically insignificant campaigns. Indeed, some factors encouraged it to increase, in certain areas. On Borneo, appalling Japanese treatment of the natives was very apparent, as were the first inklings of the catastrophe that had befallen the Australian POWs sent there.[119] Captain Combe wrote from Borneo in June 1945: 'The natives gave us information about the treatment of Australian prisoners of war in this area but I can give you no details beyond saying the treatment meted out was atrocious and makes one hope vindictively that Japan itself is bombed to smithereens'.[120]

Similarly, in the late war Aitape–Wewak campaign, cannibalism was seen more often than in earlier operations. An officer whose battalion had lost members to cannibalism argued: 'The frequent evidence of Japanese atrocities had a remarkable effect on the troops. It developed a feeling of disgust that caused men to enter battle with a greater determination to eliminate the enemy'.[121]

This 'feeling of disgust' about atrocities largely explains much of the unusually murderous behaviour of Australians. As early as the Milne Bay battle, Australians were taking the attitude that the enemy's mercilessness required a reply in kind.[122] The Japanese may have expected this. A Japanese prisoner who had participated in the landing told an Australian captain that:

> the ill-treatment and torturing of Australian troops was done by order of their officers so that the Japanese soldiers would fight and not surrender, because the same things would be done to them now that these atrocities had been committed on the Australians.[123]

If that was the intention behind atrocities, some of which occurred within 50 metres of Japanese headquarters at Milne Bay, it succeeded insofar as encouraging Australian retaliation.[124]

Thus, the lack of prisoners taken by Australians owed much to resentment of atrocities,[125] especially among men who had witnessed the result. A variation occurred during the 2/6th Battalion's campaign at Wau, where some of the men had originally been intended to reinforce the 2/22nd Battalion that was so hideously treated in New Britain. This group required much convincing on the wisdom of keeping alive a captured Japanese officer.[126] Cam Bennett, who fought in the Wau–Salamaua and Aitape–Wewak areas with the 2/5th Battalion, argued that Japanese attitudes to their captives 'divorced them from any consideration whatever' whenever Australians had a chance to kill these 'barbarians'.[127]

Unwillingness to take prisoners sometimes resulted from a simple desire to revenge the death of mates. An infantryman on Bougainville wrote: 'Our fellows wont [sic] take prisoners. I've seen them kill two or three now in cold-blood. I took a dim view of it the first time, but when you see your mates go, well I'd do it myself now'.[128]

The circumstances of jungle warfare also militated against the taking of Japanese prisoners. The fact that in the Kokoda campaign both sides took virtually no prisoners partly reflects the problems of guarding prisoners in extraordinarily difficult terrain. Ken Clift said that captured Japanese would have escaped, and that there was 'a tacit agreement' that men who surrendered would be shot. He claimed that fifty-three Japanese were shot on one occasion 'after being taken beyond 16th Brigade H.Q.',[129] although it is difficult to imagine fifty-three Japanese POWs being gathered in one location during that campaign, let alone being shot en masse. However, to men with no respect for the humanity of their enemy, the practical difficulties of the situation probably made killing them on the spot seem reasonable.

Even if there was an element of choice about deciding to kill the enemy, some jungle fighting offered no such opportunity. In the fighting at Sanananda, an Australian chaplain wrote not with anger but with resignation that the escaping crew of a burning Australian tank were shot because 'in this area it was *impossible* for Nippon to take prisoners'.[130] Because enemies were hidden and ambush was a constant possibility in the jungle, there were few opportunities for the niceties of offering surrender: men had to shoot first and ask questions later. Much of the firing was 'on the blind', by groups shooting in the area of any observed movement.[131] As Private John Butler wrote after firing at movement in the New Guinea jungle, the practice had to be 'no challenge, no beg-pardons in this country'.[132] A battalion historian said of New Guinea, 'Here it was literally the law of the jungle that counted – kill or be killed'.[133]

This logic of jungle warfare was conducive to hatred of the enemy who, like oneself, could not afford to treat one chivalrously as a potential prisoner. It was another factor that made the hatred of Australian soldiers for the Japanese very different from that of their civilian compatriots. The filthy mud, the decomposing vegetation, the pouring rain, the appalling humidity and the eerie sounds of the jungle also contributed to the hatred of the enemy, with whom the place was identified.[134] It was a place where soldiers fought in small groups, in isolation. The frightening enemy, with their apparent enthusiasm for death and the menacing environment in which they were encountered, made for a personal hatred for the Japanese that was peculiar to the soldiers who faced them.

CHAPTER SEVEN

THE JAPANESE

QUESTIONS OF QUALITY

For all their passionate hatred of the Japanese, Australians were frequently impressed by Japanese soldiering abilities. Postwar Australian publications, including unit histories and personal reminiscences, have acknowledged Japanese military prowess, but some Australians also offered praise during the war.[1] Their tributes were rarely unqualified, but they were given. On Bougainville in the last month of the war, Lieutenant-Colonel Harry Dunkley wrote of the enemy with not only sarcasm and grim humour, but respect: 'Our gentle opponents live on bamboo shoots + such like eked out with very little rice + some native foods. (not to mention a stray bit of steak off one of their unfortunate brethren) *They fight well despite it*'.[2] In December 1942, a brigadier whose troops were suffering heavy casualties in attempting to advance at Sanananda wrote home: 'This Jap is a nasty little devil. He just wont [sic] get out of his holes; and, his holes are so hard to pinpoint in the jungle'.[3] In a neighbouring unit three weeks later, Trooper Ben Love made a similar, more openly generous, comment on the Japanese forces entrenched just 40 metres away: 'How these Nips have stood the shelling rain, + lack of food these last 2 weeks is a "plurry marvel"'.[4] The following week he conceded: 'He is a tough nut to crack, this so often despised little yellow chap'.[5] During the fighting around Mubo in May 1943, General Mackay described the Japanese in the area as 'tenacious and stout fighters', who were holding their own against the Australians.[6]

103

As these accounts suggest, Japanese tenacity made an impression on Australian observers. It did so throughout the war. On Balikpapan in July 1945, Gunner Hack said with grudging admiration of the defenders that 'they are damned stubborn. They're cheeky devils too – one night they crept in close to where we were + set booby traps on their own dead we'd killed the evening before'.[7] As implied, the Japanese made impressive tactical use of jungle terrain. Training notes drawn up after the Milne Bay fighting emphasised the 'skilful fieldcraft' of the Japanese, particularly their use of tree snipers who were so well hidden as to be invisible until they fired.[8] An Australian soldier's awe at Japanese expertise in tree-sniping was published in a wartime collection of letters: 'They are beauts at getting up the coconut trees and sniping', wrote the veteran of Buna, who said of the trees 'I can't climb them stripped, yet they can take a machine-gun up one'.[9] An infantry lieutenant on New Britain admitted another Japanese skill in using the jungle: 'The Japs are great on ambushes and of course have the initiative all the time because we have to go and root the bludgers out'.[10]

The positions from which Japanese had to be 'rooted out' drew greatest respect, as they were often the result of great ingenuity and effort. Well-constructed defences, making good use of the uniquely difficult terrain of the tropics, were encountered in every campaign from the Kokoda Track onwards.[11] Private Rolleston wrote home about the strongpoints that had cost the lives of many of his comrades in an advance at Buna: 'These pill boxes were amazingly strong as they were several feet thick and made of cocoanut [sic] logs with 45 gallon drums filled with sand in between, and full of men and machine guns. Besides that they were well concealed by having grass etc growing on the top'. He also talked of Japanese weapon-pits being 'so well hidden you would almost put your feet down them before you seen them'.[12] Defences of this quality, seen in the first major Australian offensive against the Japanese, were still spoken of with awe in later offensives. In November 1943, a large patrol of the 22nd Battalion entered enemy territory near Finschhafen. The unit history recorded:

> It was obvious that this was Jap country. Along either side of the track were many weapon pits cleverly sited and expertly dug. They were exactly circular, as if marked out by compass with the sides plumb vertical. And they were finished to perfection with clever camouflage to an extent that they were quite unnoticeable until one had come abreast of them.[13]

In June 1945, an artillery commander said of the fighting at Tarakan: 'The infantry did a magnificent job against some of the best defences, fox holes, tunnels and concrete pillboxes I have ever seen'.[14] Two weeks later, Private Wallin in northern New Guinea said of evacuated Japanese positions: 'Looking at the fox holes and pillboxes this morning the only possible way to get him out is by bombing'.[15] Notes used in training Australians for jungle warfare conceded that the ability of Japanese to dig or burrow into the side of hills was 'remarkable'.[16]

The Japanese made excellent use of jungle terrain for offensive as well as defensive purposes. During the Malayan campaign, an Australian NCO noted wryly: 'There is ... plenty of jungle but jungle is not impassable as Hon Jap is past proving to our side's cost'.[17] Private Frank Hole was in a weapon-pit facing a rubber plantation in Malaya when he suddenly noticed a company of Japanese moving through the trees. On being fired at, they formed a line and charged the 2/20th Battalion positions. Hole described what followed:

> The Japs were moving very quickly from tree to tree, making the most of the cover provided, and it was very difficult to get a sight on any target. Although I fired several bursts from the Bren in the general direction of the Japs I doubt very much if I hit anyone ... The charge finished at the edge of the rubber plantation on the opposite side of the road and the Japs went to ground along a shallow drainage trench. They were very adept at making the most effective use of any cover available and even though they were no more than 25 feet away I could not see any sign of a Jap.[18]

It was only natural that Australians should be impressed by Japanese military prowess in the first year of their contact, as the Japanese won most battles in that period. The Japanese victories in New Britain, Ambon, Timor and Java were inevitable given the great numerical disparity, as well as the naval and aerial imbalance, between the sides.[19] However, the Australian reverses in Malaya, Singapore and, for a time, in Papua were due not only to numerical and material inferiority but also to the defenders' inability to prevent their experienced Japanese opponents from repeatedly outflanking and threatening to surround them. Even veterans of the Middle East faced early reverses: when the 2/14th Battalion went into action on the Kokoda Track, it suffered more than twice as many killed on one day, 30 August 1942,

as in its five weeks of campaigning in Syria.[20] There is little con-
temporary evidence of high regard for Japanese methods in the early
campaigns. Censorship would have made it difficult to praise the
Japanese in letters, but, also, to most Australians the thought of praising
the efforts of an enemy who was defeating them would have been
anathema. They were embarrassed about defeat by a supposedly inferior race, and preoccupied with maintaining morale by understating
the enemy's prowess rather than dwelling on it. However, they were
also concerned to explain away their defeats or difficulties, and from
their reversals emerged a notion of Japanese supermen or super-
soldiers.

Defeat of the Japanese at Milne Bay and on the Kokoda Track
damaged that image. A soldier writing home after the Milne Bay
fighting could assert: 'As for their troops, we do not class them as
fighters. It must have been their large numbers that won their other
battles'.[21] Nevertheless, the super-soldier concept was a resilient one.
On 29 September 1942, nearly a month after Milne Bay and just after
the Japanese had begun retreating along the Kokoda Track, a soldier
training in Queensland for service in the tropics mused: 'We get articles
read to us on the Jap's tactics, and one has to believe that he is a pretty
tough opponent, hiding in trees, swamps etc and fighting to the last
man and death'.[22] As late as 1945, the training syllabus at the jungle
warfare training school at Canungra, in Queensland, laid down that on
Day 2 recruits should be told that the concept of the Japanese 'super-
soldier' was a myth.[23]

When soldiers of the 9th Division entered the war against the
Japanese in 1943, they expected to meet a truly formidable opponent.
Jack Craig told of his unit's first night of operations in New Guinea,
made difficult by the thought: 'who was to know, leaves falling from
trees, night birds pecking off berries + numerous other noises were the
Japs. infiltrating to cut our throats in our shallow weapon pits *as we
were told so much about back in Australia*'.[24]

During the following weeks, Craig's comments on the Japanese
he encountered reflected changes in his attitude and the diversity of his
Japanese opponents. In his unit's first day of combat against the
Japanese, at Scarlet Beach, he was involved in an action in which 'a
heap of Japs screaming "banzai"' and charging down a track were
annihilated at no cost to the Australians.[25] A week later Craig noted in
his diary that even though his unit had been told from recent experience

that 'the Jap will not fight', their Japanese opponents in the area had so far fought well, and were marines, 'the best in the Jap army'.[26] Yet three weeks further into the campaign he reported inept Japanese tactics. On patrol, he met soldiers from another battalion, the 2/28th, who did not want to be relieved from their front-line position on the Sattelberg Track because:

> they were having a great time knocking off Japs as they attack 6 abreast down the Track. They say it is like shooting sitting rabbits … They have been warned by their C.O. that the man that shoots "Merv's" bugler will be courtmartialled. He blows his bugle just before his attack + during it. The attacks are always attempted at exactly the same time.[27]

A few weeks later Craig again emphasised the positive soldierly qualities of the enemy: 'The Jap is sure making a stand here + taking some shifting. It looked so easy at the start but gets harder every day'.[28]

Like all armies, the Japanese had units of varying strength, experience and ability, but the differences in quality between its soldiers were perhaps more striking than those in any other army faced by the Australians. Brigadier Porter, who in 1943 was Chief Instructor at the LHQ Training School, divided Japanese into three main groups: 'the provincial soldier', who lacked initiative, was of poor physique and 'not a particularly good fighter'; the 'intellectual type', including the strong, aggressive and well-trained marines; and a very large and varied group between those two extremes.[29] There were great variations in quality within campaigns, both between units, as experienced in Craig's campaign, and over time, as victory or defeat brought changes in morale and physical condition.[30] There was also a striking difference in quality between the Japanese faced by Australians in 1942, and those faced later. In the foreword to the official history of the campaigns from April 1943 to mid 1944, when Australian forces had the upper hand, David Dexter said: 'Any soldier who fought the Japanese cannot but have respect for them as fighters, *even though, with the tide turning against them, they did not fight it out to the last, as on the Papuan beaches*'.[31] As Dexter's own account showed, many soldiers in those campaigns did fight it out to the last, but it is true that the Japanese generally did not fight as hard or as effectively in those campaigns as in the earlier New Guinea operations.[32]

Sergeant Clive Edwards, a 7th Division veteran of Syria, Kokoda and Gona, mused as he left the Ramu Valley in January 1944 that the campaign there had been his easiest of the war. Disease had been a bigger threat than the enemy, who had inflicted far fewer casualties than in the Kokoda and Gona fighting.[33] However, he made only indirect criticisms of the Japanese effort, unlike many Australians who served in campaigns from 1943 and wrote disparaging remarks about their enemies. After the 9th Division's first efforts against them, at Lae, a unit diarist asserted: 'The enemy has done nothing to entitle him to our respect during the operation'.[34]

Sergeant Tom Derrick, who won a Victoria Cross against the Japanese and was later killed by them, wrote scornfully after the fall of Lae: 'Just under a fortnight to take the place from a never surrender fanatical enemy – hooey – our greatest problem was trying to catch up with him'.[35] No doubt there was some self-satisfaction and relief that pre-campaign fears had proven unfounded. The Japanese did fight the 9th more stubbornly later, around Sattelberg, where Derrick won his VC.[36] However, the scorn owed something to genuine surprise at the enemy's inability or unwillingness to hold very defensible positions.[37] Private Butler reported in September 1943 that his comrades were exasperated at the Japanese practice of shooting until 'you get near enough to turn them yellow', when they would flee or surrender. They considered the Japanese 'a fool of a fighter and not worth a cupful of cold water'.[38] Private Keys wrote home proudly in October:

> When we came up here we were told how bad the conditions were + what a wonderful fighter the Jap is. Well, Min, the conditions here are 100 per cent better than in the desert ... [The Jap] has had everything in his favour, such as high ground, etc. + every time we've met him we have belted him + he has run.[39]

In December 1943, near the end of the 9th Division's campaign, a diarist wrote: '*As usual* he's only fighting rearguard actions and pulls out as soon as we arrive in strength'.[40] Similar criticisms were made in the last year of the war. For example, in May 1945 Frank Legg sent a despatch from Tarakan reporting the capture of the main objective of the campaign, the airstrip, and observed: 'Why the Jap, after furiously defending the approaches to the strip, should now apparently abandon the heights which are the key to our success in this campaign, is a mystery'.[41]

By the last year of the war, Japanese forces were generally being defeated with greater ease than in earlier campaigns. Private Dove's matter-of-fact description of his first campaign, on the Danmap River, read: 'We had an easy time cleaning them out from the river to the Hills. we had a few Boys killed, but nothing near the total of the Japs after two weeks fighting here we killed little over one Hundred Japs'.[42]

In circumstances where casualty rates were running at more than ten to one against the Japanese, a sense of contempt had much to feed on.[43] In April 1944 an artilleryman on New Britain explained the reason for the attenuated Japanese effort during the late war:

> to all intents and purposes the war here in New Guinea is over. There are still plenty of Japs here but in such a bad state that they've no more fight left in them. I've often wondered what the effect of a blockade is on a people but after seeing them I don't wonder any more.[44]

In March of the following year, a lieutenant of the 2/3rd Battalion pointed out that the soldiers they were facing were not in the same class as the men they had faced in the Owen Stanley mountains – and for good reason, as the Japanese had lost communication with Tokyo and had little or no food.[45]

Another explanation for Japanese poor performance, as well as a cause for criticism, was the inadequacy of their weapons. In the Lae campaign, 'Diver' Derrick wrote: 'Their weapons are definitely inferior to ours, being old & crude yet effective. I cannot see how they can possibly have a chance at all'.[46] From 1942 it was asserted, with good reason, that Japanese weapons were inferior in quality.[47] From 1943, they were also gravely limited in quantity.[48]

The way the Japanese used their weapons was one of several supposed deficiencies that Australians regularly mentioned. A perceived technical weakness was discussed late in 1943 by an Australian infantryman who claimed in a letter: 'The Jap is a poor fighter + rotten shot + it is an accident if one gets hit'.[49] Perhaps such claims of poor shooting were designed to soothe the fears of the letter's recipient, but they are so common in the literature as to leave no doubt that they contained some truth.[50] The poor shooting was probably largely due to the inadequacies of the main Japanese rifle, the Arisaka Type 38. The Japanese themselves were said to have joked that the weapon was useful only for committing suicide.[51]

There are numerous Australian stories like that of a cavalry troop whose first victim at Balikpapan was a Japanese who missed a shot at point-blank range on Pope's Track, or the two infantrymen advancing at Buna who were suddenly fired at and missed by a Japanese in a foxhole just a few metres away.[52] Shortly before his capture on Singapore, an Australian infantryman attributed his survival and that of his mates to two factors: the Lord was on their side, and the Japanese shot poorly.[53] In bloody fighting near Mersing Bridge in Malaya in January 1942, a private whose wounded shoulder was being dressed was heard to say: 'Let me get back there – those Japs couldn't hit a bag of shit at a hundred yards'.[54] A former schoolteacher, Lieutenant A.H. Robertson, was less earthy, but summed up common attitudes and experiences when he wrote nonchalantly during the fighting at Wau: 'I have a very low opinion of the Japs as rifle shots. Most of our wounded copped it at very close range, or just through sheer bad luck. I have been missed so many times that I have quite lost faith in their marksmanship'.[55] The official history of the late 1943 and 1944 campaigns said that Japanese skill in ambush and general fieldcraft was frequently vitiated by inaccurate shooting.[56] In a list of 'weaknesses' of the Japanese soldier, read to Australian recruits at Canungra in 1945, the first item was 'His *marksmanship* is poor'.[57] Another listed criticism was the Japanese lack of caution, which many campaigning soldiers noted.[58]

A private wrote of his unit's surprising introduction to Japanese forces on the Kokoda Track: 'Along they came blaring bugles and making all the weird noises under the sun'.[59] Although Japanese forces sometimes moved with stealth, an Australian wartime correspondent expressed the common opinion when he called the Japanese 'an inveterate chatterer' and said that their talk had frequently cost Japanese their lives.[60] The official historian talked of 'blithely chattering' Japanese soldiers cycling into a bloody ambush at Gemencheh in the very first Australian action against Japanese troops.[61] Such incidents were repeated elsewhere in Malaya, and also in New Britain, Ambon and Timor; they continued to occur when the Japanese were on the defensive.[62]

Not only their loudness, but their attacks or counterattacks which followed such noise, raised questions about Japanese military efficiency. As mentioned above, bugle blasts and yelling often warned that Japanese were about to attack. It was believed that the yelling was intended to inspire courage in those shouting or to keep troops in a straight line – and to frighten the Australians.[63] The last effect was not often achieved: indeed, such attacks were frequently so naively direct as to be almost comical. One veteran described as humorous several features of Japanese attacks early in the Lae campaign. After each futile attack petered out, the survivors did not stay where they were but tried to walk back to their starting-line, 'like bowlers in a cricket match'. Inevitably some were killed while casually retreating. One Japanese officer was behind a tree, so intent on swinging a sword and yelling that 'he failed to notice a grenade fall between his feet'.[64] In October 1943 Corporal Jones wrote home concerning a Japanese bugle he had acquired as a souvenir: 'Almost every time they attack they blow this bugle. We think its [sic] very amusing. Handy warning too'.[65] The following day, a diarist wrote contemptuously: 'The Japs attacked one of our Bn positions in his usual mad mob rushes, over a thousand *dead* Japs were found in the area, we suffered three casualties'.[66] The figures were exaggerated, but the contempt for Japanese tactics was real.[67]

Many Australians considered that other aspects of Japanese tactics were also inept. Not only did Japanese frequently abandon crucial ground, they also showed an inflexibility that offset their determination.[68] Indeed, it was often said that part of the reason for the eventual Allied tactical success against the Japanese was the former's willingness to learn and adapt, unlike the unwavering Japanese adherence to traditional methods, which quickly became predictable.[69] The Australian readiness to adapt is shown in the fact that they adopted the Japanese tactic of pinning or 'fixing' a force from the front then encircling it with the forces following: this became standard Australian practice in New Guinea.[70] A good example of Japanese inflexibility concerns the supply parties sent along the Bonga–Wareo track to support their front-line forces at Wareo in November 1943. The Australian 2/32nd Battalion placed Vickers machine guns in positions enfilading the track, and became 'almost hysterical with joy' as day after day groups of Japanese continued to walk along the track – heedless of the piles of Japanese corpses around them – to their deaths. Australian onlookers were 'speechless with astonishment' that the Japanese did not change their approach, and that the soldiers in the forward positions did not warn their compatriots of the danger.[71] Cam Bennett recalled from the Wau–Salamaua operations another example of this perceived Japanese inflexibility. His company had captured a ridge, and repeatedly found itself shooting Japanese stragglers trying to crawl up to their positions. He was sure that the Japanese must have known the position was in Australian hands, and explained:

> Either they had no brains at all or were simply being obedient to the irrational Japanese trait of carrying out orders regardless of circumstances. This inability to vary a plan or an order and to exploit changed situations was a cardinal Japanese failure.[72]

Japanese self-sacrifice in battle often seemed to have no tactical value. The war diary of the 39th Battalion said of fighting near Gona on 12 December: 'Three enemy were killed making for our positions, but most of them died from a fanatical and *very often pointless* determination to remain in their posts until they were killed'.[73] Osmar White made a similar observation in 1945, that Japanese posts would often fight to the death rather than surrender, when a better alternative might have been to improvise, survive and succeed.[74] In other words, courageous fighting could be poor tactics.

The bravery of Japanese soldiers came under psychological attack in other ways. In every campaign, Australians were confronted with extraordinary Japanese bravery. Sometimes it involved spectacular efforts, like that of the Japanese soldier who jumped on a tank at Buna and shot the tank commander and gunner through the slit before being killed by the numerous Australian infantry nearby.[75] At other times the courage was more prosaic, as in the Tarakan caves that Australians blew up with explosives when the Japanese occupants would not surrender.[76] Colin Kennedy told of a 'born soldier' in his unit who, after shooting several Japanese emerging from a hut on the Kokoda Track, confided: 'There was one wounded bloke trying to get to a machine gun. I just couldn't let him reach it'. Kennedy commented that the NCO plainly 'admired the stricken man's bravery'.[77] Yet the do-or-die courage of Japanese soldiers did not necessarily raise the military prowess of Japanese in Australian eyes. As discussed, the Japanese willingness to die appeared bizarre to most Australians. Also, men found it difficult to determine whether Japanese were 'fanatically brave or idiotically stupid'. Their bravery often seemed to be fanaticism or madness rather than traditional military heroism. 'They are game blighters – or mad' wrote a diarist as his battalion inched forward on Bougainville in March 1945.[78] Many Australians saw Japanese courage in the face of death not as an expression of courageous soldiering, but as indicating an alien outlook.

Some considered the Japanese suicidal approach after 1942 as a sign not of courage, but of a loss of morale.[79] From that time, the 'super-soldiers' conceded ground and sustained casualties at such a high rate that it became easy for some to dismiss any suggestion of military prowess. Even in the terrible year 1942, some found evidence of inferior Japanese courage. An artilleryman and World War I veteran wrote from Malaya in February: 'Many times we have had to fight with the Infantry, surrounded on all sides but the "yellow stinkers" wouldn't stick to their job, once we faced them with bayonets'.[80] After describing a successful bayonet charge by 2/16th Battalion men on the Kokoda Track, H.D. Steward said 'Out in the open, cold steel and man to man, the Australians discovered then a Japanese weakness they would exploit again and again'.[81] Ironically, the Japanese themselves put great emphasis on use of the bayonet, and were confident of their skill
with that man-to-man weapon.[82] 'Man-to-man' measurement was as important to Australians fighting the Japanese as when fighting their other enemies.

COMPARING THE JAPANESE TO OTHER ENEMIES AND TO AUSTRALIANS

Some months after his capture at Singapore, an Australian gunner wrote in his diary about the surrender:

> Do you remember seeing a Gazette about the surrender of the Italians + as far as the eye could see was a continual string of them with quite a small number of Aussie guards. I laughed too at this film, but I wont [sic] again. We were just the same, – I dont [sic] think we even had a guard over us – as far as the eye could see was a marching mass of Aussies.[83]

What a blow to Australian martial prestige! Recovering it was very important to Australian soldiers. Within eighteen months of the fall of Singapore, the scorned Italians were used as a yardstick again. The author of a wartime brochure produced by the Department of Information claimed that the typical first comment made to him by Australians fighting in New Guinea was the 'contemptuous but convincing' remark: '"The Jap is a worse fighter than the Eyetie"'.[84] A veteran of Tobruk and Alamein declared during the Lae campaign: 'As for the Jap – impressions so far rate him a little below standard of the Itie'.[85] During the same campaign, Private John Butler quoted men of the 2/28th Battalion as saying 'the Jap's only a fourth rate Italian'.[86]

Inevitably, some veterans extended the comparison to the 'real enemy' in the Middle East. 'As a fighter the Jap might be a little better than the Italian,' Private Keys conceded in October 1943, 'but he can't compare with the Jerry'.[87] Clearly, such an opinion depended on the Germans fought. Ten months earlier an Australian who had been with the victorious 6th Division in Greece said after fighting at Kokoda and Sanananda that 'I think NIP a better fighter than Fritz'. This may have been a common attitude among 6th and 7th Division veterans of the Middle East who fought the Japanese in 1942.[88] On the other hand, men in the 6th Division had experienced only defeat against the Germans in Greece and Crete, and the one brigade of the 7th Division that faced Germans, the 18th Brigade, had found them tough opponents in Tobruk. They also had to face the Japanese at their formidable best – at Milne Bay and Buna. An interesting comparative comment from a member of that brigade concerned Buna, where the soldier who was quoted in Chapter 6 as marvelling at the Japanese tree-climbing ability wrote with relief that thankfully Japanese were 'not extra good shots, *not like the Hun*'.[89] Those with the task of training soldiers to fight the Japanese felt the same about their technical proficiency. At Canungra, recruits were told that 'the Jap is NOT like the German whom we have become accustomed to fighting. He is NOT as good a soldier'.[90]

Most 9th Division veterans, who generally faced stiffer opposition from the Germans at Tobruk and Alamein than from the Japanese in their later campaigns, would have agreed with that judgment. One battalion history described Middle Eastern veterans who had occupied positions evacuated by Japanese in late 1943 shaking their heads in bewilderment and asserting, 'The Germans would never give up a post like this'.[91] Allan Dawes reported a similar pronouncement after the amphibious landings at Finschhafen, and added the inevitable conclusion to this Australian way of thinking:

> 'If they'd been Germans, they'd never have let us on that beach – never,' I heard on all sides from veteran Western Desert fighters. 'No Jap would ever have got this place, if *we* had been where they were, and they had been the invaders'.[92]

As the passage suggests, comparisons with Italians and Germans were part of an exercise which concluded with the idea that at the top of the

Australians pose with their handguns and rifles in front of five dead Japanese at Gona, in December 1942. The Japanese were killed by a grenade. The Australian who threw it had been surprised by an enemy who, from only a few metres away, hurled his rifle with fixed bayonet. The photo shows the murderously grim atmosphere of the battles on the Papuan beachheads. (AWM 013881)

'Shooting wounded Japanese, Timbered Knoll', drawn in 1943 by Ivor Hele.
(Ivor Hele, Shooting wounded Japanese, Timbered Knoll 1943, charcoal,
53.5 X 50.2 cms, AWM ART33838)

Soldiers had to examine dead Japanese for documents, as these men of the 2/17th Battalion are doing in Brunei (North Borneo) in June 1945. Some men used the opportunity to look for personal souvenirs as well. (AWM 109317)

Grim-faced members of a patrol look at a Japanese machine-gun post, and the gunner they killed, in the Ramu Valley in November 1943. (AWM 016025)

Aftermath of one of the suicide attacks that bewildered Australians. These four Japanese were among thirty-one killed on Labuan Island when they infiltrated the beach maintenance area during the night of 21 June 1945. (AWM 109695)

At Bandjermasin, Borneo, on 17 September 1945, Major-General Uno is humiliated by Australian Lieutenant-Colonel Robson of the 2/31st Battalion. Uno twice tried to present his sword to Robson, who insisted that the weapon be placed on the ground instead as a sign of submission. (AWM 118033) hierarchy of armies was the one that could beat all enemies – the Australian army. Another example of that way of thinking appeared in the diary of an NCO involved in the preceding operations. In September 1943 Lance-Corporal Clothier described an attack in which a neighbouring unit suffered only eight casualties and inflicted forty in capturing a steep, heavily overgrown position. He concluded: 'If we had been in the same position Nip wouldn't have got it if he tried for 10 years'.[93]

Such contemptuous poses were readily adopted from 1943. Australian victory was certain and the odds were greatly against the Japanese, who were suffering life-threatening shortages of food and other supplies. A superior attitude had been more difficult to maintain through most of 1942, with all its military disasters. Yet even in that period Australians clung to a belief that, man for man, they were better soldiers than the enemy. Even as they lay down their arms in Singapore, they felt that they were yielding to 'a force which they counted as less than their equals'.[94]

The Australians considered the Japanese as less than equals on the basis of experience as well as prejudice. Lieutenant-Colonel Anderson, who was unusually well-versed in jungle warfare and who won a Victoria Cross for his actions in Malaya, argued that Australian units at Muar had shown 'a complete moral ascendancy' over the Japanese, superior bushcraft and fire control, and dominance in hand-to-hand fighting.[95] Similarly, a lieutenant involved in the brief fighting on Ambon reported that 'In individual combat the enemy troops were no match for our men'.[96]

Explanations for defeat are exemplified in a letter written by an Australian signalman in the midst of the fighting in Malaya: 'Our chaps are fighting like madmen against great odds. If we could only get some more planes quickly the Japs would be driven back to where they came from. Their infantry is no match for our boys'.[97] The letter shows elements common to Australian discussions of their terrible defeats in 1942: complaints about numerical inferiority and lack of air support, and assertions that Australians were better soldiers than the Japanese. Australian defeats were explained by factors external to their soldiering ability. Paradoxically, Australian victories later in the war tended to be explained by their soldiering abilities; external factors such as their numerical preponderance, aerial superiority, and the Japanese lack of supplies, were largely ignored.[98]

The Australians who were defeated in Malaya and Singapore in early 1942 rightly pointed to the absence of air cover and the bungling of those in charge, but they rather exaggerated the numbers against them and (to a more justifiable extent) their own effectiveness in reducing the odds.[99]

Some non-participants, usually inspired by inter-unit rivalry, regarded the 8th Division as responsible for its own disasters, but generally the Australian excuses were accepted by those who were not present. It would in fact be very harsh to blame the Australians for their defeats at Japanese hands in 1942. In Malaya, for example, no Commonwealth units fought more successfully than the Australians, who not only showed a degree of willingness to die in battle that was unusual in that combined force, but also suffered far fewer battle deaths than they inflicted on the enemy.[100] Frank Hole recalled that when he was in Malaya, a report of the 2/30th Battalion's successful ambush at Gemas was the first encouraging news they had heard in the war and 'the first indication that the Jap soldier was not invincible'.[101] However, the efforts of some Australian soldiers and units against the Japanese gave little to boast about.[102] The most damning and controversial evidence of this relates to large-scale desertion among Australians during the siege of Singapore. A controversial British wartime report on the fall of Singapore apportioned a very large part of the blame to Australian indiscipline, even concluding: 'For the fall of Singapore itself, the Australians are held responsible'.[103] This was an exaggeration, as implied by the fact that although the Australians represented only 14 per cent of the Allied ground forces on the island they comprised 73 per cent of the defenders' battle deaths.[104]

The early defeats were largely responsible for persistent worries about the relative quality of the Japanese.[105] Australians carried not only heavy physical loads on the Kokoda Track, but also two myths about the Japanese: that of the super-soldier and that of the short-sighted, buck-toothed incompetent.[106] The campaign put both illusions into perspective. By the end of 1942, there was a firm conviction that although the enemy was fanatical and tough, Australians were superior fighters.[107] Australians achieved something special against the Japanese in 1942: Sir William Slim declared that the news of the Japanese defeat at Milne Bay was a great morale-booster to British troops in Burma, who acknowledged that 'of all the Allies it was Australian soldiers who first broke the spell of the invincibility of the Japanese Army'.[108]

General MacArthur believed the credit belonged less to the Australians than to his strategic foresight, and wrote to General Marshall: 'The enemy's defeat at Milne Bay must not be accepted as a measure of relative fighting capacity of the troops involved'.[109] Looking back in 1945 on the campaigning that ended on the Papuan beaches in 1943, Osmar White felt that Australian bragging about tactical superiority was misplaced, for 'Allied ground troops were not yet the man-for-man equal of the Japanese in jungle fighting'.[110] Most Australian soldiers would probably have disagreed with MacArthur and White: the matter was impossible to prove, but the renewal of Australian pride was psychologically beneficial.

Australian naivety about the issue of 'who was best' persisted, for example in the expression heard in 1942–43: 'Wait till we get them into the open'.[111] Presumably the supposition was that on open ground, in an even fight, Australians would show their superiority. However, Japanese soldiers were not foolish enough to fight on open ground in a jungle-clad country. War was never played on the level field, literally or figuratively, that the Australians wanted.

As many of the examples imply, Australians in the 1943–45 campaigns were convinced, either from the start or in the course of the campaigns, of their superiority. Even a modest soldier such as Clive Edwards added this postscript to a letter: 'Dad, it is true that, on every occasion that we have clashed we have done more damage to the Jap than he to us'.[112] Despite the fact that in all the campaigns they won against the Japanese Australians had numerical and air superiority, and were fighting with Allied assistance against an enemy very short of supplies, they assumed that the two forces could be compared.

NOT TO BE TAKEN LIGHTLY

In March 1945, Clive Edwards was in Australia, training as an officer, when he saw a film shown in camp. He enjoyed the movie, largely because of the humorous remarks made by other soldiers in the audience. He singled out as 'particularly good' an incident in the film: 'They were describing how one American crept up on a Jap machine gun post and killed 15 Japs single handed and the machine [projector] suddenly cut out + one wag piped up "Even the machine couldn't swallow it"'.[113]

As the anecdote suggests, the Japanese were not a negligible enemy. In battle they were treated with great caution, and when the tide had turned irrevocably in favour of the Allies, there was a terrible grimness about campaigns against the Japanese. In a passage concerning the one-sided fighting on the Danmap River, Private Dove told how the Japanese had killed and eaten one of his best friends.[114] There was no room for complacency in such circumstances. Similarly, Lieutenant Robertson, who had written of his loss of faith in Japanese marksmanship, also told his wife: 'Of course I still intend to take all possible precautions, as it is only foolishness to do otherwise'.[115] Thousands of Australians killed by Japanese small-arms fire provided mute testimony that its effectiveness was not to be underestimated.[116] The Japanese demanded respect as soldiers; they did not receive it as human beings.

CHAPTER EIGHT

THE JAPANESE

EMPATHY, COMPASSION AND INCOMPREHENSION

In March 1945 an artilleryman in action on New Britain wrote in a letter home: 'when you stop to think war is a pretty rotten business, here we are throwing shells at the Japs + hoping they blow them to bits and although we call them little yellow –! yet they're human just as we are'.[1] It was unusual for an Australian to write in such a detached manner about the Japanese, but such detachment and even sympathy were evident: a commentator who suggested that Allied soldiers had images of Japanese as superhuman, subhuman and inhuman, but not as humans like themselves, is not entirely accurate.[2] Sometimes Australians showed empathy with the enemy: saying they knew what it was like to have dysentery as the Japanese did; imagining their discomfort under Australian gunfire; picturing their reaction as an amphibious invading force came towards them; or saying in the Aitape–Wewak region that living there for three years as the Japanese had done would be 'pure hell'.[3]

While Japanese who survived to become prisoners never aroused Australian sympathy as did those captured in the Middle East, sometimes they did touch emotions other than anger or contempt. The appearance of starved men could draw comments like 'poor devils', and even gestures such as the provision of food, water or covering.[4]

The murderous treatment meted out to Japanese prisoners was not morally acceptable to all. Captain J.J. May was responsible for loading wounded men onto air transports from the Wau airfield during the bitter fighting there in January 1943. He was approached one day to make room for six Japanese prisoners who would soon arrive, bound together, to be taken to Port Moresby for questioning. The Japanese did not arrive at the expected time, and eventually:

> A soldier appeared with his rifle slung over his shoulder and looking at the ground told me that they would not be coming. I blew off what the bloody hell do you mean you ask us to make room for you and now you dont [sic] want it. One could sense something was wrong and it very shamefacedly came out, they had been killed, a soldier had opened up on them with a Tommy gun and shot the lot. The boys and I were pretty aghast at this and we said they had been tied up; the poor messenger was also rather stricken and tried to explain how it happened. A soldier that opened up had his mate killed alongside him during the night. It somehow cast a dark shadow over us including the poor B who had to tell us.[5]

This story shows a belief that the Japanese were fellow men, and that in some circumstances killing them was immoral.

The emotions of those who did the killing were also tested. An Australian who had just killed a 'walking Japanese skeleton' at Sanananda described him as a 'rather poor specimen of humanity'.[6] Even such grudging admissions, however, acknowledged the enemy's humanity, and soldiers who killed Japanese tended to think more than usual about this point. An Australian who had ambushed and killed two Japanese soldiers at Sanananda reflected: 'it was pure murder'.[7] Captain May reported a conversation with a wounded sergeant who had been on patrol near Wau when confronted by a Japanese officer wielding a sword. In a slow country drawl and with a tone that made clear his regret, the sergeant told May, 'I think he must have been an M.O. [medical officer] or something and I had to shoot the poor bastard'.[8] Phil O'Brien told of falling into a foxhole which contained a Japanese soldier, into whom he fired his entire Bren gun magazine; on turning the man over, O'Brien discovered that he had previously been shot through the forehead 'and strange as it may seem I felt relieved that it had not been my burst of Bren gun fire that had ended his life'.[9]

Occasionally when Australians examined corpses they saw evidence of the civilian side of their enemy. Fearnside wrote of an incident in New Guinea in 1945 when his platoon ambushed and killed a lone, emaciated Japanese soldier. He said that although they were immune to compunction about such homicidal acts, searching the body brought

a haunting emotional impact. They found two objects: one was a rudi-
mentary map of Australia, apparently torn from a child's atlas, which
gave rise to the thought that the Japanese was lost and had imagined
himself in Australia. The other object was a faded photograph of a
beautiful Japanese girl. Such images brought home the fact that the
enemy too had a civilian, peaceful background.[10] The shared humanity
of the enemy was brought home to another Australian when a native
ally on Borneo brought him the head of a Japanese, still wearing its
spectacles.[11]

However, such fellow-feeling could vanish under the pressure of
events. In January 1945 a 6th Division infantryman who wrote in his
diary one day about how his unit had fed prisoners and protected them
from angry natives, could write immediately after an ambush of his
unit: 'What little pity one had for the animal cravens we had here as
prisoners yesterday has now vanished'.[12] Like the man who killed the
six bound prisoners after his mate was killed, the stresses of jungle
warfare soon swallowed feelings of altruism towards the source of
anxiety.

The end of the war, and the consequent pain suffered by the
Japanese, does not seem to have softened many Australian hearts.
Indeed, some gloried in Japanese discomfort. An artilleryman who
witnessed a surrender ceremony on Borneo reported that 'after five
years of fighting and hardship we had the pleasure of watching the Japs
come in with bowed heads, humiliated and ready to lay down all to
their victors'. He added that 'pains had not been spared to impress
these Japanese delegates that they were definitely and without doubt an
inferior race of beings'.[13]

At a surrender ceremony in Bougainville an Australian guard
described how his mates had a joke at the expense of a Japanese guard:

> I had to laugh at the boys, they threw the Jap guard a cigg, he bent
> down and picked it up, talked a bit in jap lingo and smiled, then
> the boys started, they swore at him and called him all the names
> they could think of, and all the jap did was stand there like an ape
> grinning perhaps he only new [sic] his own lingo.[14]

While some gloried in Japanese humiliation, others found Japanese surrender unsatisfactory. An infantryman in New Guinea asserted
that Australians knew the Japanese and their treachery, and suspected a
trick.[15] An artilleryman on Borneo complained in September 1945 that

Japanese atrocities were coming to light yet Australians would be
punished if they even hit a Japanese, and that Australians were for-
bidden to take watches or other items from the 'skunks' even though
many such items had obviously been stolen by the Japanese in the first
place. Also, the Japanese were now eating better than they had been in
years. He concluded: 'It is galling to us'.[16]

Captain Gordon Combe was present at two surrender ceremonies
on Borneo, and his reports on them illuminate Australian attitudes. He
shared the laughter of his comrades in Beaufort when the Japanese
general, Akashi, fell head-over-heels as he climbed off a truck. During
the other ceremony, in Papar, Combe experienced mixed emotions.
Before the Japanese officer was invited into headquarters, the Australian brigadier in charge of proceedings showed his feelings by smiling
and saying 'Bring the b...s in'.[17] Such a comment on such an occasion
is hard to imagine in relation to any enemy other than the Japanese. At
the time, Combe kept quiet his own feelings about the occasion.
However, he confided to his wife:

> the yellow creatures were marched in again and we had a staff
> conference. I was sitting a yard away from them and just had to be
> quietly civil. I couldn't help thinking of a grand chap of ours who
> was killed when a grenade burst on his chest. I felt almost guilty,
> sitting there quietly, knowing what atrocities his race had per-
> petrated – echoes of the darkest ages. I feel they are not humiliated
> enough.[18]

Much Japanese behaviour echoed the darkest ages, but Australian
attitudes towards them also drew on old fears and prejudices.

Steve Sullivan, an Australian NCO, took some men to look around
the battlefield of Slater's Knoll, Bougainville, during the fighting there
in March 1945. On finding a wounded Japanese, several of Sullivan's
comrades suggested they kill him. Sullivan objected. 'I knew all about
the Japs and their treatment of prisoners', he recalled, 'but to my mind
that is not good enough reason to kill a man in cold blood. *We are
not Japs*'.[19] The language he used to explain why he could not kill a
defenceless human being reflected the very attitude that allowed many
other Australians to do the opposite: Australians were not Japanese.
A gulf separated them. Ironically, as Sullivan perceived, actions such
as killing Japanese prisoners brought their behaviour closer.

Although Sullivan prevented his comrades from killing the prisoner
he was very cautious while capturing him, well aware of the Japanese

inclination to die rather than surrender.[20] That preference, together with Japanese military weakness and the Australian eagerness to kill, made for a terrible Japanese carnage in the final campaigns.[21] In the last year more than 22 000 Japanese died in battle against Australians, who lost just over 1500 in action. Australians killed twice as many Japanese in these strategically pointless campaigns as they themselves lost in all their fighting in World War II. There were nearly three times as many Japanese deaths in action in the final campaigns as there were among Australians in Japanese captivity.[22]

At the end of the war with Japan, as at the start, most Australians regarded the Japanese with contempt. However, much had happened in the interval. The Japanese had passed from being figures of fun to figures of awe and then to figures whose humiliation was a source of joy. The conflict had been ghastly, for its ghoulish setting, its mutual incomprehension and its inhumanity. The common theme was hatred. It is disturbing to speculate about the postwar psychological effects of the experience, particularly among Australian participants in the 'extermination' that characterised the last campaigns of the war.[23]

JAPANESE ATTITUDES TO AUSTRALIANS

Japanese propaganda fostered racist hatred and demonisation of all enemies, and naturally Australians were a target.[24] The hatred felt by Japanese soldiers who met Australians on the battlefield was probably intensified by the course of their campaigns after mid 1942. There is evidence that many raged at the 'arrogance' and 'impudence' of the Australian and American troops who attacked them, and at their own impotence against Allied aircraft.[25] A Japanese lieutenant wrote soon after the fall of Lae and Salamaua in September 1943: 'The feelings of every officer and man throughout the Army are churning with a desire to massacre all AMERICANS and AUSTRALIANS'.[26]

Massacres of Australians did occur, when the Japanese had the opportunity, in the early campaigns. Japanese treatment of their prisoners who survived to reach prison camps has appalled the world ever since, and presumably it reflected a degree of hatred and contempt. Certainly explanations that such things happen in all wars, that such treatment was culturally acceptable in Japan, or that the guards were the refuse of the Japanese forces, ring hollow.

The treatment of captives who were killed on the spot is also difficult to understand. Sometimes it was done in a matter-of-fact way. There are accounts such as these two Japanese diary extracts concerning the killing of an Australian officer near Buna: '28th August 1942 (BUNA) 1804 hours – Captured one Australian officer and killed him' and '28th August – Captured one Australian officer. Decapitated him'.[27]

It was perhaps official policy that led to the atrocities against Australians at Milne Bay, in order to make the Japanese rank and file believe there was no turning back. Yet at other times, atrocities were committed in a frenzied, spontaneous manner.

A grim pragmatism emerged in a Japanese prisoner's explanation of the killing of Australian prisoners in Papua: 'he knew of no reason as PsW are not supposed to be killed but thought it was due to difficulty in keeping them, feeding them etc, coupled with the fear that they might escape or be released by our troops'.[28] Those reasons are similar to ones used by some Australians.

Occasionally, Japanese showed chivalrous respect for the Red Cross or for enemy wounded, and one Japanese said that the executions of Australian men and women at Buna were reportedly a dreadful sight.[29] Japanese attitudes to killing varied, as did Australian attitudes.

Japanese thoughts on the military prowess of Australians are somewhat easier to fathom. Like the Australians, Japanese troops criticised their foes, and heard criticism of them from higher quarters. Before the war, the Japanese army had been particularly scathing of the Anglo–American military capacity – much as the Australians and their allies were towards Japanese – and this probably led to early underestimates of Australians as foes.[30] To many Japanese the early campaigns may well have vindicated that perception, although even in defeat Australians won some praise. For example, a Japanese wartime account of fighting at Ayer Bemban, in Malaya, said that despite continued Japanese attacks, 'the [Australian] warriors continued suicidal resistance like wounded boars'.[31] It described an Australian counterattack, which won them a brief respite before retreating: 'the enemy, defying death, strangely and impudently counter-attacked with bayonets along the whole line'.[32] Similarly, a propagandistic Japanese article about the Japanese capture of Ambon said that the 'desperate resistance of the Australians after the breakthrough was not to be despised'.[33] Although these accounts were not exactly fulsome praise of an 'impudent' and 'suicidal' – not to say fanatical – enemy, it is difficult to imagine Australian wartime publications being even that generous.

The fighting in Papua in 1942 led the Japanese to offer further praise of their enemy as fighters. In August the main contingent of the Japanese forces assigned to advance across Papua and capture Port Moresby received instructions before sailing from Rabaul. The instructions depended on information based on clashes which had occurred earlier at Rabaul and Kokoda, and included the assertion that 'The fighting spirit of the Australian infantry soldier is strong'. This spirit was said to be superior to that of the American troops in the area. The instructions highlighted Australian marksmanship, and the skilful Australian use of cover and grenades.[34] On 11 August, a Japanese lieutenant on the Kokoda Track conceded: 'Although the Australians are our enemies, their bravery must be admired'.[35]

A Japanese intelligence summary written in November, possibly in reference to the Milne Bay operations, said that the Australian soldier's 'will to resist is strong and though we attack him, he resists further'.[36] It also told of Australian skill in the use of hand grenades, and a diary written at about the same time at Gona said 'Their firing is very accurate'.[37] A Japanese diary entry, written at this desperate point, admitted: '27th November – Strength of Australian soldier is superior to that of Nippon soldier'.[38] The fighting during this period seems to have surprised many Japanese, who found their own heavy losses, and the enemy's courage and ability, a shock.[39] In January 1943, the last diary entry a Japanese private made before his death bemoaned the lack of reinforcements and supplies and included the comment: 'Things are happening just as the enemy said'.[40] The 'enemy' may have been Americans: Japanese did not always distinguish between their enemies.[41]

Naturally, while the campaigns were in progress, Japanese officers distributed instructions and information that emphasised the weaknesses of the Australian enemy. While Australians were scoffing at poor Japanese marksmanship, a comment appeared twice in a Japanese report on fighting on the Huon Peninsula that 'Sniping at the enemy is easy and gives substantial results'.[42] In an echo of the Australian assertions that Japanese did not like 'cold steel', Japanese soldiers were told after the Milne Bay battle: 'Enemy lacks fighting spirit in hand to hand combat'.[43] A pamphlet captured the following year said that 'The enemy cannot stand up to hand-to-hand fighting or charges'.[44] Not only could they not face charges, according to the official line, they also could not make them. 'Against our positions they will not charge while the position is defended, even though within grenade throwing distance', according to some 'lessons' distributed to Japanese soldiers following fighting in the Huon Peninsula.[45] These criticisms of Australian courage were directed towards the conclusion that the Australians, with their 'materialistic civilisation', were spiritually weaker than the Japanese.[46]

A sergeant-major reflected on the Jivevaneng battle: 'The enemy relies on heavy weapons and puts his faith in arms of all types, but spiritually, in the moment of final decision, he has nothing and seems shallow and weak'.[47] He did not explain the fact that the Australians defeated all Japanese attempts to shift them from their defences at Jivevaneng. However, such conclusions about 'fighting spirit' were crucial to the morale of the Japanese, who were well aware that in material terms they could not match the Australians and Americans.[48] As a corporal conceded in another report on the Jivevaneng fighting: 'The enemy has many times our fire power'.[49] The Japanese often referred to the prevalence of automatic weapons among the Australians.[50] They needed to believe in what General Adachi, commander of the forces in eastern New Guinea, called 'the unique and peerless spiritual superiority of the Imperial Army'.[51] A good example of the belief that Japanese spiritual superiority would guarantee victory over Australian and American material superiority appeared in a diary found near Wau in February 1943:

> Kept body and soul together by eating raw potatoes and dreamed of tomorrow's victory under enemy planes, under enemy bombardment, and under constant enemy assaults. Who would have such thoughts under these circumstances but Japanese soldiers? No one can stop us in our efforts to surmount difficulties. No doubt this is the way we Japanese always think.[52]

Not all Japanese felt so confident against the enemy's military might, especially as Japanese defeats became common. In a memoir of the New Guinea campaign, from September 1943 to the end of the war, Ogawa Masatsugu recalled:

> I came to feel the Australian military was very strong indeed. They didn't want to have infantry battles. They wanted to leave the fighting to mechanized power. The Japanese had only infantry.

Our artillery had almost no ammunition. If we fired even one shell, hundreds came back at us. 'Please don't fire at them,' we'd pray to our guns from the trenches.[53]

This assessment was most obviously true in the last year of the war, when the usual Australian approach to a defended enemy position was 'probe it – blast it – then occupy it'.[54] Interestingly, many Japanese reports spoke with horror not only of enemy artillery and aircraft, but also of automatic weapons and, especially, the humble mortar.[55] Some Japanese conceded that Australian strength did not always depend on support weapons. An American handbook on the Japanese, distributed in 1944, reported a Japanese comment that 'Australians are excellent guerilla fighters'.[56] That evaluation was presumably based on experiences against Australian independent companies in Timor and New Guinea.

Perhaps partly because of the impersonality of this 'mechanised' war, Ogawa Masatsugu apparently felt little antipathy towards Australians. He said: 'The "enemy"? I often wondered what that meant. We didn't hate the enemy. We seemed to fight them only because they showed up'.[57] Indeed, he drew a contrast between conditions in China, where the dead fell in man-to-man conflict with a 'real enemy', and New Guinea, where 'we didn't know what was killing us'. His chief recollection of the fighting there was of suicides and mercy killings administered by Japanese to Japanese.[58]

Masatsugu was rather scathing about Australian infantry, saying of the early success in the counterattack of October 1943: 'I was amazed how weak the Australian soldiers seemed'. Australians supposedly ran when attacked, and returned to mop up only after artillery, aircraft and exhaustion had robbed the Japanese of their ability to resist.[59] His comment is an echo of a wartime comment from a lieutenant, who said after fighting in the Jivevaneng area that when Australians advanced, whenever 'an adequate concentration of LMG, rifle, and grenade-discharger fire is put up against them, they will scream with panic and flee'.[60] These unflattering depictions differ from a diary entry reportedly found on a dead Japanese during the same campaign. Jack Craig reported that the entry ran: 'It is the first time in any campaign we have had to admit defeat & it is with tears in our eyes we see the Australians still advancing on us + pushing us back + back'.[61]

A similar attitude emerged in an account written immediately after the war by another participant in the Japanese offensive. In a letter to an Australian officer, Captain Timomoto praised his own troops' bravery but also said: 'The fighting abilities of the Australian army around Finschhafen impressed us very much … we were unable to occupy the territory your troops so bravely held'.[62] The letter may have been intended chiefly to flatter rather than inform, as may a Japanese staff officer's postwar report that in the operations in New Britain 'The Australian tactics were very steady and the Australian men were very persevering'.[63] However, a similar report by Japanese staff who had fought the Australian 17th Brigade in northern New Guinea did not hesitate to criticise the Australians for being overcautious and not repeating their successful earlier tactics of penetrating the Japanese front and sitting on Japanese supply lines.[64] Such a combination of praise and blame gives reason to believe the testimony of a Japanese platoon commander after his capture on Tarakan. He said that, although some Australians ran away when faced by ambushes on the feature called 'Joyce', the Australians generally were 'courageous'.[65]

If the generous words with which Japanese acknowledged their Australian opponents' prowess had been matched by chivalrous actions on the battlefield, much that transpired between the two sides would have been different.

CONCLUSION

In the diary he kept during the fighting at Milne Bay, Private Ron Berry recorded on 6 September 1942 that a fellow member of the 2/9th Battalion, 'Cammo' Williams, had been wounded in the mouth and head. The wounds had been incurred in an extraordinary fight: 'He met a Jap officer who had a pr of Binoculars and Cammo wanted the Binocs, and they shot it out. Cammo with a rifle and the Jap officer used a revolver. Cammo won the duel'.[1] A man-to-man struggle, won by the Australian. An individual 'duel' like this was unusual, even in the isolating circumstances of jungle warfare, yet it epitomised the archetypal struggle that exercised the minds of Australian soldiers: a 'Jap officer', the most hateful Japanese military figure, overcome in bitter struggle by the common Australian soldier, 'Cammo', in his desire for souvenirs. One could argue that Australians saw the whole war in terms of the 'digger' outfighting the enemy in duels, then taking their booty.

At about the same time as Berry was writing, a veteran of the desert campaign made a similar comment. Captain John Boas, who had lost much of his right elbow to a German shell at Tel el Eisa in July, reflected in his hospital bed that a typical Australian entering the July battle had felt a 'confidence in himself, as an individual superior to his opponent, that … is one of the chief factors contributing to his unshakeable morale'.[2]

In 1941, the Australian army's first year of action, the 6th Division's immense haul of prisoners in Libya and the 9th Division's success

against German troops (previously undefeated) at Tobruk established
not only confidence in self, comrades and leaders but also a belief that
each Australian was equal to several, if not many, Italians or Germans.
Similarly, the 7th Division's victories in Syria and the 8th's initial
successes in Malaya confirmed their members' self-evaluation. A conviction that, man-for-man, Australians were better soldiers than their
opponents, and indeed their allies, persisted throughout the war.[3]

A serious drawback in any attempt to argue that, however, was
that Australians were prominent in the forces crushed by the Germans
in Greece and Crete, and utterly defeated by the Japanese in the Far
East. Australians involved in those campaigns were all too aware that
their defeat was a potential blot on the AIF's escutcheon: that the
evacuation from Greece occurred on Anzac Day was a coincidence that
increased the embarrassment of many. The defeated Australians tried
hard to explain that they were not to blame. The enemy's numerical and
material superiority, especially their aerial dominance, were the usual
explanations. However, some non-participants, usually inspired by
inter-unit rivalry, considered that the 6th and 8th Divisions were
responsible for their disasters. Partly as a result of the later defeat,
concern about the fighting quality of the Japanese persisted until
personal experience dispelled it in 1942–43.

Generally, however, the Australian excuses for the disasters
of 1941 and 1942 were accepted by those who were not present.
Accepting the excuses meant that soldiers were still able to believe, in
February 1942, that 'the AIF [was] the best army in the world'.[4]

Although Australians tended to claim that their victories were due
to individual martial superiority, their defeats were generally ascribed
to other factors. Enemy soldiers used similar explanations for their
defeat at Australian hands. A Japanese lieutenant near Sattelberg wrote
in 1943, 'even the privates voice the same opinion. "If only we had
airplanes"'.[5] Change the place to Greece or Malaya and the writer
could have been Australian. The argument that material inferiority
contributed to defeat had considerable validity, unlike enemy soldiers'
arguments that Australians were successful because they were 'mad'
or 'drunken'.

It seems obvious, even without taking into account the impressive
casualty rates, that man-for-man the Australians were more efficient,
thoughtful and eager than their opponents in the first Libyan and
1943–45 South-West Pacific campaigns. It would also be unfair to

blame the Australians for their defeats in Greece and Crete in 1941 or in Asia in 1942. The example of Malaya, where Australians not only fought bravely but also suffered fewer battle deaths than they inflicted, has been mentioned.[6]

However, it is undeniable that in Malaya and elsewhere, the efforts of some Australian front-line soldiers were militarily undistinguished. Every unit had its share of men who were, to use one veteran's description, 'a bloody nuisance'.[7] Moreover, for various reasons – especially great or overwhelming adversity, or lack of training or experience – a few entire units or subunits were unable to function in combat as intended. This book does not discuss such reasons in detail, as doing so would place unnecessary and hurtful emphasis on the exercise of comparisons.

The main problem with such comparisons is not the lack of uniformity of effort or their internal and external divisiveness, but the fact that there are too many variables to make them valid. In most campaigns, Australians fought side by side with troops of other nationalities, and in no campaign were they entirely unassisted by their allies. In addition, all Australian victories over the Japanese were won with numerical and air superiority, against an opponent who was usually desperately short of supplies. Air and naval power were nearly always important factors in Australian campaigns.[8]

Further, it is difficult if not impossible to determine fairly what was typical of the enemy troops, and thus what we should compare with the Australians. This is particularly the case with the Australians' main enemy, the Japanese. For example, the Japanese were at their best against the Australians in 1942; the Australians were probably at their peak in terms of supplies, training and experience in 1945. How do we compare them?

We can say that the sheer determination of Australia's mainly volunteer soldiers was indispensable to their success, notably at Alamein and in Papua. There is also no doubt that Australians, even when defeated, were regarded as formidable fighters not only by their allies but also by their enemies. Indeed, we could argue that, other things being equal, the typical Australian front-line soldier was a fighter unsurpassed in World War II. Yet other things were never equal, and although some Australians liked to portray battle as a game or a boxing-match, the sides never met the preconditions for a fair sporting contest: equality of numbers and weight of hitting power. One

Australian's comment that the war would not be too bad if there were no aircraft or artillery – factors which usually favoured the Australians – was a neat expression of the fact that armies are not like boxers or cricket teams.[9]

In New Guinea, where it is hard to imagine a sport which could conceivably be likened to the vicious and ungentlemanly fighting, Trooper Love commented about untried reinforcements arriving at the front: 'The glorious game of war is going to give them a nasty jar'.[10] In struggling with jarring fear and singular squalor, and by learning that combat could be fully understood only by the initiated, the typical Australian soldier probably grasped that war was no game.

Yet Australians' tendency to use sporting metaphors was understandable. Theirs was a culture in which sport was central. Sport itself also models war in many ways, not least in the central importance of victory and defeat.

Furthermore, in spite of the obvious deficiencies of the approach to war and enemies which seeks to place them in a hierarchy, the character of a nation's army is largely determined by the contrast between it and its opponents' armies. Success against an opponent builds morale, tradition and self-esteem; defeat lowers morale and feeds self-doubt and internal division. The character of the Australian army in World War II owed much to its ability to be the winning side in most of its campaigns. Had it experienced only defeat, never victory, against any of its four opponents, there can be little doubt that its character would have changed.

One element that did change as a result of contact with the various enemies was soldiers' attitudes toward them. The shared horrors involved in contact stimulated compassion and understanding in at least some Australians.[11] Other impressions had nothing to do with empathy. The Italians and Vichy French were often more 'dinkum' than expected, but a very large proportion of soldiers felt that their enemies were 'dirty' fighters. The Germans emerged as the most consistent soldiers – a worthy yardstick – with whom Australians felt best able to identify at a technical level. As human beings, though, the Germans were often seen as victims of brainwashing.

However, they were far closer to the Australians than were the Japanese, whom the Australians generally placed second in the hierarchy of ability but last in terms of 'decency' or 'chivalry'. The murderous consequences of the mutual incomprehension and intolerance of what has rightly been called a 'race war' in the Pacific are a salutary lesson on the horrific potential of racism.[12]

The Vichy French were third and the Italians fourth in the Australians' hierarchy of ability. The Italians' place at the bottom derived mainly from their perceived lack of courage, a quality which Australians, like all soldiers, saw as the *sine qua non* of good soldiering.

Private Crawford, a thoughtful Australian who fought at Alamein, was able to distance himself from that view of courage and argue that the bravery exalted by the military is not a Christian form of courage: 'at best this courage is something perverted to drive a man on to the killing of his fellow-men, not the courage to stand alone against disease and poverty and disaster that have made the history of civilized peoples'.[13]

Other Australians also saw the immorality of war, and of inflicting suffering on their fellow human beings. Ultimately, though, most would have agreed with Lieutenant Gordon Combe's comment at Alamein that, to Australians, the war epitomised a paradox: the sin of killing was practised in pursuit of a righteous cause.

In the midst of the battle of El Alamein, Crawford and some mates buried six Germans and said a few words over their graves. As they walked away, one of the party said, 'That's more than we did for our own blokes'.[14] Men could not mourn much for an enemy when there were always some of their 'own blokes' to mourn. Ultimately they could not afford to care much about the enemy's lives, at least while hostilities were in progress.

We can speculate on the feelings about their enemies that Australian soldiers carried into peacetime. Animosities appear to have softened. The hostile comments made about Rommel and the Germans in a fine Australian book about Alamein in 1947 would be inconceivable in a book written now on that subject; they were less harsh even in battalion histories published in the postwar decades. Rommel and the Afrika Korps have become subjects of reverential treatment.[15] However, the Italian army long remained a subject of humour in Australian life: I well remember as a boy in the 1960s hearing jokes like 'What is the shortest book in the world?' 'The book of Italian war heroes' and 'How many gears does an Italian tank have?' 'Four. One forward and three reverse.' On the few occasions the Vichy French are mentioned so is the fact that Australians defeated the French Foreign

Legion – ignoring the facts that the Australians met only one small unit of the Legion, and that another Legion unit was fighting alongside the Australians.

Opinions about the Japanese have undergone the greatest revision, although this is not necessarily surprising as there was so much to revise. Television programs that offer the Japanese view of Kokoda as well as the Australian, or that feature both Japanese and Australian film stars, have sought to 'humanise' the Japanese enemy. Understandably, many veterans cannot bring themselves to forgive, but to others 'life goes on' and Japanese cars and televisions form part of their lives just as they do for most Australians. A remarkable story of forgiveness is that of Kenneth Harrison, an anti-tank gunner who was captured in Malaya. He endured three years of captivity and, despite the fact that most of the Japanese he came across were 'barbaric and sadistic', he experienced a surprising postwar change in outlook.[16] His hatred for the enemy disappeared and, the more he read, the more he became convinced that Japanese were 'possibly the bravest soldiers of all time'.[17] He rejected as 'too convenient' the argument of his friends that Japanese were not brave but 'fanatical', and even entitled his war memoir *The Brave Japanese*.[18] In a gesture of respect and reconciliation, he concluded that if he were to fight in another war he would like to be in an Australian battalion, flanked on both sides by Japanese battalions.[19]

Such praise is exceptional, and depends on detachment and reflection that are difficult for soldiers until their wars are over. However, even when the war against the Japanese was over, very few Australian soldiers could achieve Harrison's degree of detachment.

This book ends with an anecdote that emphasises not the all-too-obvious divisions between enemies, but their shared humanity. During the Battle of El Alamein, Sergeant John Lovegrove was wounded by a German stick grenade and taken to an underground Australian main dressing station a couple of kilometres behind the lines. Stretcher cases arrived from all over the battlefield. Doctors assessed the seriousness of each case on merit, regardless of nationality. Lovegrove was placed on a stretcher between an aged Italian soldier with a throat wound, and a young blond German with a shattered forearm – and assisted both men to drink the coffee dispensed by Salvation Army chaplains. It was after midnight and, as Australian, British, German and Italian wounded lay side by side, there was a tangible sense of relief that their battle was over. But, said Lovegrove, there was something else too: 'a compassion and equality was evident between men who, such a short time earlier that night, were locked in mortal combat'.[20] It is unfortunately unlikely that such an uplifting feeling would have existed had there been wounded Japanese instead of wounded Germans and Italians, but it is encouraging that sometimes the pain of war can give way to, and even foster, compassion and equality.

APPENDIX A

FIFTH COLUMNISTS

An unusual group of Australian enemies come under the heading 'fifth columnists'. The term originated in the Spanish Civil War, when the Nationalist General Mola told the Republican defenders of Madrid that he had not only four columns of troops outside the city but also one within, waiting to rise in his support.[1] The expression gained wide currency early in World War II when, in various countries attacked by Germany, there were fears, heightened by German propaganda, of German sympathisers undermining the defence.[2]

To Australians, the term meant enemy agents or soldiers operating behind the lines.[3] It has been said that 'fifth columnists were largely a myth', and that almost all their supposed activities were 'figments of the imagination'.[4] Although the Australians usually fought only in sparsely populated areas, suspicion of subversive agents was very prevalent among them. This apparently occurred in World War I also: it has been said that Australians at Gallipoli were afflicted with 'spy mania'.[5] Paul Fussell is probably correct to say that 'espionage, sabotage and treason' are popular in all wars, partly because they are interesting but also because they explain why victory is so long in coming.[6] This Appendix considers traitors and spies of all kinds, as encountered or suspected by Australian troops.

FIFTH COLUMNISTS IN THE MIDDLE EAST

By April 1941, at the latest, rumours about enemy fifth columnists were rife among Australian troops in the Middle East. On 6 April, the 9th

Division was engaged in the retreat that became known as the 'Benghazi Handicap'. During the retreat two senior British generals, Neame and O'Connor, with British and Australian troops, were captured in an ambush near Derna. A rumour grew in the 9th Division that those men had been directed into the ambush by a German dressed in the captured uniform of an English provost. The official history declared that the belief, like those that had grown in similar circumstances in France in 1940, was unfounded, despite being 'almost universally held' within the division.[7] On the other hand, the official medical history said that a man dressed as an Australian with a slouch hat directed twelve ambulances, and later the generals and others, into the German ambush.[8]

In Greece, at about the same time, men of the 6th Division near Vevi were said to be watching rather anxiously as Greek civilian refugees passed through the British lines. The 2/4th Battalion, which was in the front line, had to detach one of its rifle companies to guard an Allied headquarters, so great was the concern that the Germans might use fifth columnists.[9] A major in the 2/7th wrote in his diary of 'extensive' precautions being taken against fifth columnists.[10] According to Gullett, the Australians in Greece were warned of ruses involving military policemen, like the one suspected at Derna. Indeed, he averred that in the retreat through Greece, his company of the 2/6th Battalion was once misdirected by a fake military policeman. After detecting their mistake the company returned to the fake checkpoint and, Gullett asserted, an Australian officer shot the German.[11] The acting commander of that battalion also described an incident on 26 April, when a suspected fifth columnist claiming to be Greek was handed to the Australian Provost Company. The official report said the suspect was 'somewhat roughly handled in an effort to extricate truth from him'.[12] The commanding officer of another Australian unit, the 2/2nd Field Regiment, asserted soon after the campaign that on the night of 8 April 'German 5th columnists' had cut the regiment's signal lines in ten places.[13]

Even before arriving in Greece, the CO of the 2/8th Battalion lectured his men on the activity of fifth columnists there: he pointed out that the German consulate was still active in Athens, where several thousand Germans lived.[14] On 19 April, a diarist in the 2/8th wrote that he had gone forward to join comrades defending the Brallos Pass only to find that they had retreated, on the orders of a brigadier. The soldier noted parenthetically: '(afterwards discovered he was a fifth column)'.[15] Although the story sounds unlikely, the 2/8th Battalion history also reported that late on 19 April a brigadier in a car bearing the number 94 had indeed given a traffic control sergeant from the unit orders to withdraw from the pass. Brigade HQ informed the unit that no such orders had been issued by the brigadier: to the battalion it was 'yet another indication' of fifth column work.[16] According to the 2/7th Battalion report on 18 April, the unit captured twelve fifth columnists, two of whom were found breaking bottles on the road and carrying sticks of gelignite.[17]

Cam Bennett was with the 2/5th Battalion as they marched the last few kilometres to the beach from which they were to be evacuated from Greece. While Bennett's party paused at a dilapidated building, a civilian approached them. He explained that he was a naval officer, and asked Bennett for details of his unit and the number to be evacuated. Tired and uncertain, Bennett refused to tell the man, who shrugged and walked off. An Australian sergeant from another unit observed the incident from the side of the road, and told Bennett that he suspected the civilian was a fifth columnist. Pulling out a revolver, the sergeant demanded that the civilian identify himself. Though the civilian's explanation satisfied Bennett, the sergeant replied 'Like hell. You're a German bastard and I'm going to shoot you'. Insisting that Bennett, an officer, follow him, the sergeant took the man to the side of the building and told him to say anything he had to say. The civilian stood erect, gave a Nazi salute and said 'Heil Hitler'. The sergeant shot him in the upper chest. On the man's body was a book containing numbers and details of Allied units.[18]

These anecdotes from Greece strongly indicate that the fears of fifth column activity were not always 'figments of the imagination'. They made a very strong impression on soldiers who fought there. A private in the 2/2nd Pioneers, soon to see his first action in Syria, wrote to a friend that, according to Australians recently returned from Greece, 'our biggest enemy is 5th columnists'.[19]

The Syrian campaign offered many opportunities for fifth column work, but there are few examples of it. There was a suspicion early in the campaign that the accurate Vichy French artillery fire against the inland attack was being directed by spies with signalling equipment. An official article on the topic said vaguely that 'Measures were taken to suppress this'.[20] Three Australians captured by the Vichy French were told during interrogation the name of the ship on which they had come to the Middle East and the date on which it sailed: clearly, the enemy had accurate knowledge of at least some troop movements.[21] When the 9th Division was in Syria in 1942, the issue of spies arose. Soon after his arrival, one infantryman talked of the need to look after prisoners, including 'some Nazi spies, who will probably be shot'.[22] Later that year, another diarist recorded that four spies had been shot at Aleppo prison.[23] One battalion history called the presence of fifth columnists a 'disturbing aspect of life' in Syria, but supported it only by asserting that such agents several times cut the battalion's telephone lines.[24] Another battalion history reported the unconcerned amusement of troops in May 1942 when they were told that two men who had inspected water-carts and company cook-house lines the day before had been spies posing as hygiene personnel.[25]

Yet on campaign the previous year, 9th Division troops had been more willing to listen to spy stories, such as the one concerning the Benghazi Handicap. Suspicions continued during the siege of Tobruk; indeed when Australians and other British troops entered the fortress at the end of the Handicap, a German fifth columnist who claimed to be a native was arrested at a roadblock into the town. According to the battalion history, the man was wearing a mixture of Italian uniform and civilian clothes, so his failure to convince is perhaps not surprising.[26] During the siege, the 2/23rd Battalion newsletter laughingly suggested that German propaganda leaflets had been dropped because someone told them the defenders were short of paper: 'probably Schmitt the Spy'.[27]

However, the question of spies was not considered comical by everyone. Private John Butler, also in the 2/23rd, wrote in his diary just after the defeat of the 18th Brigade's attempt to recapture lost territory: 'the enemy knew of the attack, in fact it was whispered a false order was sent to our leader ordering him to withdraw and consolidate his position'. Butler concluded, 'It is all so mystifying and upsetting'.[28] He also said that a German officer had called on members of the 2/24th Battalion to surrender, calling out 'You are "A" or "B" Coy (whoever he was addressing) 2/24th, I call on you to surrender'.[29] Such stories had an impact on the battalion. When three men and an English signals officer approached Butler in order to tap a line the following day, Butler's lieutenant was called. The Australian officer grabbed one of the men, put a revolver to his chest and searched all four. Only when an Australian recognised the English officer did the tension dissolve. When a soldier told Butler 'It's damned ridiculous, the man is obviously an Englishman', he replied that 'Being an Englishman signifies nothing these days'. Butler concluded a long diary note about how vital such challenges could be with the words 'Suspect – Suspect and suspect'. Later that day he declared that the key to German information-gathering had been discovered: when the Australians withdrew from a certain point in the line, they did not sever their telephone wire.[30]

Five months later, as the Australian part in the siege drew to a close, the first civilian enemy agent was captured at Tobruk: a Libyan, who with another agent had been ordered to ascertain Allied dispositions. The man was not captured by the Australians but the enemy attack for which he was gathering information was supposed to fall on the 2/13th Battalion, the last Australian battalion in the fortress. The Australians waited for the assault, which never came.[31]

In the Australians' last campaign in the desert, in July–November 1942, concerns about enemy spying remained very strong. With the approach of the great British offensive at El Alamein in October 1942, concern about maximising surprise inevitably made security a big issue. Lance-Corporal Jack Craig wrote in his diary early that month of a talk, where speakers had emphasised the importance of a great battle that lay ahead. 'We were also told a lot about espionage + spies', Craig reported.[32] An artilleryman, David Goodhart, recalled that only two days before the opening of the battle, his regiment received a talk on security.[33] He stated that fifth column work was 'rife' and not only among the 'wogs', who were barred from moving west of Amiriya. Since the defeat of the Bulimba operation in September, he maintained, the Australians were less inclined to scoff at stories of German infiltrators dressed as Australians. These were 'ardent young Nazis who had grown up in Australia, gone to school there, in fact, and who spoke the dinkum language better than we did'. Goodhart's evidence for this is very thin: a story that a soldier dressed in British uniform was unable to produce his paybook and, although he knew the password, was probably a spy. Goodhart also asserted that the Germans knew every movement of the AIF in Egypt.[34] A ballad told how Vernal Vera, Axis female spy, got such information from Cairo to Rommel.[35]

FIFTH COLUMNISTS IN THE WAR AGAINST
THE JAPANESE

In December 1940, even before the 2/43rd Battalion sailed for the Middle East, its men heard a lecture on 'security of information', with vivid illustrations of fifth column activities in Australia. Lieutenant Rupert Hamer told companies about the visit of a German count, and how valuable information might be allowed to leak to the enemy through careless contacts with institutions at home.[36] After the war 'at home' began in earnest, with the entry of Japan, concern about fifth column activity became great among Australian soldiers in the Pacific.

Suspicion of Asiatic motives fell on fertile soil in Malaya, where Australians of the 8th Division awaited a Japanese attack for most of 1941. An Australian sergeant wrote home in November: 'I think that fifth column work here is certainly of high standing'. The evidence he gave was that an educated Malay had asked him whether Australians mixed pig fat with Australian butter. 'Imagine what that would mean to a Moslem', he told his correspondent.[37] At Christmas, with the campaign begun, the sergeant found his views confirmed as he looked back on what had gone wrong. In explaining 'Jap methods' in another letter, he said, 'Firstly they prepared for the campaign by gaining a first hand knowledge of the campaign and "white anting". The Malays have been won over a great deal + furnish guides etc which are essential'.[38]

The sergeant was certainly not alone in believing that there was a large-scale Japanese fifth column in Malaya.[39] The commander of the 8th Division, General Bennett, told brigade, battalion and other commanders on 23 December that units had to adopt ruses to counter fifth column activity.[40] Four days earlier, men of the 2/20th Battalion had been doing just that near Mersing. Patrols found evidence of fifth column activity: there were signs, made of strips of material 2 metres wide and placed on rooftops, pointing to Australian army and gun positions.[41] An NCO of the 2/26th Battalion recalled that in January, after the Australians had become engaged in the fighting, his men caught a fifth columnist using a white flag to direct Japanese aircraft to the Australian positions. The man was apparently executed.[42] In February, as the campaign came to a tragic close at Singapore, an Australian gunner wrote in his diary that, as they neared surrender or death, they were running out of ammunition. For this he blamed bombing and fifth columnists.[43] Another Australian wrote in his diary, apparently on or immediately after the surrender, the heading 'Reasons we were pushed back were'. The first he listed was 'Infiltration + getting behind us – 5th columnists – snipers behind lines, flour on road, arrows on roof'.[44] Even allowing for the Australians' rationalising required by Japanese successes in early operations, clearly the Japanese did make some use of fifth columnists in Malaya and Singapore.

In the immediate aftermath of Singapore, suspicion of natives reached a peak. A month after the fall of Singapore, a 6th Division officer in Ceylon wrote in his diary that Buddhist priests, potential fifth columnists, were not to be trusted.[45] In April, another Australian in Ceylon stated gloomily: 'We hear stories of fith [sic] Column operating here, and I feel myself that the place is lousy with Japs. One is always passing different natives that have more than just a little Japenese [sic] blood in them'.[46]

In the Pacific islands that became central to Australia's war in 1942, Australians also suspected or saw local assistance given to the Japanese. On New Britain soon after the Japanese invasion, Lieutenant Dawson saw evidence that natives had helped the Japanese find their way to and along a track which was the only means of escape for an Australian company. He also saw the Japanese shaking hands with a very happy local German missionary.[47]

An American wartime handbook said of Japanese methods of attack that 'the employment of advance agents and fifth columnists is standard practice'.[48] Once the Japanese were forced onto the defensive, such methods became less important in Australians' thoughts. However, Private Murphy, of the 2/23rd Battalion, twice mentioned spies in his 1943 diary. On the tablelands in Queensland in May, he confided to his diary: 'It is beleived that their [sic] are quite a few spies in these tablelands and it is a known thing that somewhere within eight miles of this camp their [sic] is an enemy radio station in communication with the enemy'.[49] In October, Murphy was in action with the battalion in New Guinea. He noted an instance of Japanese espionage: 'Another Jap was caught spying well behind our lines again today, the second in a few days, they have been dressed in Aussie clothes wearing our hat and have both been caught looking the artillery over'.[50]

In the British army, 'security' was considered an essential principle of war. Soldiers had to be careful of possible enemy action, and although in some instances their suspicions now appear ludicrous,

Private Butler doubtless had a point about the need to 'suspect'. Fifth columnists were often only shadows without substance, representing the fears of men facing defeat and all its frightening uncertainties. However, they were real often enough to invalidate the claims that they were 'mythical' and that their work was a mere figment of Australian imagination. Even if fifth columnists had not existed it would probably have been necessary to invent them, as they provided such good evidence that the enemy was treacherous and unsporting.

APPENDIX B

ORDERS OF BATTLE OF AUSTRALIA'S ENEMIES

This Appendix lists the main formations that fought Australians under the banners of the four nationalities. Usually enemy troops were members of divisions, but others were in units attached to corps. Units below divisional level, which were very numerous, are included only when divisional-size units were not employed in the campaign, notably in Syria and the South-West Pacific Area. In some campaigns, especially against the Japanese, Australians fought only remnants or parts of formations. Only enemy formations that came into direct contact with Australians have been listed. The main sources consulted were the seven volumes of the army series in the Australian Official History.

ITALY

Libya 1941 (including capture of Bardia, Tobruk and Giarabub oasis)
Corps: XX, XXII, XXIII
Divisions: 17th (Pavia), 60th (Sabratha), 61st (Sirte), 62nd
    (Marmarica), 63rd (Cyrene), 64th (Catanzaro), 1st Blackshirt,
    2nd Blackshirt[1]
Siege of Tobruk 1941
Corps: XXI
Divisions: 17th (Pavia), 25th (Bologna), 27th (Brescia), 102nd
    (Trento) Motorised, 132nd (Ariete)
El Alamein 1942
Corps: XX, XXI

144

Divisions: 60th (Sabratha), 101st (Trieste) Motorised, 102nd (Trento) Motorised, 133rd (Littorio)

GERMANY

Siege of Tobruk 1941
Corps: Deutsches Afrika Korps
Divisions: 5th Light, 15th Panzer, Afrika zbV (later called '90th Light')
Greece 1941
Corps: XVIII Mountain, XL Panzer
Divisions: 2nd Panzer, 5th Panzer, 72nd, 6th Mountain, 7th Air, Leibstandarte SS 'Adolf Hitler', possibly 9th Panzer
Crete 1941
Corps: XI Fliegerkorps (Air Corps)
Divisions: 5th Mountain, 7th Air
El Alamein 1942
Corps: Deutsches Afrika Korps
Divisions: 15th Panzer, 21st Panzer, 90th Light, 164th Light

VICHY FRANCE

Note: The troops defending Syria were divided into regiments rather than divisions.
Syria 1941
Regiments: 22nd Algerian, 29th Algerian, 24th Colonial, 7th Chasseurs d'Afrique, 6th Foreign Legion, 1st Moroccan Spahis, 17th Senegalese, 16th Tunisian, possibly 6th Chasseurs d'Afrique

JAPAN

Malaya 1942
Army: XXV
Divisions: Imperial Guards, 5th
Singapore 1942
Divisions: Imperial Guards, 5th, 18th
New Britain and New Ireland 1942
144th Infantry Regiment

Ambon 1942
38th Division HQ, 228th Regimental Group, 1st Kure SNLF (Special Naval Landing Force)
Timor 1942
228th Regimental Group, 3rd Yokosuka SNLF
Java 1942
Divisions: 2nd, possibly 38th
Kokoda Track
41st Regiment, 144th Regiment, 15th Independent Engineer Regiment
Milne Bay
3rd Kure SNLF, 5th Kure SNLF, 5th Yokosuka SNLF, 10th Naval Landing Corps
Buna, Gona, Sanananda
21st Independent Mixed Brigade, 41st Regiment, 144th Regiment, 170th Regiment, 229th Regiment, 15th Independent Engineer Regiment, 5th Sasebo SNLF, 5th Yokosuka SNLF
New Guinea 1943–45
Army: XVIII
Divisions: 20th, 41st, 51st
Bougainville 1944–45
Army: XVII
Divisions etc.: 6th Division, 38th Independent Mixed Brigade
New Britain 1944–45
Army: 8th Area
Divisions: 17th, 38th
Borneo 1945
Army: XXXVII
North Borneo: 4th Independent Mixed Regiment, 56th Brigade
Balikpapan: 22nd Naval Base Force, 454th Battalion
Tarakan: 2nd Naval Garrison Force, 455th Independent Mixed Battalion

Notes

INTRODUCTION

1 The topic of relations in prisoner of war camps is beyond the scope of this work. To examine Australians' attitudes to these nationalities as captors and captives is a related but essentially different task. This book also concentrates exclusively on the army.

2 Marshall, *Men Against Fire*, pp. 44–5.

3 White, *Green Armour*, p. 200. This is discussed in detail below.

4 Why the defeats and victories occurred is discussed in the relevant sections below.

5 Baker, *The Australian Language*, pp. 166, 177.

6 Gray, *The Warriors*, p. 160.

7 Grossman, *On Killing*, pp. 24–5, 34–6.

8 Marshall, *Men Against Fire*, p. 50. He later revised these estimates for the Korean and Vietnam Wars; ibid., p. 35; Watson, *War on the Mind*, p. 44.

9 For example, interviews with Alwyn Shilton (ex 2/5 Bn) and Jack Caple (ex 2/24) on 19/2/99. For further discussion of the Marshall thesis, see Johnston, *At the Front Line*, pp. 85–7; Holmes, *Firing Line*, p. 325.

10 Bourke, *An Intimate History of Killing*, pp. 1, 37, 244, 373. Acknowledging that attitudes differed between wars and enemies: p. 374.

11 Pte J.H. Ewen, 61 Bn, D1/4/45.

12 Holmes, *Firing Line*, p. 361.

13 On civilians, see Gray, *The Warriors*, p. 132. Enemy civilians are discussed in Appendix A.

14 ibid., pp. 134, 137.

15 The Middle East is defined here as including Greece and Crete, as it was in wartime publications such as *Active Service*.

CHAPTER 1: THE ITALIANS

1 Knox, 'The Italian Armed Forces', pp. 163, 170; Sullivan, 'The Italian Soldier in Combat', pp. 179–81, 184, 187.
2 Knox, 'The Italian Armed Forces', pp. 162, 170, 172; Sullivan, 'The Italian Soldier in Combat', p. 187.
3 Sullivan, 'The Italian Soldier in Combat', p. 178.
4 These figures include 6th Division casualties from 12 December 1940 to 5 January 1941: Long, *To Benghazi*, p. 203n.
5 Quoted in Knox, *Mussolini Unleashed*, p. 256.
6 Some forces in Savige's brigade group had contact with Germans, and possibly Italians, in the February–9 March period: Long, *To Benghazi*, pp. 285–6.
7 See, for example, Wilmot, *Tobruk 1941*, p. 232; Lewin, *The Life and Death of the Afrika Korps*, p. 73.
8 Maughan, *Tobruk and El Alamein*, p. 165.
9 von Mellenthin, *Panzer Battles*, p. 164; Maughan, *Tobruk and El Alamein*, pp. 574–6.
10 Pte A. Ulrick, 2/2 Bn, L24/10/40.
11 Pte J.K. Atock, 2/7 Bn, L6/10/40.
12 For example Spr J.G. Cannam, 2/8 Fd Coy, L23/3/41; Pte J.M. Butler, 2/23 Bn, D17/8/41; Wilmot, *Tobruk 1941*, p. 5; Cpl R.F. Hoffmann, HQ 16 Bde, L1/2/41.
13 Butler, D13/1/41.
14 Lt G. Gill, 2/48 Bn, L9/2/41 (my emphasis).
15 Cannam, L23/3/41.
16 Wilmot, *Tobruk 1941*, p. 4.
17 Capt G. Laybourne Smith, 2/3 Fd Regt, L3/2/41; Fancke, *Mud and Blood in the Field*, p. 232.
18 Cpl M. Chellew, 2/13 Bn, quoted in Shelton Smith, *The Boys Write Home*, p. 51 (my emphasis).
19 Atock, L11/1/41 (my emphasis).
20 Hoffmann, L1/2/41.
21 Examples in Gullett, *Not as a Duty Only*, p. 19; Givney, *The First at War*, p. 113.
22 Long, *To Benghazi*, pp. 198, 203; Gullett, *Not as a Duty Only*, p. 1.
23 Sgt R. da Fonte, 2/8 Bn, D21/1/41 (my emphasis). See also Long, *To Benghazi*, p. 229; Knox, *Mussolini Unleashed*, p. 256.
24 Examples in Caccia-Dominioni, *Alamein 1933–1962*, pp. 72, 74, 82–3, 213.
25 Maughan, *Tobruk and El Alamein*, pp. 655–6; Lucas Phillips, *Alamein*, p. 135.
26 Pte J. Ritchie, 2/32 Bn, quoted in Yeates & Loh, *Red Platypus*, p. 34; Maughan, *Tobruk and El Alamein*, p. 575, Trigellis-Smith, *Britain to Borneo*, p. 92; IWM AL866/6, Panzerarmee Afrika, Tagesmeldungen, 17 July 1942.

27 Lt C.H. Cawthorne, 2/43rd Bn, quoted in Yeates & Loh, *Red Platypus*, p. 34.
28 Gullett, *Not as a Duty Only*, p. 13; Givney, *The First at War*, p. 113.
29 Spr R. Beilby, 2/1 Fd Coy, D3/1/41.
30 Pte A.Wallin, 2/2 AGH, D7/1/41, reporting the words of a wounded participant. See also Givney, *The First at War*, p. 113. The artillery was the best arm of the Italian army: Sullivan, 'The Italian Soldier in Combat', p. 185.
31 Positive about Italian equipment: Pte G. Nowland, 9 Div AASC attached to 2/15 Bn, D-/5/41; Ulrick, L15/2/41; Walker, *Middle East and Far East*, p.142; Givney, *The First at War*, p. 136.
32 Johnston, *At the Front Line*, p. 110; Wilmot, *Tobruk 1941*, p. 4; Combe, Ligertwood & Gilchrist, *The Second 43rd*, p. 27.
33 Long, *To Benghazi*, p. 183n. See also Haywood, *Six Years in Support*, p. 28; Pte P. Partington, 2/5 Bn, D3/1/41. On grenades see Combe, Ligertwood & Gilchrist, *The Second 43rd*, p. 26; Wilmot, *Tobruk 1941*, p. 229; Gnr P. Russell, 2/2 Fd Regt, L23/2/41.
34 Atock, L10/3/41. Similar: Pte E. MacLeod, 2/11 Bn, L6/4/41; da Fonte, D27/1/41. Numerous soldiers reported being fired on with dud Italian shells.
35 L/Cpl R. Turner, 2/11 Bn, L8/3/41. Similar: Lt C. Chrystal, 2/4 Bn, D4/1/41; Ackland & Ackland, *Word from John*, p. 82.
36 Lt E. Wilmoth, 2/8 Bn, L7/3/41.
37 Ulrick, L15/2/41.
38 Cpl C. Greenwood, 2/17 Bn, D11/4/41. Some Australians did criticise technical aspects of the defences: Givney, *The First at War*, p. 113; Long, *To Benghazi*, pp. 205–6; Wilmot, *Tobruk 1941*, p. 7.
39 MacLeod, L6/4/41 (my emphasis). Similar comments that Italians should have done better: Beilby, D7/1/41; Lt W. Sherlock, 2/6 Bn, L24/1/41; Hay, *Nothing Over Us*, p. 91.
40 Pte R.L. Hoffmann, 16 Bde, L1/2/41. Similar: Hay, *Nothing Over Us*, p. 98.
41 Sigmn T. Neeman, 17 Bde Sigs, L-/1/41.
42 Laybourne Smith, L4/2/41.
43 D30/3/41. Feeble: Pte R. Aldridge, 2/13 Bn, L early 1941. Similar: Lt E. Lecky, 20 Bde Sigs, L7/7/41.
44 Butler, D16/4/97.
45 D25/4/41.
46 Gill, L28/4/41.
47 Lt G. Combe, 2/43 Bn, L19/7/42, quoted in Combe, 'My Three-Score Years and Ten', Part I, p. 190 (my emphases).
48 Pte L. Murphy, 2/23 Bn, D30/10/42. See also Goodhart, *We of the Turning Tide*, p. 151.
49 Sgt R. Bourke, 2/1 Bn, L-/1/41; Butler, D16/4/41; Pte C. Keys, 2/15 Bn, L20/9/41. See also Liddell Hart, *The Rommel Papers*, p. 262.
50 Fancke, *Mud and Blood in the Field*, p. 171.

51 ibid., p. 237. This letter was probably fictional.
52 ibid., p. 216. Other humour on Italian cowardice: pp. 98, 137, 140–1, 164, 232, 334.
53 Filthy and unhygienic: Walker, *Middle East and Far East*, p. 188; Wilmot, *Tobruk 1941*, p. 169. Dirt and contempt: Share, *Mud and Blood*, p. 34. Contempt: Sgt C. Symington, 2/17 Bn, D19/4/41; Bourke, L-/1/41.
54 Not liking bayonet: Pte A. Armstrong, 2/13 Bn, D-/4?/41; Nowland, D19/5/41; Hoffmann, L1/2/41; Glenn, *Tobruk to Tarakan*, p. 44. Fainting: Serle, *The Second Twenty-Fourth*, p. 199.
55 WOII C. Craig, L-/12/42. Bardia and Tobruk: Wilmot, *Tobruk 1941*, p. 40; Hoffmann, L27/1/41.
56 Wallin, D7/1/41.
57 Bentley, *The Second Eighth*, p. 33.
58 Long, *To Benghazi*, pp. 178, 185, 229. Also Graeme-Evans, *Of Storms and Rainbows*, p. 168; Hay, *Nothing Over Us*, p. 121; Lt F. Coffill, 7 Div Amn Sub Park, D4/1/41; Lt J. Cumpston, HQ 26 Bde, D16/5/41; Charlton, *The Thirty-Niners*, pp. 111, 124; Jones, 'A Volunteer's Story', p. 58; Bennett, *Rough Infantry*, p. 61. Where these accounts describe specific incidents, none appear to be ones described elsewhere.
59 Pte J. Davies, 2/33 Bn, L-/5/41. Reporting incidents heard.
60 Goodhart, *We of the Turning Tide*, p. 66.
61 Clift, *Saga of a Sig*, p. 41. See also Barter, *Far Above Battle*, pp. 68–9; Barrett, *We Were There*, p. 251.
62 D29/3/41.
63 Russell, L23/2/41.
64 Ulrick, L12/1/41.
65 Long, *To Benghazi*, p. 200.
66 Cannam, L23/3/41.
67 Capt. C. Golding, 2/1 Bn, L6/2/41.
68 Givney, *The First at War*, p. 111.
69 Long, *To Benghazi*, p. 200.
70 ibid., p. 165n; Beilby, D21/1/41.
71 Long, *To Benghazi*, p. 265.
72 Beilby, D3/1/41.
73 Use of this concept: Beilby, D7/1/41; Greenwood, D11/4/41; Cpl A. Hackshaw, 2/11 Bn, D5/1/41. Similar: Atock, L28/1/41; Butler, D16/4/41; Glenn, *Tobruk to Tarakan*, p. 44.
74 L4/2/41.
75 Maughan, *Tobruk and El Alamein*, p. 182.
76 Bentley, *The Second Eighth*, p. 25.
77 L12/1/41.
78 C. Craig, L-/12/42; Cpl J. Craig, 2/13 Bn, D8/11/42; Shelton Smith, *The Boys Write Home*, p. 61. Similar in Libya: Keys, L20/9/41; Jones, 'A Volunteer's Story', p. 38. Docility: Wallin, D10/1/41. On Germans also driving themselves into imprisonment in trucks: Butler, D6/11/42.

79 Laybourne Smith, L1/2/41. Similar: Murphy, D22/11/41; Neeman, L-/1/41; Gnr H. Sunley, 2/1 Fd Regt, D?/1/41; Wallin, D16/1/41; WOII H. Williams, 2/24 Bn, L3/6/41; Cpl D. Plank, 2/2 MG Bn, L9/11/42. Italians looking unhappy: Wallin, D4/1/41.
80 Share, *Mud and Blood*, p. 37; Goodhart, *We of the Turning Tide*, p. 66.
81 Pte A. Currie, 2/23 Bn, L2/4/41.
82 L14/3/41.
83 Three other forms of assistance deserve mention. At Bardia, Italian doctors helped to treat Australian wounded: Walker, *Middle East and Far East*, p. 138; Barter, *Far Above Battle*, p. 64. During the siege of Tobruk, Italian stretcher-bearers 'did a prodigious amount of work apparently willingly' in the 6th AGH there: Kyle, 'The Treatment of Wounded', p. 460. Another form of help which pleased but did not impress Australians was the willingness of Italian prisoners to give information about enemy positions: Glenn, *Tobruk to Tarakan*, p. 71; Masel, *The Second 28th*, p. 47.
84 L/Cpl A. Jones, 2/43 Bn, L3/4/41.
85 L-/1/41; Sgt J. Lovegrove, 2/43 Bn, D25/10/42; Shelton Smith, *The Boys Write Home*, p. 14. Sympathy and pity: Long, *To Benghazi*, p. 200; Butler, D16/4/41 and 8/8/41; Lt F. Coffill, D5/1/41; Murphy, D30/10/42; Pte W. Richardson, 2/1 MG Bn, L12/1/41; Pte R. Zuckur, 2/24 Bn, L-/5?/41; Ackland & Ackland, *Word from John*, p. 82; Bennett, *Rough Infantry*, p. 161.
86 There were especially difficult logistical problems in catering for prisoners at Tobruk: Long, *To Benghazi*, p. 239; Hay, *Nothing Over Us*, p. 130; Barter, *Far Above Battle*, pp. 68–9. An officer in charge of Australians who were guarding the prisoners criticised the indiscipline and selfishness of POWs who feigned extreme thirst and passed Red Cross armbands around to get preferential treatment with food and water: Maj H. Thomas, 2/7 Bn, D23/1/41; Bolger & Littlewood, *The Fiery Phoenix*, p. 52.
87 MacLeod, L6/4/41. See also Beilby, D3/1/41; Wallin, D7/1/41.
88 Chapman, *Iven G. Mackay*, p. 198. No hesitation: Wilmot, *Tobruk 1941*, p. 24. See also Haywood, *Six Years in Support*, pp. 152–3.
89 Some Australian soldiers expressed antagonism towards Italians at home: Aldridge, L20/8/41; Pte W. Fairbrother, 2/10 Bn, D11/6/40; Pte J. Trimble, 2/3 Bn, L17/7/40.
90 Golding, L6/2/41. Hodge was the company commander. See also Macksey, *Beda Fomm*, p. 104. Impersonal attitude: Pte R. Robertson, 2/2 Bn, L15/12/42.
91 Wartime report by Pte S.L. Carroll, 2/11 Bn. Small fry: Gill, L14/3/41. Satellites: Fancke, *Mud and Blood in the Field*, p. 171.
92 Aldridge, L early 1941; Fancke, *Mud and Blood in the Field*, pp. 435, 516.
93 Crawford, 'Forward from El Alamein', p. 199.
94 AWM 3/2632, Middle East Military Censorship Fortnightly Summary, 4–17/11/42.
95 Caccia-Dominioni, *Alamein 1933–1962*, p. 87.
96 ibid.

97 Moorehead, *African Trilogy*, p. 86. See also Barter, *Far Above Battle*, p. 52.
98 Russell, L23/2/41.
99 Moorehead, *African Trilogy*, p. 96. See also 2/48 Bn newsletter, *Khamseen Chronicle*, 30 August 1942, in 2/48 Bn War Diary and 9th Australian Division Intelligence Summary 281, 29 August 1942.
100 Bulletproof: Long, *To Benghazi*, p. 178; Beilby L19/1/41. Italians impressed: Charlton, *The Thirty-Niners*, pp. xviii, 111.
101 Masel, *The Second 28th*, p. 115.
102 Capt L. Bolner, 46th Trento Artillery, quoted in Caccia-Dominioni, *Alamein 1933–1962*, p. 230 (my emphases).
103 Goodhart, *We of the Turning Tide*, p. 99.
104 For more detail see Johnston, *At the Front Line*, pp. 64–6.
105 During battle: da Fonte, D22/1/41; Partington, D3/1/41. After battle: Bdr H. Adeney, 2/2 Fd Regt, L12/1/41; Hoffmann, L1/2/41; Bennett, *Rough Infantry*, p. 55.
106 Negroes: Walker, *Alam Halfa and El Alamein*, p. 290. Masses of armour: Knox, *Mussolini Unleashed*, p. 255.
107 Capt J.S. Cumpston, 2/23 Bn, D6/7/42; Share, *Mud and Blood*, pp. 105, 108.
108 Fearnside, *Half to Remember*, p. 143.
109 Fearnside, *Bayonets Abroad*, p. 252.
110 Brown, *Retreat to Victory*, p. 193.
111 Caccia-Dominioni, *Alamein 1933–1962*, pp. 70, 81, 82, 229.
112 ibid., pp. 70, 229.
113 Greene & Massignani, *Rommel's North African Campaign*, p. 133.
114 ibid. The action concerned was at Tobruk on the night of 30 April 1941, when the Australians suffered heavy casualties in German attacks: Wilmot, *Tobruk 1941*, pp. 129–30.

CHAPTER 2: THE GERMANS: THE REAL ENEMY

1 The Australians suffered several hundred casualties in this retreat, but no consolidated figure appears to be available. See Maughan, *Tobruk and El Alamein*, pp. 76–108. Not all casualties are mentioned there.
2 The term 'Nazi' was not as common as 'Hun' or 'Jerry'. Other terms used were 'Gerald', 'Heenie' and 'Herman'.
3 Cpl J. Craig, 2/13 Bn, D26/10/42 (my emphasis). His account seems to be largely accurate.
4 Hackshaw note in D5/1/41, clearly written after the later campaigns.
5 For example: Pte C.P. Keys, 2/15 Bn, L4/10/43; Share, *Mud and Blood*, p. 312; Jones, 'A Volunteer's Story', p. 249. But see Johnston, *War Diary 1942*, p. 120n.
6 Some soldiers in Greece saw little of the Germans except their airmen: Bennett, *Rough Infantry*, p. 82.

7 Cpl N.B. Campbell, 2/5 Bn, L2/5/41. Also on German ingenuity: Pte J.M. Butler, 2/23 Bn, D12, 31/5/41; Maughan, *Tobruk and El Alamein*, p. 268; Pte C.J. O'Dea, 2/28 Bn, D14/9/42.

8 Sgt C. Greenwood, 2/17 Bn, D16/9/41.

9 Pte E. Lambert, 2/15 Bn, D1/11/42. Similar: Maj L.A. Fell, 2/24 Bn, D30/4/41.The '88' gun was particularly feared.

10 In Maughan, *Tobruk and El Alamein*, p. 268. Similar: Greenwood, D3, 5/7/41; Pte L.F. Williams, 2/11 Bn, L3/11/41.

11 D5/5/41. This may be a simplification of the way the Afrika Korps worked, but the Axis combined arms coordination was at this stage undoubtedly better than that of Commonwealth forces. See Lewin, *The Life and Death of the Afrika Korps*, p. 70; von Mellenthin, *Panzer Battles*, p. 64. A hostile commentator's admission that Germans were 'professionals' in their approach: Goodhart, *We of the Turning Tide*, p. 219.

12 L2/11/41.

13 Symington, D18/4/41. Similar: Jones, L22/5/41; Murphy, D23/8/42; 2/48 Bn War Diary, 12/7/42.

14 Hackshaw, D20/5/41.

15 Nowland, D-/5/41.

16 Pte J.H. Abraham, 2/48 Bn, D23/7/42.

17 Pte F.M. Paget, 2/28 Bn, D27/10/42.

18 D31/10/42. Similar on German courage: L/Cpl L. Clothier, 2/13 Bn, D24/10/42, quoted in Gillan, *We Had Some Bother*, p. 99; Goodhart, *We of the Turning Tide*, pp. 174, 241.

19 Maughan, *Tobruk and El Alamein*, pp. 675, 705; Glenn, *Tobruk to Tarakan*, p. 146; Share, *Mud and Blood*, p. 171.

20 A/Sgt Fairbrother, 2/28 Bn, D31/10/42. In July 1942, German tanks had been instrumental in the virtual destruction of his battalion, at Ruin Ridge.

21 Serle, *The Second Twenty-Fourth*, p. 72. Similar: Long, *Greece, Crete and Syria*, p. 120; Pte L. Murphy, 2/23 Bn, D28/7/42; Pte R. Zuckur, 2/24 Bn, L-/5/41.

22 Butler, D26/6/42, also D28/7/42, 18/2/43. Also on Germans as good fighters: O'Brien, 'A Rat of Tobruk', p. 16; Barrett, *We Were There*, pp. 302, 308; Barter, *Far Above Battle*, p. 134.

23 Lt Gill, L28/4/41; Pte R. Robertson, 2/2 Bn, L15/12/42.

24 Gill, L15/7/42; Jones, 'Volunteer's Story', p. 196; Goodhart, *Turning Tide*, p. 174.

25 Hordes: Anon, 2/3 Bn, L ?/?/41(after Greece); Armstrong, D4/4/41; Neeman, L1/5/41. Tactical faults: Armstrong, D9/4/41, Lt-Col W. Cremor, 2/2 Fd Regt, L16/6/41; Bentley, *The Second Eighth*, p. 58; Holt, *From Ingleburn to Aitape*, p. 97; Masel, *The Second 28th*, p. 111; Long, *Greece, Crete and Syria*, pp. 59, 87, 114; Maughan, *Tobruk and El Alamein*, pp. 182, 374n.

26 Aldridge, L early 1941. See also references in note 25.

27 Pte C. Keys, 2/15 Bn, L21/4/41.

28 AAV: MP508/1, File No. 17/715/120; Sgt R. da Fonte, 2/8 Bn, D12/4/41;
    Pte A. Wallin, 2/2 AGH, D2/5/41, reporting what he was told by
    participants.
29 Capt C. Chrystal, 2/4 Bn, L2/11/42.
30 WOII C. Craig, 2/13 Bn, L-/12/42; L/Cpl A. Jones, 2/43 Bn, L22/5/41.
31 Pte A. Armstrong, 2/13 Bn, D4/4/41. Other criticisms in Capt G.
    Laybourne Smith, 2/3 Fd Regt, L8/5/41; Cpl C.W. Mears, 2/17 Bn,
    D6/9/42.
32 Pte W. Lock, 2/2 Pnr Bn, L7/5/41; Wallin, D6/5/41 (both reporting stories).
    New Zealanders believing the same: McLeod, *Myth & Reality*, p. 32.
33 Paget, D28/10/42.
34 Jones, 'A Volunteer's Story', p. 76.
35 Ellis, *The Sharp End of War*, p. 293. The notion is peremptorily rejected in
    McGuirk, *Afrikakorps*, p. 83.
36 Bdr H. Adeney, 2/2 Fd Regt, L6/5/41; Sgt R. Robertson, HQ 1 Aus Corps,
    L19/5/41.
37 Long, *Greece, Crete and Syria*, p. 277.
38 D4/6/41.
39 ibid., 29/10/42. Similar: Long, *Greece, Crete and Syria*, p. 277; Glenn,
    Tobruk to Tarakan, p. 129.
40 Exceptions: Cpl J.G. Cooper, 2/28 Bn, D-/6?/41; Gill, L9/2/41; Lt G.
    Combe, 2/43 Bn, L9/1/42.
41 C. Craig, L-/12/42.
42 Butler, D17/5/41.
43 Nowland, D-/5/41 (my emphasis).
44 L28/4/41 (my emphasis). Also Lovegrove, D25/10/42; Boas, 'Memoir',
    p. 270; Fearnside, *Half to Remember*, p. 55; Share, *Mud and Blood*, pp. 73,
    177; Holt, *From Ingleburn to Aitape*, p. 117.
45 Shelton Smith, *The Boys Write Home*, p. 45 (my emphasis). Similar:
    Cremor, L16/6/41; Pte S. O'Brien, 2/7 Fd Amb, L-/7/41; Fancke, *Mud and
    Blood in the Field*, p. 279.
46 Laybourne Smith, L8/5/41; Bennett, *Rough Infantry*, p. 80, Clift, *Saga of
    a Sig*, p. 75.
47 There are so many accounts of such occurrences that there can be little
    doubt that the practice existed: Armstrong, D9/4/41; Butler, D10/7/42;
    Mears, D25/10/42; Symington, D18/4/41; Maughan, *Tobruk and El
    Alamein*, pp. 165–6; Glenn, *Tobruk to Tarakan*, p. 156.
48 Hospitals: Butler, D30/5/41, 17/8/41; Sgt E.J. Little, HQ 76 Base Sub-Area
    (Tobruk), D6/4/41, 4/5/41; Bennett, *Rough Infantry*, pp. 84, 161–2;
    Maughan, *Tobruk and El Alamein*, p. 240; Gnr M.H. Dooley, 2/12 Fd Regt,
    D25/10/42; Walker, *Middle East and Far East*, pp. 193, 213. Ambulances:
    Butler, D16, 22/7/42; Hay, *Nothing Over Us*, p. 157; Mears, D25/10/42.
    Mears claimed that a German tank knocked out two ambulances. Perhaps
    the Germans suspected the ambulances of carrying weapons, a practice in
    which they themselves apparently sometimes engaged. Stretcher-bearers:
    Butler, D22/7/42; Pte R. Berry, 2/9 Bn, D28/5/41; Masel, *The Second 28th*,

p. 111; Combe, Ligertwood & Gilchrist, *The Second 43rd*, p. 52; Glenn, *Tobruk to Tarakan*, p. 149.

49 S. O'Brien, L-/7/41.

50 Pte T.C. Derrick, 2/48 Bn, D5/8/41 (my emphasis).

51 For example: Berry, D25/4/41; Maughan, *Tobruk and El Alamein*, p. 671; Givney, *The First at War*, p. 184; Combe, Ligertwood & Gilchrist, *The Second 43rd*, p. 40; Trigellis-Smith, *Britain to Borneo*, p. 112.

52 Butler, D22/7/42; Pte J. Davies, 2/33 Bn, L-/5/41 (reporting stories). Other treachery: Hetherington, *The Australian Soldier*, p. 57; Pike, *What We Have ... We Hold!*, p. 42.

53 Armstrong, D-/5/41.

54 Australians: J. Craig, D8/11/42. Enemy dead: AWM 3/2632, Middle East Field Censorship Summary 4–17/11/42; Dooley D26/10/42 (mentions that dead Italians were mined). None of these sources say Germans were responsible, though they seem the more likely source, as German booby-traps abounded at Alamein: C. Craig, L-/12/42.

55 2/48th Bn War Diary, Intelligence Summary for 16/7/42; Masel, *The Second 28th*, p. 41n; Farquhar, *Derrick V.C.*, pp. 104–5. AWM 54, File No. 526/6/1, interview with Lt R.G. Penny, p. 7.

56 Greece: Bentley, *The Second Eighth*, p. 59. Crete: 2/8 Bn report, '11 Platoon "B" Company, 2/8 Battalion, Crete Campaign', by Lt H. Coulston; Various, *Active Service*, p. 59. Long, *Greece, Crete and Syria*, p. 225n talks of this as only a 'rumour' based on misunderstanding of an incident involving New Zealanders, yet the incident recounted by Coulston is a separate one.

57 Boas, 'Memoir', p. 134.

58 D26/7/42. Other callous actions: Glenn, *Tobruk to Tarakan*, p. 124; Cpl K.B. MacArthur, 2/15 Bn, D19/4/41. Germans' reputation for callous behaviour: Givney, *The First at War*, p. 209.

59 Bennett, *Rough Infantry*, p. 92; Clift, *Saga of a Sig*, p. 69; Griffiths-Marsh, *The Sixpenny Soldier*, p. 171.

60 Cpl C.G. White, 2/1 MG Bn, L30/4?/41; Pte R.F. Cameron, 2/1 Bn, L3/5/41. Similar: Campbell, L2/5/41; Lt J.B. Harkness, 2/2 Bn, L11/5/41; Pte R. Robertson, 2/2 Bn, L19/5/41; Cremor, L16/6/41. Enemy aircraft as the explanation: WOII C.H. Robertson, 2/3 Fd Regt, L12/7/41; Pte L.F. Williams, 2/11 Bn, L-/10/41.

61 Long, *Greece, Crete and Syria*, pp. 182–3.

62 Lt W.R. Dexter, 2/6 Bn, D18/4/41. Dexter said that the RMO and chaplain told him that the Anzacs had accounted for 18 000 Germans in one day. In 1985, Bennett acknowledged that the Germans had in fact 'outclassed' the Australians in Greece: *Rough Infantry*, p. 79. New Zealanders: McLeod, *Myth & Reality*, p. 32.

63 L16/6/41.

64 Wallin, D6/5/41. Similar: Lock, L7/4/41 (re Greece); Sgt R.H. Bourke, 2/1 Bn, L-/7?/41(re Crete).

65 Long, *Greece, Crete and Syria*, p. 316. The casualty rate had been very much in the Australians' favour at Retimo: ibid., p. 275.

66 R. Robertson, L19/5/41. Also White, L30/1/41; Clift, *Saga of a Sig*, p. 77.
67 Pte C.A. Gullidge, 9 Div AASC, D11/5/41.
68 Heckmann, *Rommel's War in Africa*, p. 83. A similar description of Australians of the 2/28th after Ruin Ridge appears in Fearnside, *Half to Remember*, p. 137.
69 Heckmann, *Rommel's War in Africa*. The tanks had been stopped mainly by British tanks and artillery, though Australian anti-tank guns were also involved: Maughan, *Tobruk and El Alamein*, p. 152.
70 AWM 54, Item No. 519/7/26, 'Lessons of Second Libyan Campaign: 9th Division Training Instruction', p. 4; Maughan, *Tobruk and El Alamein*, pp. 150, 167; Heckmann, *Rommel's War in Africa*, p. 113.
71 D16/4/41. See also Maughan, *Tobruk and El Alamein*, p. 137; Wilmot, *Tobruk 1941*, pp. 107, 111.
72 L15/7/42.
73 On Tobruk, see Maughan, *Tobruk and El Alamein*, p. 384.
74 Soldier quoted in Lt J. Cumpston, HQ 26 Bde, D20/10/42.
75 For example: Gill, L25/4/41; Keys, L16/7/41; Wallin, D6/5/41; Zuckur, L-/10?/41; Coulston, 'Crete Campaign'; Various, *Active Service*, p. 39; Shelton Smith, *The Boys Write Home*, p. 88; AWM 54, Item No. 883/2/97, Middle East Field Censorship Summary, 19–25/11/41; Notes by Lt-Col H.H. Hammer on El Alamein, 2/48 Bn War Diary, November 1942.
76 Pte J.C. Jones, L13/5/41. Similar: Armstrong, D9/4/41; Keys, L15/12/42; Middle East Field Censorship Summary, 17–23/12/41.
77 Gammage, *The Broken Years*, p. 98. Australian prowess with the bayonet in World War I: ibid., p. 259.
78 Charlton, *The Thirty-Niners*, p. 176. Also Long, *Greece, Crete and Syria*, p. 252; Maj H. Thomas, 2/7 Bn, D26/5/41. New Zealanders: McLeod, *Myth & Reality*, pp. 98–103.
79 Maughan, *Tobruk and El Alamein*, pp. 559, 714, 734; Wilmot, *Tobruk 1941*, p. 150.
80 Maughan, *Tobruk and El Alamein*, pp. 149, 582, 689.
81 Pte R. Grant, 2/17 Bn, L-/-/41 (my emphasis). See also Wells, *'B' Company Second Seventeenth Infantry*, p. 67; Wilmot, *Tobruk 1941*, pp. 97–8.
82 D16/4/41. On Crete, the Germans made a similar complaint – that the Australians waged 'unethical warfare' by shooting paratroops before they landed, ignoring the fact that the paratroops were firing their own submachine guns as they descended: Randolph, 'An Unexpected Odyssey', p. 21.
83 D19/5/41.
84 Schmidt, *With Rommel in the Desert*, p. 164.
85 Gammage, *The Broken Years*, p. 257.
86 Nowland, D19/5/41. Similar New Zealand experience: McLeod, *Myth & Reality*, p. 100.
87 Gilbert, *The Imperial War Museum Book*, p. 23.
88 Fancke, *Mud and Blood in the Field*, p. 27.
89 Legg, *War Correspondent*, p. 35.

90 Pte R. Aldridge, 2/13 Bn, L5/1/42. Also on youthfulness: Butler, D15/7/42; Goodhart, *We of the Turning Tide*, p. 151.
91 L. Williams, L3/11/41. Also on 'good shooting': Mears, D28/10/42.
92 Lt R.L. Newbold, 2/2 Fd Regt, L1/5/41. Similar: Laybourne Smith, L7/5/41.
93 Goodhart, *We of the Turning Tide*, p. 142.
94 Williams, L3/11/41. Similar: S. O'Brien, L-/7/41.
95 Aldridge, L22/12/41.
96 Charlton, *The Thirty-Niners*, p. 176.
97 Butler, D17/5/41.
98 J. Craig, D29/10/42. Similar: Symington, D14/4/41; Serle, *The Second Twenty-Fourth*, p. 199.
99 Givney, *The First at War*, p. 184.
100 Combe, Ligertwood & Gilchrist, *The Second 43rd*, p. 40.
101 Berry, D25/4/41; Cumpston, D16/5/41.
102 L. Williams, L3/11/41; Cpl A. Hackshaw, 2/11 Bn, DR20/5/41.
103 Hackshaw, DR20/5/41. When between 120 and 300 Germans were killed and only three were captured in the famous bayonet charge of that campaign, there were German accusations that some of the dead were killed after the action: Long, *Greece, Crete and Syria*, p. 255. See also Randolph, 'An Unexpected Odyssey', p. 24.
104 D23/10/42 (original capitals). According to Goodhart, a desert maxim said that it was unwise to take prisoners after dark: *We of the Turning Tide*, p. 151. In fact, Australians took numerous prisoners at night, when they undertook most of their attacks.
105 Joyce, 'As I Saw It', p. 19. Earlier that day, men from Joyce's battalion had shot dead five German prisoners who sought to escape: Share, *Mud and Blood*, p. 190.
106 Crawford, 'Forward from El Alamein', p. 123. See also Barrett, *We Were There*, p. 251; Share, *Mud and Blood*, p. 176.
107 Trying to escape: Share, *Mud and Blood*, p. 190.
108 Armstrong, D-/5/41 (original emphasis). Similar: Jones, 'A Volunteer's Story', p. 192.
109 D26/7/42. Similar: Butler, D22/7/42, 28/10/42.
110 Lovegrove, D25/10/42.
111 Fearnside, *Half to Remember*, p. 55.
112 Share, *Mud and Blood*, p. 73.
113 D19/5/41 (my emphasis).

CHAPTER 3: THE GERMANS: MUTUAL RESPECT

1 R.J.G., 'Ali Baba's Diggers', in *Parade* (Middle East weekly newsletter), 8/8/42, quoted in 2/48 Bn War Diary, August 1942.
2 The watch incident: Glenn, *Tobruk to Tarakan*, p. 129.
3 Lemaire, 'A Boy from Balmain', p. 26.

4 Bosgard, 'The Benghasi Handicap', p. 3. Similar: Barter, *Far Above Battle*, p. 134; Heckmann, *Rommel's War in Africa*, pp. 112–13.
5 D16/6/41. Similar: O'Brien, 'A Rat of Tobruk', p. 16. The concern accorded men by Germans in the field sometimes contrasted sharply with that received further back. For example: Jones, 'A Volunteer's Story', p. 304. An example of callous German treatment of Australian prisoners in Greece appears in Shelton Smith, *The Boys Write Home*, p. 72.
6 Pte L. Williams, 2/11 Bn, L3/11/41 (original parentheses). See also Pte R. Anson, 2/17 Bn, L21/8/42; Serle, *The Second Twenty-Fourth*, p. 190; Crawford, 'Forward from El Alamein', pp. 204–5; 2/3rd Pnr Bn War Diary, 15/11/42.
7 Williams, L3/11/41.
8 Quoted in Capt J.S. Cumpston, 2/23 Bn, D1/10/42.
9 Masel, *The Second 28th*, p. 88n. However, in some cases at Alamein 'the enemy' buried four or five Australians in one hole: AWM 54, Item No. 527/6/9, '26 Brigade Report on Operations Oct–Nov 1942'.
10 Douglas Lade, interview with the author, 15/10/98.
11 Crawford, 'Forward from El Alamein', p. 204.
12 D15/4/41. See also Gillan, *We Had Some Bother*, p. 199.
13 Martin, 'My Adventures as a Prisoner of War', pp. 1–2.
14 Walker, *Middle East and Far East*, p. 382; Long, *Greece, Crete and Syria*, p. 265; Givney, *The First at War*, pp. 191, 199.
15 D17/5/41. Similar actions: Lt C. Chrystal, 2/4 Bn, D26/5/41; Combe, Ligertwood & Gilchrist, *The Second 43rd*, p. 125; Glenn, *Tobruk to Tarakan*, p. 178; Wilmot, *Tobruk 1941*, p. 186.
16 Shelton Smith, *The Boys Write Home*, p. 55. He told of saving another wounded German, who gratefully handed him souvenirs.
17 AWM 54, Item No. 526/6/10, 20 Bde Report on Ops 'Lightfoot'. This 'enemy' included Italians. Similar: 2/11 Fd Amb War Diary, 2/11/42.
18 Coulston, 'A Regimental Aid Post in Tobruk', p. 495; Walker, *Middle East and Far East*, pp. 272, 289; Long, *Greece, Crete and Syria*, p. 266n.
19 Maughan, *Tobruk and El Alamein*, pp. 325, 722.
20 Cpl C.W. Mears, 2/17 Bn, D31/10/42. Similar: Maughan, *Tobruk and El Alamein*, p. 323. Examples of Australian concern for German wounded: Jones, 'A Volunteer's Story', p. 150; Farquhar, *Derrick V.C.*, p. 119.
21 Maughan, *Tobruk and El Alamein*, p. 325; Wilmot, *Tobruk 1941*, p. 200.
22 Combe, Ligertwood & Gilchrist, *The Second 43rd*, pp. 67–8.
23 ibid. Other truces: Anson, D26/5/41; Glenn, *Tobruk to Tarakan*, p. 117; Long, *Greece, Crete and Syria*, pp. 265, 290.
24 Wilmot, *Tobruk 1941*, p. 124.
25 Knowing it: Pte J.M. Butler, 2/23 Bn, D4/6/41.
26 Farquhar, *Derrick V.C.*, p. 54 (my emphasis); Gillan, *We Had Some Bother*, p. 16 (my emphasis). A German account which criticises romantic ver-sions of the 'chivalrous' campaign: Heckmann, *Rommel's War in Africa*, pp. 145–6.
27 Combe, Ligertwood & Gilchrist *The Second 43rd*, p. 69.

28 Masel, *The Second 28th*, p. 41.
29 Fearnside, *Half to Remember*, p. 61; T.L. Murphy, letter to the author, 23/11/88.
30 Maughan, *Tobruk and El Alamein*, p. 384; Wilmot, *Tobruk 1941*, p. 209; Heckmann, *Rommel's War in Africa*, p. 145.
31 D25/8/42. Also: Stokes, 'Taradale to Tarakan', pp. 216–17.
32 D26/8/42. Other violations: Wilmot, *Tobruk 1941*, p. 209; Crawford, 'Forward from El Alamein', p. 44.
33 Quoted in Cumpston, D22/10/42.
34 Sgt S.R. Ferrier, 9 Div Cav Regt, L7/8/42.
35 Pte G. Nowland, 9 Div AASC attached to 2/15 Bn, D11/5/41.
36 Butler, D23/8/41. He saw Italians doing the same: D8/9/41. The practice also occurred in World War I.
37 D24/5/41, quoted in Gillan, *We Had Some Bother*, p. 83.
38 Schmidt, *With Rommel in the Desert*, p. 52. Similar Australian behaviour: Pte T.C. Derrick, 2/48 Bn, D18/7/42; Nowland, D10/5/41; Graeme-Evans, *Of Storms and Rainbows*, p. 176.
39 Fearnside, *Half to Remember*, p. 54.
40 ibid., p. 56.
41 L14/10/41.
42 Shelton Smith, *The Boys Write Home*, p. 17. Germans calling out abuse: Butler, D25/8/42.
43 Crawford, 'Forward from El Alamein', pp. 203–4.
44 Randolph, 'An Unexpected Odyssey, pp. 24–5.
45 Givney, *The First at War*, p. 205.
46 Gammage, *The Broken Years*, p. 257. Sporting metaphors: ibid., p. 301.
47 D13/6/41.
48 D28/5/41.
49 Cpl N.B. Campbell, 2/5 Bn, L2/5/41. Similar: Pte R. Robertson, 2/2 Bn, L19/5/41.
50 Shelton Smith, *The Boys Write Home*, p. 68. Similar: Hetherington, *The Australian Soldier*, p. 63.
51 Hospitals: Fancke, *Mud and Blood in the Field*, p. 34. Comrades: Glenn, *Tobruk to Tarakan*, p. 129. Not returning: ibid., p. 99.
52 A similar point is made in McLeod, *Myth & Reality*, p. 82.
53 For example: Anson, D28/8/41; Fearnside, *Half to Remember*, p. 100.
54 L26/1/42 (my emphasis).
55 Crawford, 'Forward from El Alamein', p. 35.
56 Haywood, *Six Years in Support*, p. 153; Barrett, *We Were There*, p. 309.
57 Goodhart, *We of the Turning Tide*, p. 71.
58 Wells, *'B' Company Second Seventeenth Infantry*, p. 64.
59 Fearnside, *Half to Remember*, pp. 109–10.
60 Pte L. Murphy, 2/23 Bn, D30/10/42. Similar: Oakes, *Muzzle Blast*, p. 148; Share, *Mud and Blood*, p. 176.
61 Combe, 'My Three-Score Years and Ten', p. 187.
62 Oakes, *Muzzle Blast*, pp. 97–8.

63 Jones, 'A Volunteer's Story', pp. 201–2. Similar: Anson, L21/8/42, 9/11/42.
64 Lt A.G. Hirst, 2/3 A-Tk Regt, L6/11/42.
65 For example: L/Cpl J. Craig, 2/13 Bn, D27/8/42; Pte C.J. O'Dea, 2/28 Bn, D10/9/42.
66 Joyce, 'As I Saw It', p. 19.
67 Capt G. Laybourne Smith, 2/3 Fd Regt, L7/5/41. Other pity: Lt G.T. Gill, 2/48 Bn, L1/6/41; Pte A. Hackshaw, 2/11 Bn, D20/5/41.
68 D15/4/41.
69 Pte R. Berry, 2/9 Bn, D24/5/41.
70 D14/7/42.
71 ibid., p. 104.
72 D28/8/41. The shot was fired by Poles, and some of the joy was clearly theirs.
73 Serle, *The Second Twenty-Fourth*, p. 220.
74 Combe, 'My Three-Score Years and Ten', p. 342.
75 L15/7/42.
76 Capt R.S. Shillaker, 2/48 Bn, L2/9/42.
77 Crawford, 'Forward from Alamein', p. 35 (my emphasis).
78 MS 9553, 17 Brigade Report on Campaign in Greece and Crete, p. 95.
79 Hackshaw, DR20/5/41.
80 Glenn, *Tobruk to Tarakan*, p. 37; Sgt C. Symington, 2/17 Bn, D16/4/41.
81 Lewin, *The Life and Death of the Afrika Korps*, p. 75.
82 Irving, *The Trail of the Fox*, p. 113; Liddell Hart, *The Rommel Papers*, p. 132. See also Schmidt, *With Rommel in the Desert*, p. 52.
83 Liddell Hart, *The Rommel Papers*, pp. 132–3.
84 Young, *Rommel*, p. 125.
85 ibid.
86 ibid., p. 126.
87 Maughan, *Tobruk and El Alamein*, p. 267.
88 Crack: Carell, *Foxes of the Desert*, p. 22. He added: 'Their sniping was superb'. Incredible accuracy: Heckmann, *Rommel's War in Africa*, p. 125.
89 Butler, D17/5/41. Similar on German attitudes: Glenn, *Tobruk to Tarakan*, p. 37; Maughan, *Tobruk and El Alamein*, p. 401; Serle, *The Second Twenty-Fourth*, p. 75.
90 Wells, *'B' Company Second Seventeenth Infantry*, pp. 68–9.
91 Schmidt, *With Rommel in the Desert*, p. 109. There were no Australians in the vicinity.
92 Liddell Hart, *The Rommel Papers*, pp. 225–6. Similar: Glenn, *Tobruk to Tarakan*, pp. 136–7.
93 von Mellenthin, *Panzer Battles*, p. 167. Similar: Schmidt, *With Rommel in the Desert*, p. 164.
94 Crawford, 'Forward from El Alamein', p. 124.
95 Lewin, *The Life and Death of the Afrika Korps*, p. 75. Similar: Clark, *The Fall of Crete*, p. 90. Heckmann, who clearly admired the Australians'

fighting qualities at Tobruk, nevertheless called them 'roughneck and totally unmilitary': *Rommel's War in Africa*, p. 147.

96 Heckmann, *Rommel's War in Africa*, p. 83.

97 Serle, *The Second Twenty-Fourth*, p. 73.

98 DR20/5/41.

99 Crawford, 'Forward from El Alamein', p. 73.

100 Tobruk: Combe, Ligertwood & Gilchrist, *The Second 43rd*, p. 63. Rommel: Goodhart, *We of the Turning Tide*, p. 162.

101 DR20/5/41.

102 ibid. Similar: Long, *Greece, Crete and Syria*, p. 307.

103 Serle, *The Second Twenty-Fourth*, p. 73. Sometimes Germans did not differentiate Australians from the English. Members of Australia's 2/13th Battalion were ordered to yell 'Australians coming' during their charge on the German positions at Ed Duda, in order to frighten the enemy. When the charge began, the Germans instead called *'Engländer kommen'* (Englishmen coming): Maughan, *Tobruk and El Alamein*, p. 477. A report on an action on Crete called Australian forces 'English': Long, *Greece, Crete and Syria*, p. 255.

104 Cumpston, *The Rats Remain*, p. 17; Maughan, *Tobruk and El Alamein*, p. 638.

105 Maughan, *Tobruk and El Alamein*, p. 638. This comment played upon the reputation of Australians among the British: Johnston, *At the Front Line*, pp. 145–6.

106 In Cumpston, D22/10/42.

107 *Panzerarmee* intelligence summary of 10 October 1942, in Appendix A to 9 Div Intelligence Summary No. 353.

108 In 2/24 Bn War Diary for November 1942, Intelligence Summary No. 62 (from a captured Italian document written between 30 September and 20 October 1942).

109 Baillieu, *Both Sides of the Hill*, p. 21. This was in a letter to an Australian. General Bayerlein, Chief of Staff of the Afrika Korps, said that the British were the toughest troops. 'Then came the New Zealanders, Australians and South Africans': Jewell, *Alamein and the Desert War*, p. 126. *Panzerarmee Afrika* was a title given to the German–Italian forces in North Africa.

110 A private, quoted in Cumpston, D19/10/42.

CHAPTER 4: THE VICHY FRENCH

1 A full list of the Australian units who participated in the campaign is in Long, *Greece, Crete and Syria*, p. 338n. The 18th Brigade was in Tobruk at this time.

2 ibid., p. 338n; Long, *The Six Years War*, p. 87.

3 Long, *Greece, Crete and Syria*, p. 334. Over half of the 34 000 ground troops allotted to the entire campaign were Australian: McAllester & Trigellis-Smith, *Largely a Gamble*, p. 14.

4 There were also 10 000 Levantine troops, 'of doubtful value': ibid., p. 334; Mollo, *The Armed Forces of World War II*, p. 144.

5 Long, *Greece, Crete and Syria*, p. 328. Also on walkover: McAllester & Trigellis-Smith, *Largely a Gamble*, p. 31.

6 ibid., p. 332.

7 This paragraph is based on Long, *Greece, Crete and Syria*, p. 337.

8 ibid., p. 351.

9 ibid., p. 356n.

10 ibid., p. 354.

11 ibid., p. 355.

12 Laffin, *Forever Forward*, p. 37.

13 Uren, *1,000 Men at War*, pp. 41–2. Laffin said that the 2/31st wore their slouch hats to frighten the French: *Forever Forward*, p. 37. The 2/14th men took their helmets, but did not actually wear them on the first day: Russell, *The Second Fourteenth Battalion*, p. 43. See also Various, *Active Service*, p. 62; Long, *Greece, Crete and Syria*, p. 352.

14 Long, *Greece, Crete and Syria*, p. 526.

15 Pte A.K. Wright, 2/16 Bn, L-/7?/41.

16 Crooks, *The Footsoldiers*, p. 35.

17 ibid.

18 ibid., p. 36.

19 L-/7/41.

20 Long, *Greece, Crete and Syria*, p. 435.

21 Bennett, *Rough Infantry*, p. 107.

22 A. Shilton, letter to the author, 12/2/98.

23 Crooks, *The Footsoldiers*, p. 106.

24 ibid., p. 73.

25 ibid., p. 109.

26 Long, *Greece, Crete and Syria*, pp. 483–4n. A story of Vichy French firing on a white flag appears in McAllester & Trigellis-Smith, *Largely a Gamble*, p. 115.

27 Long, *Greece, Crete and Syria*, p. 496.

28 McAllester & Trigellis-Smith, *Largely a Gamble*, p. 73. This story does not appear in the official history.

29 Shilton, letter to the author, 12/2/98. These events occurred on 7–8 July.

30 Steward, *Recollections of a Regimental Medical Officer*, p. 47.

31 Long, *Greece, Crete and Syria*, p. 411.

32 Pte D. Hughes, 2/4 Fd Amb, D16/6/41. He said that he thought the Vichy French respected the Red Cross flag.

33 Steward, *Recollections of a Regimental Medical Officer*, p. 44.

34 Russell, *The Second Fourteenth Battalion*, p. 71; Long, *Greece, Crete and Syria*, p. 459n.

35 O'Brien, *Guns and Gunners*, p. 125; Long, *Greece, Crete and Syria*, p. 487n; Steward, *Recollections of a Regimental Medical Officer*, p. 53.

36 Long, *Greece, Crete and Syria*, p. 486n.

37 Pte J.M. Butler, 2/23 Bn, D1/11/41.

38 Crooks, *The Footsoldiers*, p. 115; Long, *Greece, Crete and Syria*, p. 452n.
39 Various, *Active Service*, p. 62.
40 For example, Long, *Greece, Crete and Syria*, p. 483.
41 See, for example, McAllester & Trigellis-Smith, *Largely a Gamble*, pp. 90–1, 99, 119–21, 153.
42 Various, *Active Service*, p. 62.
43 ibid.
44 Long, *Greece, Crete and Syria*, p. 375.
45 Quoted in McAllester & Trigellis-Smith, *Largely a Gamble*, p. 229.
46 Crooks, *The Footsoldiers*, p. 62.
47 ibid. Similar praise of enemy: McAllester & Trigellis-Smith, *Largely a Gamble*, p. 40.
48 Bennett, *Rough Infantry*, p. 100. Similarly humorous: Crooks, *The Footsoldiers*, p. 91.
49 Terrible country: Cpl C.E. Edwards, 2/27 Bn, D10, 13/6/41. Gallipoli: Hughes, D20/7/41.
50 Lt W.R. Dexter, 2/6 Bn, D13/12/41. Also on strong defences: Long, *Greece, Crete and Syria*, pp. 408, 424; Russell, *The Second Fourteenth Battalion*, p. 78; Uren, *1,000 Men at War*, p. 49.
51 Pte T.L. Murphy, 2/23 Bn, D18/1/42.
52 Pte W. Lock, 2/2 Pnr Bn, L11/7/41. This appears to have been on the approaches to Damour.
53 McAllester & Trigellis-Smith, *Largely a Gamble*, p. 99.
54 Uren, *1,000 Men at War*, p. 49; Long, *Greece, Crete and Syria*, p. 367.
55 Wright, L-/7?/41.
56 Shilton, letter to the author, 12/2/98. A successful Australian bayonet charge: McAllester & Trigellis-Smith, *Largely a Gamble*, p. 186.
57 ibid., p. 187.
58 McAllester, *Men of the 2/14 Battalion*, pp. 231–3.
59 Laffin, *Forever Forward*, p. 53. The Australian numbers have probably been understated and the Vichy French overstated in this anecdote. See also Long, *Greece, Crete and Syria*, p. 409.
60 Bennett, *Rough Infantry*, p. 162.
61 L-/7/41.
62 Long, *Greece, Crete and Syria*, p. 516.
63 ibid.
64 Crooks, *The Footsoldiers*, p. 120. Some 2/33rd men captured by the Vichy French were well-treated. Very diverse experiences of the battalion's prisoners at Vichy French hands: ibid., pp. 480–1.
65 Calculated from Long, *Greece, Crete and Syria*, p. 519. Only 5668 of the 37 700 Vichy French troops joined the Free French.
66 ibid., p. 529.
67 Russell, *The Second Fourteenth Battalion*, p. 78n.
68 Most fighting against Australians: Porch, *The French Foreign Legion*, p. 478. They also fought Foreign Legionnaires on the Free French side: ibid.

69 AWM PR00527, Papers of S.H.W.C. Porter, Folder 17, Porter's account of Syrian campaign.
70 McAllester & Trigellis-Smith, *Largely a Gamble*, p. 71.
71 ibid., pp. 137, 179, 183, 229.
72 ibid., p. 183.
73 ibid., p. 228.
74 McAllester, *Men of the 2/14 Battalion*, p. 178. O'Day says Leport must have been well-briefed.

CHAPTER 5: THE JAPANESE: MOST ENCOUNTERED, MOST HATED

1 Calculated from 'killed or missing in action', 'died of wounds' and 'died of wounds while prisoners of war' figures in Long, *The Final Campaigns*, pp. 633–4. The totals were 3366 in the 'war against Germany' (including actions against Vichy French and Italians) and 7434 in the 'war against Japan'.
2 Calculated from ibid. If troops who died from wounds as POWs are not taken into account, the figure was more than forty times higher in Japanese captivity.
3 Sweeting, 'Prisoner of the Japanese', p. 511.
4 Wigmore, *The Japanese Thrust*, p. 382.
5 Some of the Japanese casualties were inflicted by Americans, who suffered more than 2800 casualties: Long, *The Six Years War*, p. 246. Casualties in subsequent campaigns are not listed here.
6 Lt-Col H. Dunkley, 7 Bn, L28/8/45.
7 Gnr W.C. Bird, 2/10 Fd Regt, D28/5/42.
8 D8/9/42.
9 Crooks, *The Footsoldiers*, p. 190. This was in the first week of October 1942. Similar: Johnston, *The Toughest Fighting in the World*, p. 208.
10 Johnston, *The Toughest Fighting*, p. 129; White, *Green Armour*, p. 200 (original emphasis); Crooks, *The Footsoldiers*, p. 190.
11 Sanananda: Tpr B. Love, 2/7 Cav Regt, D20/12/42. Buna–Gona–Sanananda: Chaplain R. Smith, 2/9 AGH, L10/1/43. Lae: Dawes, *'Soldier Superb'*, p. 35.
12 White, *Green Armour*, p. 216 (my emphasis). See also Givney, *The First at War*, p. 270.
13 Nalty, *Pearl Harbor and the War in the Pacific*, p. 105.
14 There are numerous other recorded occasions of units entrenched very close to Japanese positions, for example at Jivevaneng, Aitape, Tarakan, Labuan and Balikpapan.
15 McCarthy, *South-West Pacific Area*, p. 516; L/Cpl Spindler, 3 Bn, DR2/12/42.
16 ibid., D29/11/42.
17 Capt S.H. Buckler, 2/14 Bn, Ops Report, 12/10/42, p. 3. Similar: Pte Wallin, 2/5 Bn, D27/6/45; Pte Murphy, 2/23 Bn, D4/12/43.

18 PR85/235, A.C. Fielder, letter re 2/6 Bn history, 21/7/81. See also Stanley, *Tarakan: An Australian Tragedy*, p. 117.

19 Combe, 'My Three-Score Years and Ten', p. 255.

20 Gullett, *Not as a Duty Only*, p. 127; Lt Gill, 2/48 Bn, L26/1/42; Pte R. Robertson, 2/2 Bn, L15/12/42.

21 Pte M.F. Dunne, 2/9 Bn, L20/1/43 (my emphasis).

22 On the 'good German', a concept not apparently used by Australian soldiers, see Dower, *War without Mercy*, p. 8. 'Good Jap': Pte Butler, 2/23 Bn, D21/9/43; Macfarlan, *Etched in Green*, p. 118.

23 Mathews, *Militia Battalion at War*, p. 216; Kennedy, 'World War 2', pp. 3, 34. Neither unit could contrast their attitudes to European enemies, as both fought only the Japanese.

24 Gullett, *Not as a Duty Only*, p. 127. Similar: Murphy, letter to the author, 23/11/88.

25 Holmes, *Firing Line*, p. 366; McLeod, *Myth & Reality*, p. 83; Stouffer, *The American Soldier*, p. 34.

26 Haywood, *Six Years in Support*, p. 152.

27 Hay, *Nothing Over Us*, pp. 316–17.

28 D25/10/43.

29 D28/12/43.

30 *Battle of Wau*, p. 50.

31 Hunting: Dexter, *The New Guinea Offensives*, pp. 113, 278; Serle, *The Second Twenty-Fourth*, p. 350; Uren, *1,000 Men at War*, p. 181. Exterminating: Clift, *Saga of a Sig*, p. 163; Combe, Ligertwood & Gilchrist, *The Second 43rd*, p. 226; Medcalf, *War in the Shadows*, p. 85.

32 Kennett, *G.I.*, p. 63.

33 Combe, Ligertwood & Gilchrist, *The Second 43rd*, p. 231; Capt M.T. Lewis, 2/7 Cav Cdo Regt, 'Account of Balikpapan Experiences', p. 15; Medcalf, *War in the Shadows*, p. 65; Macfarlan, *Etched in Green*, p. 167.

34 Cpl J.P. O'Brien, 2/15 Bn, D6/7/45. Similar: Crooks, *The Footsoldiers*, pp. 230–1; Dexter, *The New Guinea Offensives*, p. 74; Givney, *The First at War*, pp. 303–4, 312; Long, *The Final Campaigns*, pp. 157, 277.

35 Pte Paget, 2/28 Bn, D2/7/45.

36 D27/6/45.

37 In AAV: MP729/6, File No. 51/403/466, 'Report on Employment of Tanks in Operations of 9 Aust Div in Area North of Finschhafen, New Guinea'.

38 Fancke, *Mud and Blood in the Field*, p. 497.

39 Combe, Ligertwood & Gilchrist, *The Second 43rd*, p. 185; Lt G. Combe, 2/43 Bn, L21/11/43. Similar humour: Share, *Mud and Blood*, pp. 275–6; Legg, *War Correspondent*, p. 37.

40 Bennett, *Rough Infantry*, pp. 162, 165; Charlott, *Unofficial History of the 29/46th*, p. 65; Clift, *Saga of a Sig*, p. 158; Medcalf, *War in the Shadows*, p. 95.

41 Wallin, D8/7/45.

42 Fry, *Ivor Hele*, p. 92. The drawing, ART33838, is in the Australian War Memorial.

43 Pressure: Dexter, *The New Guinea Offensives*, pp. 66, 746; Medcalf, *War in the Shadows*, p. 62; Gilmore, *You Can't Fight Tanks with Bayonets*, pp. 60–5. Garrulous: Dexter, *The New Guinea Offensives*, p. 520; Long, *The Final Campaigns*, p. 368; Mathews, *Militia Battalion at War*, p. 173; McCarthy, *South-West Pacific Area*, p. 517.

44 Gilmore, *You Can't Fight Tanks with Bayonets*, p. 147.

45 Capt J.J. May, 2/10 Fd Amb, D1/2/43. Also on unwillingness to take prisoners: Allchin, *Purple and Blue*, p. 260; Hay, *Nothing Over Us*, p. 249; Mathews, *Militia Battalion at War*, p. 172; Medcalf, *War in the Shadows*, p. 62; Serle, *The Second Twenty-Fourth*, p. 279.

46 G. Terrey, foreword to Clift, *Saga of a Sig*, p. xii.

47 Bennett, *Rough Infantry*, p. 196. Similar: Holt, *From Ingleburn to Aitape*, pp. 195, 197.

48 Dower, *War without Mercy*, pp. 70–1.

49 ibid., pp. 11, 68. He also mentioned the Australian reputation for not taking prisoners: p. 69. See also Bergerud, *Touched with Fire*, pp. 415–16.

50 Dexter, *The New Guinea Offensives*, pp. 408, 520; Crooks, *The Foot-soldiers*, p. 322; Long, *The Final Campaigns*, p. 449; AWM: Canungra Training Instructions, Serial No. 34.

51 D29/11/43. Other prisoners fearing being killed: Capt D. Fienberg, Angau, Special Patrol Report, 6/5/45; Wallin, 19/1/45; Stanley, *Tarakan*, p. 129.

52 Legg, *War Correspondent*, p. 54.

53 Wells, *'B' Company Second Seventeenth Infantry*, p. 159.

54 Lt-Col G.R. Matthews, 9 Bn, D29/11/44.

55 AWM: Field Censorship Report for Month Ending 31/1/45.

56 ibid. The report coupled talk of this desecration with references to cannibalism by the Japanese. Gold teeth and skull collection on Tarakan: Stanley, *Tarakan*, p. 140.

57 For example, AWM: Field Censorship Report for Month Ending 31/1/45; Pte C.P. Keys, 2/15 Bn, D11/8/43.

58 Givney, *The First at War*, pp. 308, 465; Pte C.D. Keys, 2/7 Indep Coy, L9/7/43; Matthews, D29/11/44; Paget, 24 Bde Carrier Coy, D25/1/44; Holt, *From Ingleburn to Aitape*, p. 199; Medcalf, *War in the Shadows*, p. 51. American examples: Dower, *War without Mercy*, p. 70, Fussell, *Wartime*, p. 120.

59 Germans: reported in C.P. Keys, L11/8/43. This practice also occurred in WWI: Gammage, *The Broken Years*, p. 225.

60 Dower, *War without Mercy*, p. 71; Fussell, *Wartime*, p. 117.

61 American: AAV: MP742/1, File No. 76/1/59. Australian: *Manual of Military Law 1941* (Australian edition), p. 245. The Geneva Convention demanded honourable treatment of the dead.

62 Stanley, *Tarakan*, p. 179.

CHAPTER 6: THE JAPANESE: SOURCES OF HATE

1 Pte F.J. Sewell, 2/19 Bn, L28/12/41. Similar: Pte C.P. Keys, 2/15 Bn, L9/12/41.
2 Sigmn T. Neeman, 17 Bde Sigs, L16/1/42.
3 D6/3/42.
4 Pte R. Robertson, 2/2 Bn, L15/12/42. Similar: Lt G. Combe, 2/43 Bn, L25/1/42.
5 Johnston, *The Toughest Fighting in the World*, p. 228 (Johnston was not present at the time). Also: Dower, *War without Mercy*, p. 71.
6 Russell, *The Second Fourteenth Battalion*, p. 123.
7 'Japanese Threat', in Dennis, *The Oxford Companion to Australian Military History*, pp. 322–4; Yarwood & Knowling, *Race Relations in Australia*, pp. 225–6, 248. Fear: Macintyre, *The Oxford History of Australia*, p. 124.
8 Dominance of such attitudes in Australian life 1890–1940: Markus, 'Racism', p. 343.
9 Nish, 'Japan at the Peace Conference', p. 3289.
10 When he sought parliamentary approval of the government's declaration of war against Japan: 'Japanese Threat', *Oxford Companion*, p. 323.
11 AAV: MP508/1, File No. 275/701/556, letter from the Prime Minister to the Premier of New South Wales, 18/3/42. See also Johnston, 'The Civilians who Joined Up', p. 5.
12 Medcalf, *War in the Shadows*, pp. 41, 49.
13 These examples from Gnr W.J. Mearns, 2/15 Fd Regt, L3/2/42; Pte J.H. Ewen, 61 Bn, D24/2/45; Lt G.T. Gill, 2/48 Bn, L10/12/41; Neeman, L4/2/43.
14 Pte E. Lambert, 2/15 Bn, D15/2/44. Americans using 'little': Fussell, *Wartime*, p. 119.
15 For example: Neeman, L17/8/43; Legg, *War Correspondent*, p. 53; Farquhar, *Derrick V.C.*, p. 143. Hygiene: Lt E. Lecky, 9 Div Sigs, L15/10/43; Pte K.R. Rose, 2/13 Bn, D17/9/43; Dexter, *The New Guinea Offensives*, p. 312.
16 Pte T.L. Murphy, 2/23 Bn, D17?/9/43.
17 In report: 'Operations Milne Bay 24 Aug–8 Sep 42, Lessons from Operations', p. 11.
18 Gnr W.C. Bird, 2/10 Fd Regt, D28/5/42. Earlier underestimates: Johnston, *At the Front Line*, p. 37; Barrett, *We Were There*, pp. 247, 309.
19 See, for example, AWM PR00527, Porter, Folder 20, Reminiscence of 1942.
20 C.P. Keys, L4/2/44.
21 Gullett, *Not as a Duty Only*, p. 127.
22 Like rats or vermin: L/Cpl F. Arthur, 2/6 Fd Pk Coy, L20/1/42; Cpl J.R. Stoner, 2/30 Bn, L26/1/42; Gnr H. Sunley, 2/1 Fd Regt, D25/12/42; Dower, *War without Mercy*, p. 71. Like animals: Pte A. Armstrong, 2/13 Bn, D10/12/43; Gullett, *Not as a Duty Only*, p. 127; Pte A.E. Wallin,

2/2 AGH, D19/1/45. Americans: Bergerud, *Touched with Fire*, p. 412. Gullett uses the image of a snake, a common image for a feared enemy: Gray, *The Warriors*, p. 148.

23 Johnston, *The Toughest Fighting in the World*, p. 207; Dower, *War without Mercy*, pp. 53, 71.

24 Butler, D27/4/43. Similar: Barter, *Far Above Battle*, p. 188.

25 See, for example, Blamey's speech in Johnston, *The Toughest Fighting in the World*, p. 207; White, *Green Armour*, pp. 218–19, 282; Fussell, *Wartime*, p. 119; Gullett, *Not as a Duty Only*, p. 127.

26 D20/9/43.

27 D21/11/43.

28 Wartime descriptions: White, *Green Armour*, p. 282; Dower, *War without Mercy*, p. 9; Shelton Smith, *The Boys Write Home*, p. 65. Aborigines: Markus, 'Racism', p. 343.

29 Barker, *Japanese Army Handbook*, p. 118.

30 Buckler, 'Ops Report', p. 3; Charlott, *Unofficial History of the 29/46th*, p. 53; Long, *The Final Campaigns*, p. 179; White, *Green Armour*, p. 166.

31 Robinson, *Record of Service*, p. 87.

32 Shelton Smith, *The Boys Write Home*, p. 131.

33 Dower, *War without Mercy*, p. 9; Fussell, *Wartime*, p. 119; Ellis, *The Sharp End of War*, p. 319.

34 Mayo, *Bloody Buna*, p. 36. Similar: Dower, *War without Mercy*, pp. 9, 11.

35 Charlton, *War Against Japan*, p. 34. The propaganda campaign: McKernan, *All In!*, p. 141. Criticism of politicians' oversimplifications: Wetherell, *The New Guinea Diaries of Philip Strong*, p. 180.

36 'Japanese Threat', *Oxford Companion*, p. 324.

37 Mongrels: Pte R.M. Berry, 2/9 Bn, D20/12/42.

38 Curs: O'Brien, 'A Rat of Tobruk', p. 14.

39 On this point see Isby, Introduction to US War Department, *Handbook on Japanese Military Forces*, p. vi.

40 Gullett, *Not as a Duty Only*, p. 127.

41 Buckler, 'Ops Report', pp. 3, 11 and 'Operations Milne Bay', p. 7; Givney, *The First at War*, p. 322; Wall, *Singapore and Beyond*, p. 75.

42 D20/1/43. Similar: Cpl J. Hawkins, 5 Army Tps Coy, D18/6/43. 'Fanatical': Barrett, *We Were There*, p. 309; Bennett, *Rough Infantry*, p. 145; Long, *The Final Campaigns*, p. 373.

43 See Johnston, *At the Front Line*, p. 225n19.

44 Barker, *Japanese Army Handbook*, p. 10.

45 Dower, *War without Mercy*, pp. 12, 72.

46 Buckler, 'Ops Report', p. 3. See also Gullett, *Not as a Duty Only*, p. 126.

47 'Japanese Threat', *Oxford Companion*, p. 323.

48 McCarthy, *South-West Pacific Area*, p. 508.

49 Paull, *Retreat from Kokoda*, p. 295; Austin, *To Kokoda and Beyond*, p. 203; Mayo, *Bloody Buna*, p. 130.

50 Fearnside, *Half to Remember*, pp. 195–6. Similar: Hay, *Nothing Over Us*, p. 440; Masel, *The Second 28th*, pp. 174–5; McCarthy, *South-West Pacific Area*, p. 484.

51 Bentley, *The Second Eighth*, p. 137.

52 D21/6/45. Similar: Medcalf, *War in the Shadows*, p. 94; Crooks, *The Footsoldiers*, p. 409; Macfarlan, *Etched in Green*, p. 147.

53 Pte F. Camarsh, 2/17 Bn, D10/1/44. Similar: Wells, *'B' Company Second Seventeenth*, p. 165.

54 Share, *Mud and Blood*, p. 415; Serle, *The Second Twenty-Fourth*, pp. 288–9, 324; Macfarlan, *Etched in Green*, p. 147.

55 Crooks, *The Footsoldiers*, pp. 399–400. This suicide was perhaps motivated by realising that he could not surrender.

56 Dexter, *The New Guinea Offensives*, p. 520.

57 ASA Intelligence Report No. 22, 30/3/45. At the time, this battalion consisted of fewer than twenty men.

58 Gilmore, *You Can't Fight Tanks with Bayonets*, pp. 97–8.

59 Bennett, *Rough Infantry*, p. 145. Examples of suicide rather than surrender: Murphy, D16/9/43; Share, *Mud and Blood*, p. 418; Crooks, *The Footsoldiers*, p. 415.

60 Long, *The Final Campaigns*, pp. 386, 451, 545, 501.

61 Crooks, *The Footsoldiers*, pp. 321–2.

62 Long, *The Final Campaigns*, p. 449; US War Department, *Handbook on Japanese Military Forces*, p. 9; AWM: Canungra Training Instructions, Serial No. 34. Dishonour: Spector, *Eagle Against the Sun*, p. 398. Japanese instructions: Cook & Cook, *Japan at War*, p. 264.

63 Maj Dunkley, 2/7 Bn, L19/12/42. Similar: Legg, *War Correspondent*, p. 41; Crooks, *The Footsoldiers*, p. 415; Brigg & Brigg, *The 36th Australian Infantry Battalion*, p. 117.

64 Maj Matthews, 14 Bde, D3/1/43.

65 Murphy, D8/11/43.

66 C. Kennedy, 'World War 2', p. 33, mentions that this occurred at least three times to his battalion. Also Budden, *That Mob*, p. 143.

67 Bentley, *The Second Eighth*, p. 186.

68 McCarthy, *South-West Pacific Area*, p. xii (my emphasis).

69 Macfarlan, *Etched in Green*, p. 95.

70 Gullett, *Not as a Duty Only*, p. 107; Bennett, *Rough Infantry*, p. 145; McCarthy, *South-West Pacific Area*, pp. 442, 523.

71 Lt-Col Arnold, 2/12 Bn, quoted in McCarthy, *South-West Pacific Area*, p. 521.

72 Spector, *Eagle Against the Sun*, p. 398, makes this point about treatment of Americans. Lack of prisoners on either side: Gilmore, *You Can't Fight Tanks with Bayonets*, p. 62.

73 Tradition: Reid, *Prisoner of War*, p. 31.

74 D30/11/43. Also on giving information: Dexter, *The New Guinea Offensives*, p. 520; Long, *The Final Campaigns*, p. 368; McCarthy, *South-West Pacific Area*, p. 517. Observers were also struck by how happy

Japanese POWs seemed to be: Crooks, *The Footsoldiers*, p. 191; Uren, *1,000 Men at War*, p. 236; Murphy, D15/9/43.

75 Lt A. Crawford, 2/3 Indep Coy, L17/3/43.

76 Bergerud, *Touched with Fire*, pp. 405, 416.

77 McCarthy, *South-West Pacific Area*, p. xii. Also on inhumanity: Bentley, *The Second Eighth*, p. 137.

78 Lt A. Crawford, 2/3 Indep Coy, L17/3/43.

79 AWM: Canungra Training Instructions, Serial No. 29.

80 Wily: A/Sgt Edwards, 2/27 Bn, D6/12/42.

81 Brig J. Field, 7 Bde, D31/8/42. Also McCarthy, *South-West Pacific Area*, p. 178. Examples from other campaigns: Bentley, *The Second Eighth*, p. 184; Combe, Ligertwood & Gilchrist, *The Second 43rd*, p. 178; Crooks, *The Footsoldiers*, p. 393; Shaw, *Brother Digger*, p. 139.

82 F.M. Paget, letter to the author, 25/10/88. Killing because of distrust: Rolleston, *Not a Conquering Hero*, p. 126; Stanley, *Tarakan*, p. 129.

83 AWM: Canungra Training Instructions, Serial No. 19.

84 Rolleston, *Not a Conquering Hero*, p. 83. Treacherous Japanese: Cpl P.J. Casey, 3 Div Pro Coy, D29/6/45; Sgt K.C. Turner, 2/6 Bn, 'Reflection on armistice', 16/8/45; Gilmore, *You Can't Fight Tanks with Bayonets*, p. 37. Other suspicion of surrendering Japanese: Murphy, D15/9/43; Mathews, *Militia Battalion at War*, p. 62.

85 Mayo, *Bloody Buna*, p. 57; Combe, Ligertwood & Gilchrist, *The Second 43rd*, p. 178. See also Harries & Harries, *Soldiers of the Sun*, p. 410.

86 Gnr J.M. Hack, 2/5 Fd Regt, L11/7/45; Barrett, *We Were There*, p. 312; US War Department, *Handbook on Japanese Military Forces*, p. 127.

87 Use mentioned: J. Craig, D29/9/43, 1/10/43; Lt-Col Matthews, 9 Bn, D27/1/45; Long, *The Final Campaigns*, p. 231; Serle, *The Second Twenty-Fourth*, p. 347; Charlott, *Unofficial History of the 29/46th*, p. 51; Givney, *The First at War*, pp. 271, 384. Hague Convention: Gilbert, *Sniper*, p. 30.

88 Ewen, D24/2/45. Medcalf told of a comrade expressing horror at the 'rotten bastards' for the practice, despite the fact that he himself regularly filed the noses off his bullets: Medcalf, *War in the Shadows*, p. 90.

89 Edwards, D6/12/42; Givney, *The First at War*, pp. 329–30; Steward, *Recollections of a Regimental Medical Officer*, p. 153; Uren, *1,000 Men at War*, p. 174. There were exceptions, notably the sparing of the hospital ship *Manunda* at Milne Bay: McCarthy, *South-West Pacific Area*, p. 184. Edwards D6/12/42 talked of some Japanese respecting the Red Cross. Japanese using the Red Cross to bring up a mortar without enemy attention: Harrison, *Ambon*, p. 53. Stretcher-bearers: Legg, *War Correspondent*, p. 227; McAllester, *Men of the 2/14 Battalion*, p. 35. Similar for New Zealanders: McLeod, *Myth and Reality*, p. 91.

90 Robinson, *Record of Service*, p. 99.

91 Christie & Christie, *A History of the 2/29 Battalion*, p. 13.

92 The sergeant was one of only two men to survive that massacre: Wall, *Singapore and Beyond*, p. 101.

93 They were left for dead, but the man who had moved actually survived: Wigmore, *The Japanese Thrust*, p. 480.

94 ibid., pp. 410, 669; Long, *The Six Years War*, p. 147.

95 Wigmore, *The Japanese Thrust*, p. 374.

96 Harrison, *Ambon*, pp. 172–7, 260.

97 At least two men survived: Wigmore, *The Japanese Thrust*, pp. 247–8.

98 Wall, *Singapore and Beyond*, p. 83. The soldier claimed to have killed the three men with grenades.

99 Lloyd & Hall, *Backroom Briefings*, p. 217.

100 Gnr R.H. McLennan, 2/1 LAA Regt, L5/5/42. On these stories, also AWM PR00527, Porter, Folder 20, Reminiscence of Port Moresby, 1942.

101 New Britain and China: Steward, *Recollections of a Regimental Medical Officer*, p. 108. He also claimed that men on Kokoda knew of the murder of white men and women from Sangara and Gona missions in July–August 1942, although details were apparently not published until May 1943: Wetherell, *New Guinea Diaries of Philip Strong*, p. 180. China: Bennett, *Rough Infantry*, p. 162. Tol story being spread: White, *Green Armour*, p. 40n; Medcalf, *War in the Shadows*, p. 92 (also says Australians had heard stories about Malaya). See also Bergerud, *Touched with Fire*, pp. 413–14.

102 War correspondents also knew of these stories: Johnston, *War Diary 1942*, p. 83.

103 D18/9/42.

104 AAV: MP742/1, File No. 336/1/1232, 'War Crimes'. Quotations are from accounts of former captains K.A. Gategood, 2/12 Bn and C. Kendall, 2/9 Bn. Some accounts were supported by photographic evidence. See also Baker & Knight, *Milne Bay*, which reprinted the findings of the Webb Royal Commission into Japanese atrocities at Milne Bay. On other atrocities at Milne Bay, see McCarthy, *South-West Pacific Area*, p. 178; Brune, *The Spell Broken*, p. 116.

105 O'Brien, 'A Rat of Tobruk', p. 16.

106 Crooks, *The Footsoldiers*, p. 145; Robinson, *Record of Service*, p. 73.

107 McCarthy, *South-West Pacific Area*, p. 263.

108 D25/11/43. In describing the same incident, J. Craig said that up to ten wounded Australians were bashed and killed: D28/11/43.

109 Dvr A.J. Bradley, School of Sigs, D30/3/45.

110 AAV: MP742/1, File No. 336/1/285. The file concerns a board of inquiry into Japanese war crimes, held at Wewak in late 1945 and early 1946.

111 Other examples from Aitape–Wewak: ibid.; Johnston, *At the Front Line*, p. 39; Holt, *From Ingleburn to Aitape*, p. 194; Wallin, 13/6/45. Papua: McCarthy, *South-West Pacific Area*, pp. 271, 526; Charlton, *The Thirty-Niners*, p. 231; Givney, *The First at War*, pp. 271, 288; Harries & Harries, *Soldiers of the Sun*, p. 343; Kennedy, 'World War 2', p. 3. Bougainville: Hawkins, D10/11/44, 7/12/44. Japanese cannibalising each other: Lt-Col

Dunkley, 7 Bn, L5/8/45; Wallin, D17/7/45; Cook & Cook, *Japan at War*, pp. 273–4. Cannibalising natives: Fienberg, 'Special Patrol Report', 6/5/45. Atrocities elsewhere: Timor: Wigmore, *The Japanese Thrust*, pp. 485–6. Balikpapan: Lewis, 'Balikpapan memoir', p. 10 (against natives), L365 (natives). Bougainville: Mathews, *Militia Battalion at War*, p. 192. Japanese killing wounded Australians: McCarthy, *South-West Pacific Area*, pp. 320, 594. Australian anger spurred by Japanese callousness: Field, D2/9/42; Wells, *'B' Company Second Seventeenth*, pp. 148–9.

112 D31/2/43.

113 Wallin, D18/6/45. Similar: Holt, *From Ingleburn to Aitape*, p. 205.

114 Givney, *The First at War*, p. 288.

115 Clift, *Saga of a Sig*, p. 154.

116 O'Brien, 'A Rat of Tobruk', p. 21.

117 Haywood, *Six Years in Support*, p. 153.

118 Gullett, *Not as a Duty Only*, p. 127.

119 Natives: Long, *The Final Campaigns*, p. 522; Capt Combe, L30/8/45.

120 L17/6/45. He was not aware that Australian prisoners were still dying from the most appalling brutality elsewhere on the island. In October 1944 there had been 2500 Australian and British POWs at Sandakan; only six survived the war: Wigmore, *The Japanese Thrust*, pp. 599–604.

121 Long, *The Final Campaigns*, p. 342.

122 Field, D2/9/42; Rolleston, *Not a Conquering Hero*, p. 99; Brune, *The Spell Broken*, p. 116.

123 AAV: MP742/1, File No. 336/1/1232. This excuse does not explain why natives were treated hideously. Another explanation – that the Japanese killed native prisoners after failing to obtain information by interrogation – also rings hollow: Baker & Knight, *Milne Bay*, p. 435.

124 Fifty metres: ibid.

125 For example, Mathews, *Militia Battalion at War*, p. 172; Barrett, *We Were There*, p. 251.

126 Hay, *Nothing Over Us*, p. 249.

127 Bennett, *Rough Infantry*, p. 162.

128 Ewen, D18/3/45. Similar: May, D30/1/43.

129 Clift, *Saga of a Sig*, p. 147. He also said of the fighting at Oivi that many Japanese 'surrendered and were exterminated': p. 158. Cases where prisoners were taken by Australians: Givney, *The First at War*, pp. 305, 307. Prisoners taken by Japanese: Russell, *The Second Fourteenth Battalion*, p. 148.

130 Hartley, *Sanananda Interlude*, p. 67 (my emphasis).

131 White, *Green Armour*, p. 201; Charlton, *The Thirty-Niners*, p. 176.

132 D15/12/43.

133 Serle, *The Second Twenty-Fourth*, p. 292.

134 This interpretation is partly inspired by Haywood, *Six Years in Support*, p. 153.

CHAPTER 7: THE JAPANESE: QUESTIONS OF QUALITY

1 Official accounts: McCarthy, *South-West Pacific Area*, pp. xii, 143, 171, 494, 531, 532–3; Dexter, *The New Guinea Offensives*, pp. xi, 304, 817; Long, *The Final Campaigns*, p. 202. Unit: Share, *Mud and Blood*, p. 277; Crooks, *The Footsoldiers*, pp. 188, 250; Mathews, *Militia Battalion at War*, pp. xi, 161. Individual: Barrett, *We Were There*, pp. 302, 309; Gullett, *Not as a Duty Only*, pp. 126–7; Steward, *Recollections of a Regimental Medical Officer*, p. 123.
2 L5/8/45 (my emphasis).
3 MS 11477, Brig S.H.W.C. Porter, 30 Bde, L20/12/42.
4 D7/1/43.
5 D12/1/43. Other praise from this period: Gnr H.C. Sunley, 2/1 Fd Regt, D20/12/42.
6 Dexter, *The New Guinea Offensives*, p. 38.
7 L11/7/45. Also on tenacity: Sigmn T.R. Neeman, 17 Bde Sigs, L4/2/43; Austin, *To Kokoda and Beyond*, p. 203; Uren, *1,000 Men at War*, p. 216.
8 'Operations Milne Bay', p. 6. Good infiltrators: Pte F.M. Paget, 2/13 Fd Coy, D6/5/45. Later criticism of Japanese use of snipers: AAV:MP742/1, File No. 323/1/1260. Criticism of fieldcraft: Buckler, 'Ops Report', p. 3.
9 Shelton Smith, *The Boys Write Home*, p.118. Japanese tree-climbing shoes and split-toed sandals helped their climbing: Barker, *Japanese Army Handbook*, p. 118.
10 Lt E.B. Le Fevre, 19 Bn, L-/3/45.
11 Austin, *To Kokoda and Beyond*, p. 189; Dexter, *The New Guinea Offensives*, p. 165; Long, *The Final Campaigns*, pp. 125, 419, 503.
12 L-/2/43.
13 Macfarlan, *Etched in Green*, p. 123.
14 Lt-Col W.J. Green, 2/7 Fd Regt, L2/6/45.
15 D16/6/45.
16 AWM, PR00527, Porter, Folder 10, Section V, n.d.
17 Sgt J. Mitchell, 2/30 Bn, L28/1/42.
18 F. Hole, 'Record of Events, East Coast, Johore', pp. 14–15. Heavily camouflaged Japanese attackers: Sgt A.J. Hill, 2/6 Bn, D22/6/43.
19 Wigmore, *The Japanese Thrust*, pp. 397, 422, 427, 437n, 489.
20 Calculated from Russell, *The Second Fourteenth Battalion*, pp. 154, 322–3; Buckler, 'Ops Report', p. 6.
21 Shelton Smith, *The Boys Write Home*, p. 123.
22 Dvr Wallin, No 2 Coy AASC, D29/9/42. Wallin served in two campaigns against the Japanese as an infantryman.
23 AWM: Canungra Training Instructions, Serial No. 62. Wartime recognition of Japanese tactical skill: White, *Green Armour*, p. 25.
24 D4/9/43 (my emphasis). See also Jones, 'A Volunteer's Story', p. 227; Glenn, *Tobruk to Tarakan*, p. 201. Some entered this campaign confidently: Dexter, *The New Guinea Offensives*, p. 328.
25 D23/9/43.

26 D1/10/43. The belief that the naval forces were the Japanese elite is a recurrent theme in Australian writing: Dexter, *The New Guinea Offensives*, p. 499; Share, *Mud and Blood*, p. 386; Medcalf, *War in the Shadows*, p. 63. Whether it was accurate is debatable: Mollo, *The Armed Forces of World War II*, pp. 263–4; US War Department, *Handbook on Japanese Military Forces*, p. 78. They were part of a corps like the American marines: Hayashi, *Kogun*, p. 203.

27 D25/10/43.

28 D7/11/43.

29 AWM, PR00527, Porter, Folder 10, 'Jungle Tactics No. 1'. Unfortunately this folder is not dated, but was clearly produced during the war, probably in 1943. See Gilmore, *You Can't Fight Tanks with Bayonets*, pp. 164–5, for a similar American analysis.

30 For example, Dawes, *'Soldier Superb'*, p. 23 (Lae–Finschhafen); Long, *The Final Campaigns*, p. 283 (Aitape–Wewak); Serle, *The Second Twenty-Fourth*, p. 332 (Tarakan); Masel, *The Second 28th*, p. 177; Robinson, *Record of Service*, p. 86. The Japanese army on New Britain fought with markedly less vigour than its armies on Bougainville and in the Aitape–Wewak region: Long, *The Final Campaigns*, pp. 269–70. Falling Japanese morale: Gilmore, *You Can't Fight Tanks with Bayonets*, pp. 74–94.

31 Dexter, *The New Guinea Offensives*, p. xi (my emphasis).

32 Example of Japanese fighting to the last: ibid., p. 619.

33 D7/1/44.

34 Dexter, *The New Guinea Offensives*, p. 391. Dexter said that not all members of the division would have agreed, even at that point.

35 D17/9/43.

36 Greater respect later: Dawes, *'Soldier Superb'*, p. 44.

37 For example: Share, *Mud and Blood*, p. 312. Unable or unwilling to hold: Dexter, *The New Guinea Offensives*, pp. 520, 563, 579, 673, 675, 719, 759.

38 D22/9/43 ('cupful' is a euphemism). See Baker, *The Australian Language*, p. 180. Also on 'panicky Japs': Murphy, D9/12/43. Japanese as easy meat: Dawes, *'Soldier Superb'*, p. 35.

39 L4/10/43.

40 L/Cpl L. Clothier, 2/13 Bn, D26/12/43, quoted in Gillan, *We Had Some Bother*, p. 112 (my emphasis). Other unnecessary surrender of ground: McCarthy, *South-West Pacific Area*, p. 468; Macfarlan, *Etched in Green*, p. 145.

41 AAV:MP742/1, File No. 264/1/1591, 'Despatch from Frank Legg', 7/5/45. Similar: Uren, *1,000 Men at War*, p. 235; Share, *Mud and Blood*, p. 368.

42 Pte R.R. Dove, 2/4 Bn, D-/12?/44.

43 Robertson, *Australia Goes to War*, p. 217.

44 Gnr G. Chapman, 2/14 Fd Regt, L24/4/44.

45 Lt B.H. MacDougal, 2/3 Bn, L20/3/45. See also Long, *The Final Campaigns*, p. 292. Tarakan troops: Stanley, *Tarakan*, pp. 129–30.

46 D16/9/43.

47 Buckler, 'Ops Report', p. 11, 'Operations Milne Bay', p. 10. Poor grenades: White, *Green Armour*, p. 200; Dexter, *The New Guinea Offensives*, p. 475; Chislett, 'Advance in the South Pacific', p. 17. Poor shells: Lt A.H. Robertson, 2/7 Bn, L31/5/43; J.P. O'Brien, D9/10/43. Impressed by enemy weapons: Bird, D28/5/42; L/Cpl H.P. Spindler, 3 Bn, D14/9/42; Crooks, *The Footsoldiers*, p. 186. Good reason: Barker, *Japanese Army Handbook*, p. 115.

48 Paget, D30/11/43; Cook & Cook, *Japan at War*, p. 271; Share, *Mud and Blood*, p. 410; Serle, *The Second Twenty-Fourth*, p. 269. Japanese were often said to use captured Australian weapons against their former owners: Share, *Mud and Blood*, p. 383; Dexter, *The New Guinea Offensives*, pp. 651, 664; Combe, Ligertwood & Gilchrist, *The Second 43rd*, pp. 175, 232; Macfarlan, *Etched in Green*, p. 141.

49 C.P. Keys, L22/12/43.

50 This was said even of Japanese specialist marksmen. The official report quoted above, on the camouflaging skill of Japanese tree-snipers at Milne Bay, concluded: 'The snipers' marksmanship was not as good as their fieldcraft': 'Operations Milne Bay', p. 6. Similarly, the soldier who had praised their tree-climbing ability wrote with relief that they were not expert shots: Shelton Smith, *The Boys Write Home*, p. 118. Accurate Japanese sniping: AAV: MP742/1, File No. 323/1/1260; Johnston, *The Toughest Fighting in the World*, p. 122.

51 Gilmore, *You Can't Fight Tanks with Bayonets*, p. 82. As a poor weapon: Barker, *Japanese Army Handbook*, p. 118.

52 Lewis, 'Account of Balikpapan', p. 13; Pte F. Rolleston, 2/9 Bn, L-/2/43. Also on poor shooting: Neeman, L4/2/43; White, *Green Armour*, p. 35; Dexter, *The New Guinea Offensives*, p. 49; Austin, *To Kokoda and Beyond*, p. 91.

53 Shelton Smith, *The Boys Write Home*, p. 99.

54 Wall, *Singapore and Beyond*, p. 43. The man, Francis 'Joe' Wilson, was awarded a DCM.

55 L21/2/43.

56 Dexter, *The New Guinea Offensives*, pp. 108, 742. Indeed, all the official histories give examples of inaccurate Japanese shooting: Wigmore, *The Japanese Thrust*, pp. 219, 278n; McCarthy, *South-West Pacific Area*, p. 168; Long, *The Final Campaigns*, p. 212.

57 AWM: Canungra Training Instructions, Serial No. 34 (original emphasis). Also Dexter, *The New Guinea Offensives*, p. 108; 'Operations Milne Bay', p. 10; AWM PR00527, Porter, Folder 10, Section V. In contrast, the Japanese artillery and mortar fire, which was very sporadic after the Singapore fighting, was often said to be uncannily accurate: Wigmore, *The Japanese Thrust*, p. 227; Spindler, D19/10/42, 7/11/42; McCarthy, *South-West Pacific Area*, p. 298; Dexter, *The New Guinea Offensives*, p. 45; Share, *Mud and Blood*, p. 289; Glenn, *Tobruk to Tarakan*, pp. 213–14, 218. Inaccurate Japanese artillery: Lt A. Robertson, 2/7 Bn, L28/5/43; Walshe, *Splinter's Story*, p. 20; Serle, *The Second Twenty-Fourth*, p. 331.

58 ibid. This was said even before Australians went into action against Japanese: S/Sgt J. Mitchell, 2/30 Bn, L25/12/41.

59 Shelton Smith, *The Boys Write Home*, p. 121.

60 Dawes, *'Soldier Superb'*, p. 20. Noisy Japanese: 'Operations Milne Bay', p. 6; A/Cpl J.A. Roxburgh, 2/30 Bn, D23/1/42; Christie & Christie, *A History of the 2/29 Battalion*, p. 47; McCarthy, *South-West Pacific Area*, p. 284. Stealth: Dexter, *The New Guinea Offensives*, pp. 515, 559.

61 Wigmore, *The Japanese Thrust*, p. 214.

62 Malaya etc.: Wigmore, *The Japanese Thrust*, pp. 246, 403, 436, 476, Harrison, *Ambon*, p. 66. Defensive: Mathews, *Militia Battalion at War*, p. 67; Long, *The Final Campaigns*, p. 222.

63 Purpose: Buckler, 'Ops Report', p. 3. Hole, 'Record of Events', p. 14; Mathews, *Militia Battalion at War*, p. 95; AWM PR00527, Porter, Folder 10, Section V.

64 Share, *Mud and Blood*, pp. 275–6. A case where it appeared to 'unnerve' Australians: Dexter, *The New Guinea Offensives*, p. 79. Noise costing Japanese lives: ibid., p. 77; Glenn, *Tobruk to Tarakan*, p. 210.

65 L22/10/43.

66 Murphy, D23/10/43 (original emphasis).

67 Actual casualties in this period: Dexter, *The New Guinea Offensives*, p. 553. Far from decrying it, some Australian units reportedly copied the idea of shouting and yelling from the Japanese: ibid., pp. 165, 172.

68 Predictable in ambushes: Le Fevre, L-/3/45. Japanese tactical errors: Le Fevre, L-/3/45; Lewis, 'Account of Balikpapan', p. 13; Wigmore, *The Japanese Thrust*, pp. 277, 314; Dexter, *The New Guinea Offensives*, pp. 80, 636; Macfarlan, *Etched in Green*, p. 88; McCarthy, *South-West Pacific Area*, p. 177; Long, *The Final Campaigns*, pp. 164, 318.

69 Uren, *1,000 Men at War*, p. 187; Dawes, *'Soldier Superb'*, p. 9; White, *Green Armour*, p. 216.

70 McCarthy, *South-West Pacific Area*, p. 386; Dexter, *The New Guinea Offensives*, p. 783; Uren, *1,000 Men at War*, p. 164.

71 Dexter, *The New Guinea Offensives*, p. 651; Trigellis-Smith, *Britain to Borneo*, p. 233. Carelessness on a track: McCarthy, *South-West Pacific Area*, p. 164; Serle, *The Second Twenty-Fourth*, p. 339.

72 Bennett, *Rough Infantry*, p. 158. Other inflexibility: AWM PR00527, Porter, Folder 10, Section V; Dexter, *The New Guinea Offensives*, pp. 503, 555; Long, *The Final Campaigns*, p. 164; Masel, *The Second 28th*, p. 137.

73 Austin, *To Kokoda and Beyond*, p. 208 (my emphasis). Similar: Gullett, *Not as a Duty Only*, p. 127; Bergerud, *Touched with Fire*, p. 413.

74 White, *Green Armour*, p. 216.

75 AWM File No. 44/1/5, 2/6 Australian Armoured Regiment, 'AFV Training Memoranda No. 2'; Pte R.M. Berry, 2/9 Bn, D18/12/42.

76 Long, *The Final Campaigns*, p. 424.

77 Kennedy, 'World War 2', p. 46.

78 Pte J.H. Ewen, 61 Bn, D17/3/45. Japanese as 'mad fools': Tpr B. Love, 2/7 Cav Regt, D11/1/43.

79 Gullett, *Not as a Duty Only*, p. 127; Dawes, *'Soldier Superb'*, p. 35. Japanese loss of morale: Dexter, *The New Guinea Offensives*, p. 187.
80 Cpl C.W. Mears, 2/17 Bn, L3/2/42. Similar: Wigmore, *The Japanese Thrust*, p. 246; Uren, *1,000 Men at War*, p. 133.
81 Steward, *Recollections of a Regimental Medical Officer*, p. 106. Also Brune, *The Spell Broken*, p. 119. Similar American attitude: Fussell, *Wartime*, p. 119.
82 Barker, *Japanese Army Handbook*, p. 49.
83 Bird, D28/5/42.
84 Department of Information, *Jungle Trail*, p. 5. This pamphlet was based on the Wau–Salamaua campaign, in which many participants had no experience of fighting Italians.
85 Lt E. Lecky, 9 Div Sigs, L15/10/43.
86 D23/9/43.
87 C.P. Keys, L4/10/43.
88 R. Robertson, L15/12/42. He had been with Corps Headquarters in Greece, and would have had a very different perspective than in Papua.
89 Shelton Smith, *The Boys Write Home*, p. 118 (my emphasis).
90 AWM: Canungra Training Instructions, Serial No. 19. The lecture continued: 'but is, as has often been described, "a cunning little rat"'.
91 Share, *Mud and Blood*, p. 312.
92 Dawes, *'Soldier Superb'*, p. 44 (my emphasis).
93 D28/9/43, quoted in Gillan, *We Had Some Bother*, p. 109.
94 Walker, *Middle East and Far East*, p. 520.
95 Wigmore, *The Japanese Thrust*, p. 246.
96 Harrison, *Ambon*, p. 66. See also Wigmore, *The Japanese Thrust*, p. 436.
97 Shelton Smith, *The Boys Write Home*, pp. 91, 97; Maj K.B. Burnside, AAMC, D21, 26/1/42; Pte K.H. Eckley, 2/20 Bn, L28/1/42.
98 External factors: Robertson, *Australia Goes to War*, p. 217.
99 Air cover: Shelton Smith, *The Boys Write Home*, pp. 91, 105. Bungling: Pte H.E. Russell, 2/30 Bn, L6/2/42; Shaw, *Brother Digger*, p. 53. Exaggeration: Shelton Smith, *The Boys Write Home*, pp. 91, 97; Wall, *Singapore and Beyond*, pp. 55–6.
100 Robertson, *Australia Goes to War*, p. 90; Wigmore, *The Japanese Thrust*, p. 271.
101 Hole, 'Record of Events', p. 9.
102 Examples in: Wigmore, *The Japanese Thrust*, p. 366; McCarthy, *South-West Pacific Area*, pp. 228, 248; Dexter, *The New Guinea Offensives*, pp. 128, 784; Long, *The Final Campaigns*, p. 264.
103 In Elphick, *Singapore*, p. 322.
104 Coates, 'Malayan Campaign', in *Oxford Companion*, p. 381. See also Parker, *Struggle for Survival*, p. 91, where Australians are described as the 'best troops among the defenders'. The allegations, and much supporting evidence, appear in detail in Elphick, *Singapore*, pp. 303–54. Australian newspapers covered the issue in early 1993.

105 The other cause of these misgivings was the scare stories told by New Guinea veterans.
106 See Johnston, *At the Front Line*, p. 37. Also on expecting a very capable enemy: Crooks, *The Footsoldiers*, p. 178; Rolleston, *Not a Conquering Hero*, p. 95. Expecting poor enemy: Austin, *To Kokoda and Beyond*, p. 16.
107 Shelton Smith, *The Boys Write Home*, p. 118; Sunley, D20/12/42; Givney, *The First at War*, p. 333.
108 In Mayo, *Bloody Buna*, p. 47. See also Harries & Harries, *Soldiers of the Sun*, p. 344.
109 McCarthy, *South-West Pacific Area*, p. 186.
110 White, *Green Armour*, p. 214.
111 Kennedy, 'World War 2', p. 1; Dept of Information, *Jungle Trail*, p. 5.
112 Sgt Edwards, L31/10/43.
113 D18/3/45.
114 D-/12?/44.
115 L21/2/43.
116 Estimate based on US rate of 32 per cent fatalities in the South-West Pacific Area caused by small arms: Nalty, *Pearl Harbor and the War in the Pacific*, p. 105. Approximately 7400 Australians were killed in action or died of wounds against the Japanese: Long, *The Final Campaigns*, p. 634.

CHAPTER 8: THE JAPANESE: EMPATHY, COMPASSION AND INCOMPREHENSION

1 Gnr G. Chapman, 2/14 Fd Regt, L10/3/45. Similar: Givney, *The First at War*, p. 385.
2 Dower, *War without Mercy*, p. 9.
3 Dysentery: Gnr H.C. Sunley, 2/1 Fd Regt, D5/10/42. He said he would pity them 'if they were not our enemies'. Gunfire: Cpl J. Craig, 2/13 Bn, D20, 24/10/43; Pte M. Herron, 2/1 Pnr Bn, L4/7/45. Reaction: Chaplain L.T. Ugalde, 53 Comp AA Regt, D1/5/45. Hell: Lt B.H. MacDougal, 2/3 Bn, L20/3/45. Other empathy: Lt-Col G.R. Matthews, 14 Bde, D6/1/43; Cpl C.E. Edwards, 2/27 Bn, D7/10/43.
4 Poor devils: Tpr B. Love, 2/7 Cav Regt, D18/1/43. Gestures: Givney, *The First at War*, pp. 305, 392; Johnston, *The Toughest Fighting in the World*, p. 208.
5 D30/1/43. See also the story told by Bill Crooks in Bergerud, *Touched with Fire*, pp. 423–4.
6 Love, D14/1/43.
7 Quoted in ibid., 31/12/42.
8 D4/2/43.
9 Letter to the author, 27/7/88.
10 Fearnside, *Half to Remember*, p. 195. Similar response to photos: Pte M. Herron, 2/1 Pnr Bn, L4/7/45.

11 Barrett, *We Were There*, p. 441.
12 Pte A.E. Wallin, 2/5 Bn, D20/1/45.
13 Gnr S.L. Beard, 2/12 Fd Regt, L18/9/45. The word 'race' may not be a biological term. Similar: Cpl L.E. Buckland, 2/7 Cdo Sqn, L14/9/45. Macfarlan, *Etched in Green*, p. 250.
14 Pte S.F. McGrath, 8 Bn, L?/9/45. Other laughter at Japanese humiliation: Masel, *The Second 28th*, p. 181.
15 Turner, 'Reflection on Armistice', 16/8/45.
16 Gnr J.M. Hack, 2/5 Fd Regt, L26/9/45.
17 Combe, 'My Three-Score Years and Ten', p. 335.
18 ibid.
19 Shaw, *Brother Digger*, p.136 (my emphasis). Similar: Barrett, *We Were There*, p. 251.
20 ibid.
21 Dower, *War without Mercy*, p. 53.
22 Note that the figure of 'twice as many' deaths relates only to deaths that were the direct result of fighting; it does not include deaths among prisoners of war, except the 106 POWs who died of wounds in imprisonment. Battle deaths in the final campaigns were roughly as follows:

	Japanese battle deaths	Australian battle deaths
Bougainville	8500	516
Aitape–Wewak	9000	442
Tarakan	1500	225
North Borneo	1300+	114
Balikpapan	2000	229
Approximate total	22 300	1526

Many more Japanese died of starvation or disease. Source: Long, *The Final Campaigns*, pp. 237, 385–6, 451, 501; Stanley, *Tarakan*, pp. 202, 220–1. Figures are not available for New Britain, but would probably have been small: fifty-three Australians were killed: Long, *The Final Campaigns*, p. 269. According to Long, 10 800 Australians were killed in action or died of wounds. 7777 Australians died in Japanese captivity: ibid., p. 634.
23 On this general issue: Gray, *The Warriors*, pp. 151–3.
24 Propaganda: Dower, *War without Mercy*, pp. 10ff; Holmes, *Firing Line*, p. 374.
25 Arrogance: AWM 55, 12/29, ATIS 1123, Notebook of 1st Lt Uchimura, 238 Inf Regt, November 1943, pp. 22, 38; AWM 55, File 1/6, Bulletin No 431, September 1943, p. 18. Air: Uchimura Notebook, p. 21.
26 ATIS 1123, Uchimura Notebook, p. 15; Gilmore, *You Can't Fight Tanks with Bayonets*, p. 80.

27 AWM 54, 423/5/29, 'A Study of the Japanese Soldier – from reports and interrogations', October 1943, p. 36.
28 AWM 55, 12/32, 22 October 1943. This account related to the fighting near Sanananda or Buna, the previous year.
29 Wigmore, *The Japanese Thrust*, p. 220; Walker, *Middle East and Far East*, pp. 477, 503; Maj K.B. Burnside, AAMC, D21/1/42, 10–18/2/42; Share, *Mud and Blood*, p. 364; McCarthy, *South-West Pacific Area*, p. 184. Other chivalry: Austin, *To Kokoda and Beyond*, pp. 60–1.
30 Scathing: Spector, *Eagle Against the Sun*, p. 38.
31 Wigmore, *The Japanese Thrust*, p. 279.
32 ibid., pp. 279, 249; Christie & Christie, *A History of the 2/29 Battalion*, p. 50; Robertson, *Australia Goes to War*, p. 90.
33 Quoted in Harrison, *Ambon*, pp. 77–8.
34 Paull, *Retreat from Kokoda*, pp. 91–2.
35 ibid., p. 80.
36 AWM 55, File 2/1, Spot Report No 36.
37 AWM 55, File 2/1, Spot Report Nos 28, 36.
38 AWM 54, 423/5/29, p. 5.
39 Uren, *1,000 Men at War*, p. 171. Japanese reconsidering Americans in this period: Miller, *Guadalcanal*, pp. 311–12.
40 Paull, *Retreat from Kokoda*, p. 305. See also Gilmore, *You Can't Fight Tanks with Bayonets*, pp. 109–10.
41 AWM 54 423/5/29, p. 5.
42 AWM 55, ATIS 1230, 'Remarks on Combat in the Jivevaneng Area', November 1943, p. 44.
43 AWM 55 File 2/1, Spot Report No 36. Also: Spot Report No 44; Current Translations, ATIS 1230, p. 45.
44 AWM 55, File 1/6, Bulletin No 431, p. 16.
45 AWM 55, ATIS 1222, 'Lessons from Katika Area Combat'. p. 64. Also: ATIS 1218, p. 55; AWM 55, Bulletin No 440.
46 Materialistic: ATIS 1123, August 1943, Finschhafen Garrison Force, p. 24. Also ATIS 1084, p. 20.
47 AWM 55, ATIS 1230, Sgt-Maj Seiki, Yamamoto unit, p. 45. Similar: ATIS 1123, Uchimura Notebook, p. 15.
48 See also US War Department, *Handbook on Japanese Military Forces*, p. 126; Gilmore, *You Can't Fight Tanks with Bayonets*, p. 82.
49 AWM 55, ATIS 1230, November 1943, Cpl Tanaka, p. 43.
50 AWM 55, ATIS 1222, p. 64; ATIS 1297, p. 39; ATIS 12/29, p. 7; Bulletin No 440.
51 AWM 55, ATIS 1181, November 1943, p. 84.
52 AWM 55, Spot Report No 77, February 1943. Similar: ATIS 1218, p. 53; ATIS 1230, p. 43; ATIS 1123, p. 22.
53 Cook & Cook, *Japan at War*, p. 271; Gilmore, *You Can't Fight Tanks with Bayonets*, p. 176.
54 Crooks, *The Footsoldiers*, p. 392 re Balikpapan, but this applied in all campaigns. For example: Long, *The Final Campaigns*, pp. 192, 381, 433, 531, 534.

55 AWM 55, ATIS 12/29, September 1943, pp. 2–8 is a compilation of many captured Japanese documents on attitudes to Allied weapons. See also ATIS 1218, February 1944, p. 53; AWM PR00527, Porter, Folder 10, Section V; Gilmore, *You Can't Fight Tanks with Bayonets*, p. 79.
56 US War Department, *Handbook on Japanese Military Forces*, p. 126.
57 Cook & Cook, *Japan at War*, p. 271.
58 ibid.
59 ibid., p. 270.
60 AWM 55 Current Translations, ATIS 1230, February 1944, p. 41.
61 D29/11/43.
62 Trigellis-Smith, *Britain to Borneo*, p. 215.
63 Long, *The Final Campaigns*, p. 268.
64 ibid., p. 369. The Japanese told of their amazement on seeing Australian strength at the end of hostilities: ibid.
65 Stanley, *Tarakan*, p. 163.

CONCLUSION

1 D6/9/42. Similar story in Glenn, *Tobruk to Tarakan*, p. 225.
2 Boas, 'Memoir', p. 238.
3 An American analyst stated that during the Vietnam War Australians had a similar, and unusual, preoccupation with comparative quality and performance: Holmes, *Firing Line*, pp. 263–4.
4 Sgt S.R. Ferrier, 9 Div Cav Regt, L8/2/42.
5 AWM 55, ATIS 1123, p. 21.
6 Robertson, *Australia Goes to War*, p. 90.
7 Cpl N.B. Campbell, 2/5 Bn, L2/5/41. See also Hay, *Nothing Over Us*, p. x.
8 The ideas in this paragraph owe much to Robertson, *Australia Goes to War*, pp. 213, 217.
9 Pte R.L. Zuckur, 2/24 Bn, L-/5?/41.
10 D10/1/43.
11 Goodhart, *We of the Turning Tide*, p. 68.
12 Dower, *War without Mercy*, p. 4.
13 Crawford, 'Forward from El Alamein', p. 210.
14 ibid., p. 205.
15 Fine book: Goodhart, *We of the Turning Tide*, e.g. p. 162.
16 Harrison, *The Brave Japanese*, Foreword and p. 279.
17 ibid., p. 279. Also acknowledging their courage: Dunlop, *The War Diaries of Weary Dunlop*, p. xvi.
18 ibid.
19 ibid.
20 D25/10/42.

APPENDIX A: FIFTH COLUMNISTS

1 Horne, *To Lose a Battle*, p. 117. 'Fifth columnists': *Oxford Companion to the Second World War*, pp. 353–4.

2 *Oxford Companion to the Second World War*, p. 354.
3 Long, *Greece, Crete and Syria*, p. 56.
4 *Oxford Companion to the Second World War*, p. 354. Similar: Horne, *To Lose a Battle*, pp. 119–20, 518.
5 Gammage, *The Broken Years*, p. 61n.
6 Fussell, *Wartime*, p. 39.
7 Maughan, *Tobruk and El Alamein*, p. 91.
8 Walker, *Middle East and Far East*, p. 184.
9 Long, *Greece, Crete and Syria*, p. 56.
10 Maj H.W. Thomas, 2/7 Bn, D13/4/41.
11 Gullett, *Not as a Duty Only*, p. 59.
12 'Report of 2/6 Aus Inf Bn's Participation of the Grecian Campaign', p. 38.
13 Lt-Col W. Cremor, 2/2 Fd Regt, L16/6/41.
14 Bentley, *The Second Eighth*, p. 48.
15 Sgt R.J.W. da Fonte, 2/8 Bn, D19/4/41.
16 Bentley, *The Second Eighth*, p. 68.
17 'Report of Activities of 2/7 Aust Inf Bn – 1 Apr–4 Jun 41', p. 57.
18 Bennett, *Rough Infantry*, p. 90.
19 Pte W. Lock, 2/2 Pnr Bn, L7/4/41.
20 Various, *Active Service*, p. 62.
21 Crooks, *The Footsoldiers*, p. 480.
22 Cpl K.B. MacArthur, 2/15 Bn, D20/1/42.
23 Pte T.L. Murphy, 2/23 Bn, D19/5/42.
24 Combe, Ligertwood & Gilchrist, *The Second 43rd*, p. 85. Similar on Palestine: Lt A.H. Robertson, 2/7 Bn, L22/2/42.
25 Share, *Mud and Blood*, p. 160.
26 Masel, *The Second 28th*, p. 18.
27 Fancke, *Mud and Blood in the Field*, p. 103. 'Schmidt the Spy' was a common term.
28 D3/5/41.
29 D8/5/41.
30 D9/5/41.
31 Maughan, *Tobruk and El Alamein*, pp. 419–20.
32 D3–4/10/42.
33 Goodhart, *We of the Turning Tide*, p. 119.
34 ibid., pp. 119–20.
35 ibid., pp. 110, 128.
36 Combe, Ligertwood & Gilchrist, *The Second 43rd*, p. 13.
37 S/Sgt J. Mitchell, 2/30 Bn, L9/11/41.
38 L25/1/41.
39 For example: Pte F.J. Sewell, 2/19 Bn, L28/12/41; Shaw, *Brother Digger*, p. 45.
40 Wigmore, *The Japanese Thrust*, p. 168.
41 Wall, *Singapore and Beyond*, p. 29.
42 Shaw, *Brother Digger*, p. 50.
43 Gnr G.W. Fletcher, 2/15 Fd Regt, D14/2/42.

44 A/Cpl J.A. Roxburgh, 2/2 Con Depot, D16/2/42.
45 Lt W.R. Dexter, 2/6 Bn, D25/3/42.
46 Pte A.E. Wallin, AASC, D15/4/42.
47 Wigmore, *The Japanese Thrust*, p. 405.
48 US War Department, *Handbook on Japanese Military Forces*, p. 121.
49 D25/5/43. A year before, such activity had also been reported in Queensland: Macfarlan, *Etched in Green*, p. 21.
50 D28/10/43.

APPENDIX B: ORDERS OF BATTLE OF AUSTRALIA'S ENEMIES

1 Blackshirt Divisions were Fascist Militia divisions.

Bibliography

This bibliography is divided into four sections: personal wartime testimonies and their authors; government and army documents; unpublished postwar reminiscences; and published works.

PERSONAL WARTIME TESTIMONIES AND THEIR AUTHORS
Only those soldiers and other wartime writers whose names are referred to in the Notes are listed. The biographical and bibliographical entries are organised as follows, with examples in brackets:

Name (X.Y. Smith), Decorations gained for wartime service (VC, DCM), Rank(s) referred to in this book (Pte to Capt – not necessarily in chronological order), Unit(s) of which individual was a member in the period covered by documents referred to (2/1 Bn and 2/1 Fd Regt). Pre-enlistment occupation (Orchardist); pre-enlistment residence (of Hay, NSW); year of birth (b. 1910). Wartime death, if applicable (KIA 1/2/43). Source of collection (AWM PR85/abc or Donor: Mrs A.B. Smith).

    Pre-enlistment details were obtained from Central Army Records Office files, almost invariably from attestation forms. For key to abbreviations of ranks, units and archival holdings, see 'Conventions and Abbreviations' guide at the beginning of the book.

J.H. Abraham, Pte, 2/48 Bn. Foreman; of Whyalla, SA; b. 1917. Donor: Mrs Joan Abraham.
H.W. Adeney, Bdr to Sgt, 2/2 Fd Regt. Wool-classer; of Camberwell, Vic; b. 1913. MS10868.
R. Aldridge, Pte, 2/13 Bn. Labourer; of Sydney; b. 1917. Donor: Mrs D. Woodlock.

Anonymous, NCO, 2/3 Bn. AWM PR85/429.

R.J. Anson, Pte, 2/17 Bn. Drover; of Canterbury, NSW; b. 1916. Donor: R.J. Anson.

A. Armstrong, Pte, 2/13 Bn. Postal assistant; of Crookwell, NSW; b. 1914. AWM PR85/165.

F. Arthur, L/Cpl, 2/6 Fd Park Coy. Wood trimmer; of Kalgoorlie, WA; b. 1903. Donor: Mrs B. Culhane.

J.K. Atock, Pte, 2/7 Bn. Chemist; of East Hawthorn, Vic; b. 1919. AWM 3DRL 6372.

S.L. Beard, Gnr, 2/12 Fd Regt. Farmhand; of Wonthaggi, Vic; b. 1917. AWM PR87/43.

R.C. Beilby, Spr, 2/1 Fd Coy. Soldier; of Perth, WA; b. 1918. MS10019.

R.M. Berry, Pte, 2/9 Bn. Labourer; of Mossman, Qld; b. 1919. AWM PR84/21.

W.C. Bird, Gnr, 2/10 Fd Regt. Van salesman; of Townsville, Qld; b. 1912. Died as POW. Donor: J. Bird, S. Stocks.

R.H. Bourke, Sgt, 2/1 Bn. Sales manager; of Potts Point, NSW; b. 1915. Died of disease 1942. AWM PR88/125.

A.J. Bradley, Dvr, NG School of Sigs. Butcher; of Hastings, Vic; b. 1922. MS9690.

L.E. Buckland, Cpl, 2/7 Cdo Sqn. Saddler stockman; of Perth, WA; b. 1920. AWM PR82/144.

K.B. Burnside, Maj, AAMC. Medical practitioner; of Toorak, Vic; b. 1913. AWM 3DRL 7665.

J.M. Butler, Pte to Cpl, 2/23 Bn. Accountant; of Red Cliffs, Vic; b. 1900. AWM 3DRL 3825 and donor: Mrs G. Butler.

R.F. Cameron, Pte, 2/1 Bn. Motor driver; of Dulwich Hill, NSW; b. 1915. KIA 25/5/41. AWM 3DRL 506.

N.B. Campbell, Cpl, 2/5 Bn. Soldier; of Toorak, Vic; b. 1915. DOW 12/7/41. AWM 3DRL 505.

J.G. Cannam, Spr, 2/8 Fd Coy. Orchard hand; of Lavington, NSW; b. 1905. MS9800.

S.L. Carroll, MM, Pte, 2/11 Bn. Labourer; of Southern Cross, WA; b. 1915. AWM 3DRL 6045.

P.J. Casey, Pte to Cpl, 58/59 Bn and 3 Div Pro Coy. Accountant; of Newcastle, NSW; b. 1917. Donor: Mrs E. Pattison.

G. Chapman, Gnr, 2/14 Fd Regt. Clerk; of Nairne, SA; b. 1918. AWM 3DRL 7523 and 3DRL 7591.

C. Chrystal, Lt to Capt, 2/4 Bn. Bank officer; of Liverpool, NSW; b. 1917. Donor: Mrs P. Chrystal.

F.S. Coffill, Lt to Capt, 7 Div Amn Sub Park. Bank officer; of Strathfield, NSW; b. 1916. Donor: F.S. Coffill, MBE.

S.H. Cook, Sigmn, 1 Corps Sigs. General carrier; of Orange, NSW; b. 1904. Donor: Mrs J. Williamson.

J.G. Cooper, Pte to Cpl, Reinft draft and 2/28 Bn. Storeman; of Swanbourne, WA; b. 1903. Donor: Mrs A.F. Ryan.

C.L. Craig, WOII, 2/13 Bn. Calibrator; of Newtown, NSW; b. 1917. Donor: J. Craig.

J. Craig, Pte to A/Sgt, 2/13 Bn. Farmer; of Ashfield, NSW; b. 1915. Donor: J. Craig.

A.W. Crawford, Lt, 2/3 Indep Coy. Salesman; of Camberwell, Vic; b. 1917. Donor: A.R.J. Causon.

W. Cremor, Lt-Col, 2/2 Fd Regt. Secretary; of Malvern, Vic; b. 1897. Donor: R.L. Newbold, via Barrett collection.

J.S. Cumpston, Capt, 2/23 Bn. Public servant; of Canberra, ACT; b. 1909. AWM PR87/147.

A.E. Currie, Pte, 2/23 Bn. Insurance agent; of Hamilton, Vic; b. 1904. Donor: Mrs E. Currie.

R.J.W. da Fonte, Sgt, 2/8 Bn. Radio salesman; of Kyneton, Vic; b. 1910. Donor: 2/8 Bn Association.

J. Davies, Pte, 2/33 Bn. Truck driver; of North Brighton-le-Sands, NSW; b. 1907. Donor: Mrs S. Davies.

T.C. Derrick, VC, DCM, Pte to Sgt, 2/48 Bn. Orchardist; of Berri, SA; b. 1914. KIA 24/5/45. AWM PR82/190.

W.R. Dexter, DSO, Lt, 2/6 Bn. Student; of Melbourne; b. 1917. AWM PR85/218.

M.H. Dooley, Gnr, 2/12 Fd Regt. Farmer; of Ivanhoe East, Vic; b. 1921. Donor: Max Parsons.

R.R. Dove, Pte, 2/4 Bn. Milkman; of Arncliffe, NSW; b. 1924. Donor: R.R. Dove.

H.L.E. Dunkley, DSO, MC, Capt to Lt-Col, 2/7 Bn, 17 Bde and 7 Bn. Schoolmaster; of Geelong, Vic; b. 1911. AWM PR84/35 and donor: Mrs L. Jones.

M.F. Dunne, Pte, 2/9 Bn. Clerk; of Port Kembla, NSW; b. 1920. Donor: Ms E. Freeman.

R.F. Eaton, Cpl, 2/28 Bn. Clerk; of Perth, WA; b. 1914. Donor: R.F. Eaton.

K.H. Eckley, Pte, 2/20 Bn. Sawmiller; of Bogan Gate, NSW; b. 1916. Donor: H. Priestly.

C.E. Edwards, Cpl to Lt, 2/27 Bn, OCTU, 1 AARD. Salesman; of Guildford, SA; b. 1917. Donor: C.E. Edwards.

J.H. Ewen, Pte, 61 Bn. Mailman; of Cootamundra, NSW; b. 1915. AWM PR89/190.

W.T. Fairbrother, Pte to A/Sgt, 2/10 Bn and 2/28 Bn. Farmhand; of Happy Valley, SA; b. 1915. Donor: W.T. Fairbrother.

L.A. Fell, Maj, 2/24 Bn. Grazier; of Metung, Vic; b. 1899. AWM 3DRL 3064.

S.R. Ferrier, Cpl to Sgt, 9 Div Cav Regt. Farmer; of Echuca, Vic; b. 1918. Donor: S.R. Ferrier, via Dr John Barrett.

J. Field, CBE, DSO, ED, Lt-Col to Brig, 2/12 Bn and 7 Bde. Mechanical engineer and university lecturer; of Hobart, Tas; b. 1899. AWM 3DRL 6937.

G. Fletcher, Cpl, 2/12 Bn. Labourer; of Roma, Qld; b. 1914. AWM PR84/189.

G.T. Gill, Lt, 2/48 Bn. Soldier; of Prospect, SA; b. 1915. KIA 23/7/42. AWM 3DRL 7945.

C.W. Golding, Capt, 2/1 Bn. Insurance agent; address unavailable, NSW; b. 1914. Donor: Miss G. Griffiths.

R.S. Grant, Pte, 2/17 Bn. Shop assistant; of Bradfordville, NSW; b. 1920. AWM PR84/163.

W.J. Green, DSO, ED, Lt-Col, 2/7 Fd Regt. Accountant; of Surrey Hills, Vic; b. 1904. Donor: Mrs E. McKean.

C.F. Greenwood, Cpl to A/Sgt, 2/17 Bn. Car spraypainter; of Mudgee, NSW; b. 1920. Donor: C.F. Greenwood.

C.A. Gullidge, Pte, 18 Bde Amn Sec and 9 Div AASC. Motor driver; of Gulnare, SA; b. 1910. Donor: Mrs E. Gullidge.

J.M. Hack, Gnr to L/Bdr, 2/5 Fd Regt. Schoolteacher; of Tenterfield, NSW; b. 1914. Donor: Miss G. Hack.

A. Hackshaw, Pte, 2/11 Bn. Truck driver; of Bencubbin, WA; b. 1912. AWM 3DRL 6398.

J.H. Hawkins, A/Cpl to L/Sgt, 5 Army Troops Coy RAE. Painter; of Warragul, Vic; b. 1899. MS9615.

M. Herron, Pte, 2/1 Pnr Bn. Apprentice compositor; of Enfield, NSW; b. 1919. Donor: M. Herron.

A.J. Hill, Sgt, 2/6 Bn. Farm labourer; of Terang, Vic; b. 1916. AWM PR85/221.

A.G. Hirst, Lt, 2/3 A-Tk Regt. Biographical details unavailable. Donor: K. Hirst.

R.L. Hoffmann, Pte (to Cpl?), 16 Bde. Journalist; of Sydney, NSW; b. 1907; d. 3/8/45. ML Document 703.

D. Hughes, Pte, 2/4 Fd Amb. Tramway employee; of Coogee, NSW; b. 1902. Donor: Ms J. Holdup.

A.A. Jones, Pte to L/Cpl, 2/43 Bn. Motor painter; of Renmark, SA; b. 1918. Donor: A.A. Jones.

J.C. Jones, Pte, 2/13 Bn. Dairy farmer; of Enfield, NSW; b. 1919. Donor: Mrs E. Crocker.

C.D. Keys, Pte, 2/7 Indep Coy. Clerk; of Dalby, Qld; b. 1918. Donor: Miss W.J. Keys.

C.P. Keys, Pte, 2/15 Bn. Linotype operator; of Dalby, Qld; b. 1907. Donor: Miss W.J. Keys.

E. Lambert, Pte (to L/Cpl?), 2/2 MG Bn and 2/15 Bn. Student radio (sic); of Balgowlah, NSW; b. 1918. MS10049.

G. Laybourne Smith, MC, Capt, 2/3 Fd Regt. Architect; of Millswood, SA; b. 1908. Donor: Mrs H. Laybourne Smith.

E. Lecky, MBE, Lt, 9 Div Sigs. Public servant (clerk); of Coolah, NSW; b. 1920. AWM 3DRL 7816.

E.B. Le Fevre, Lt, 19 Bn. Farmer; of Pyengana, Tas; b. 1917. Donor: W. Humphries.

F.H. Legg, Sgt, 2/48 Bn. Journalist and broadcaster; of Adelaide, SA; b. 1906. PRG 466.

M.T. Lewis, Capt, 2/7 Cav Cdo Regt. Clerk; of Kensington, NSW; b. 1918. Account of Balikpapan experiences, written on Borneo, September 1945. AWM 3DRL 3848.

E.J. Little, Sgt, HQ 76 Base Sub-Area. Clerk; of Ivanhoe, Vic; b. 1903. MS9643.

W. Lock, Pte, 2/2 Pnr Bn. Truck driver; of Epping, Vic; b. 1915. MS10622.

B. Love, Tpr, 2/7 Cav Regt. Tailor; of Naremburn, NSW; b. 1908. AWM 3DRL 7211.

J.H. Lovegrove, Cpl to Sgt, 2/43 Bn. Clerk; of Orroroo, SA; b. 1918. Donor: J.H. Lovegrove.

K.B. MacArthur, Cpl, 2/15 Bn. Salesman; of Mackay, Qld; b. 1902. AWM PR86/121.

B.H. MacDougal, DCM, Lt, 2/3 Bn. Salesman; of Mosman, NSW; b. 1915. AWM 3DRL 457.

E. MacLeod, Pte, 2/11 Bn. Miner; of Coolgardie, WA; b. 1905. Donor: Mr E. MacLeod, MBE.

G.R. Matthews, DSO, ED, Maj to Lt-Col, 14 Bde and 9 Bn. Public servant; of Hazelwood Park, SA; b. 1910. AWM PR87/79.

J.J. May, MBE, Capt, 2/10 Fd Amb. Dentist; of Condobolin, NSW; b. 1910. AWM PR87/135 and donor: J.J. May.

S.F. McGrath, Pte, 8 Bn. Labourer; of Mayfield, NSW; b. 1918. Donor: Mrs B. McGrath.

R.H. McLennan, Gnr, 2/1 Lt AA Regt. Bank officer; of Willoughby, NSW; b. 1904. Donor: Mrs J.W. Garrett.

W.J. Mearns, Gnr, 2/15 Fd Regt. Storekeeper; of Condobolin, NSW; b. 1906. KIA 11/2/42. AWM PR87/45 and donor: D.C. Mearns.

C.W. Mears, Pte to L/Cpl, 2/17 Bn. Shop assistant; of Queanbeyan, ACT; b. 1919. AWM PR84/379.

J. Mitchell, S/Sgt, 2/30 Bn. Assistant clerk of Petty Sessions; of Lithgow, NSW; b. 1906. Died as POW. AWM 3DRL 6451.

T.L. Murphy, Pte, 2/23 Bn. Fisherman; of Tarraville, Vic; b. 1921. Donor: T.L. Murphy.

T.R. Neeman, MM, Sigmn, 17 Bde Sigs. Gardener; of North Brighton, Vic; b. 1917. Donor: T.R. Neeman.

R.L. Newbold, Lt, 2/2 Fd Regt. Unemployed bookkeeper; of Glen Iris, Vic; b. 1914. Donor: R.L. Newbold, via Dr John Barrett.

G.T. Nowland, Pte, 9 Div AASC, incl. attachment to 2/15 Bn. Bank clerk; of Ryde, NSW; b. 1909. Donor: G.T. Nowland, via Dr John Barrett.

S. O'Brien, A/WOII, 2/7 Fd Amb. Hotel keeper; of Perth, WA; b. 1903. MS10616.

C.J. O'Dea, Pte, 2/28 Bn. Clerk; of Rockdale, NSW; b. 1920. Donor: C.J. O'Dea.

F.M. Paget, Pte, Reinft draft and 2/28 Bn and 2/13 Fd Coy. Farmhand; of Harvey, WA; b. 1920. Donor: F.M. Paget, via Dr John Barrett.

P.T. Partington, Pte, 2/5 Bn. Railway porter; of North Balwyn, Vic; b. 1918. Donor: Mrs L. Thomson.

D.L. Plank, Cpl, 2/2 MG Bn. Biographical details unavailable. AWM PR90/182.

S.H.W.C. Porter, CBE, DSO, Maj to Brig, 2/5 Bn, 30 Bde and 24 Bde. Bank official; of Wangaratta, Vic; b. 1905. MS11477 and AWM PR00527.

W. Richardson, Pte, 2/1 MG Bn. Unemployed estate agent; of East Malvern, Vic; b. 1917. Donor: W. Richardson.

A.H. Robertson, Lt, 2/7 Bn. Schoolteacher; of Bacchus Marsh, Vic; b. 1907. Donor: Mrs H. Lind.

C.H. Robertson, WOII, 2/3 Fd Regt. Life insurance agent; of Sth Perth, WA; b. 1915. Donor: N. Rowden.

R.G. Robertson, Pte to Sgt, HQ 1 Aust Corps and 2/2 Bn. Civil servant; of East Melbourne, Vic; b. 1915. AWM 2DRL 1304.

F. Rolleston, Pte, 2/9 Bn. Farm labourer; of Mackay, Qld; b. 1915. AWM 3DRL 3876.

K.R. Rose, Pte, 2/13 Bn. Labourer; of Waterloo, NSW; b. 1922. AWM PR86/298.

J.A. Roxburgh, A/Cpl, 2/30 Bn, 2/2 Con Depot. Tram conductor; of Nth Sydney, NSW; b. 1909. AWM PR84/117.

H.E. Russell, Pte, 2/30 Bn. Warehouse employee; of Canterbury, NSW; b. 1918. Died as POW 20/6/43. MS10918.

P. Russell, Gnr, 2/2 Fd Regt. Grazier's assistant; of Beaufort, Vic; b. 1919. Donor: P. Russell, via Dr John Barrett.

F.J. Sewell, Pte, 2/19 Bn. Farm labourer; of Griffith, NSW; b. 1913. KIA 1942. Donor: T. Sewell.

W.H. Sherlock, Lt, 2/6 Bn. Grazier; of Coleraine, Vic; b. 1908. KIA 29/1/43. AWM PR85/240.

R.S. Shillaker, MC, Capt, 2/48 Bn. Cadet engineer; of St Peters, SA; b. 1919. AWM 3DRL 7945.

R. Smith, Chaplain, 2/9 AGH. Salvation Army officer; of East Brunswick, Vic; b. 1921. MS10142.

H.P. Spindler, L/Cpl, 3 Bn. Farm labourer; of Central Tilba, NSW; b. 1911. AWM PR83/171.

J.R. Stoner, OAM, Cpl, 2/30 Bn. Bank officer; of Grafton, NSW; b. 1906. Donor: J.R. Stoner, OAM, via Dr John Barrett.

H.C. Sunley, Gnr, 2/1 Fd Regt. Dairy hand; of Merrylands, NSW; b. 1911. Donors: H.C. Sunley and R. Sunley.

C.G. Symington, Sgt, 2/17 Bn (attached to AAMC). Fruiterer; of Orange, NSW; b. 1907. Donor: Mrs H. Maguire.

H.W. Thomas, Maj, 2/7 Bn. Hosiery mechanic; of Armadale, Vic; b. 1916. AWM 54, Item No. 253/1/10.

J. Trimble, Pte, 2/3 Bn. Unemployed bus driver; of Bexley, NSW; b. 1909. AWM PR85/279.

K.C. Turner, Sgt, 2/6 Bn. Public servant; of Ararat, Vic; b. 1919. Reflection on armistice, August 1945. MS10346.

R.K. Turner, L/Cpl, 2/11 Bn. Baker; of Midland Junction, WA; b. 1911. AWM PR83/42.

L. Ugalde, Chaplain, 53 Comp AA Regt. Biographical details not available. MS10045.

A.J. Ulrick, Pte, 2/2 Bn. Telephonist; of Ulmarra, NSW; b. 1918. AWM PR82/177.

A.E. Wallin, Pte, 2/2 AGH, No 2 Rlwy Constr Coy, 6 Div AASC and 2/5 Bn. Railway employee; of Richmond, Vic; b. 1913. MS10172.

C.G. White, Cpl, 2/1 MG Bn. Labourer; of Renmark, SA; b. 1904. Donor: Mrs M.E. White.

H.E. Williams, WOII, 2/24 Bn. Clerk; of Melbourne, Vic; b. 1917. MS9225.

L.F. Williams, Pte, 2/11 Bn. Coffin maker; of Fremantle, WA; b. 1916. Donor: M. Barr.

E.R. Wilmoth, Lt, 2/8 Bn. Law student and radio announcer; of Horsham, Vic; b. 1917. AWM PR86/370.

A.K. Wright, Pte, 2/16 Bn. Motor driver; of Joondanna, WA; b. 1908. Donor: Mrs E. Wright.

R.L. Zuckur, Pte, 2/24 Bn. Station hand; of Moulamein, NSW; b. 1905. Died of illness 30/6/42. Donor: Mrs L. Beaumont.

GOVERNMENT AND ARMY DOCUMENTS

Only documents mentioned in the Notes are listed.

ASA Intelligence Report No 22, dated 30/3/45. Donor: C. Crouch.

Australian Archives (Vic), Department of the Army; MP508/1, General Correspondence 1939–1942.

—— Department of Defence (II) and Department of Army; MP729/6, Secret Correspondence files, multiple number series (Class 401), 1936–1945.

—— Department of Defence (III), Army Headquarters; MP742/1, Correspondence files, multiple number series, 1943–1951.

Australian War Memorial, AWM 3DRL 6599, 'Aus. Trg Centre Jungle Warfare Canungra Training Syllabus Precis & Instructions', as at February 1945. In collection donated to the AWM by Lt-Col P.D.S. Starr, ED.

—— AWM 3DRL 999, 'Ops Report by Capt S.H. Buckler, A Coy 2/14 Aust Inf Bn, att 126 Regt USF – 12 Oct 42'.

—— AWM PR85/314, Capt D. Fienberg, Angau, 'Special Patrol Report', 6 May 1945.

—— AWM 52, 8/3/24, War Diary of 2/24th Infantry Battalion.

—— AWM 52, 8/3/36, War Diary of 2/48th Infantry Battalion.

—— AWM 52, 8/6/3, War Diary of 2/3rd Pioneer Battalion.

—— AWM 52, 11/12/20, War Diary of 2/11 Field Ambulance.

—— AWM 54, Item No 175/3/4, Field Censorship Reports by 1 Australian Field Censorship Company (AIF), Dec. 1944–July 1945.

—— AWM 54, Item No 423/11/18 Part 5, 9th Australian Division Intelligence Summaries Nos 246–358.

—— AWM 54, Item No 519/7/26, 'Lessons of Second Libyan Campaign – 9th Division Training Instruction'.

—— AWM 54, Item No 526/6/10, 20 Brigade Report on Ops 'Lightfoot'.

—— AWM 54, Item No 527/6/9, '26 Brigade Report on Operations Oct.–Nov. 1942'.

—— AWM 54, Item No 883/2/97, 'Middle East Field Censorship: Part 1, Summary of British Troops in Egypt and Libya 1941; Part 2: Weekly Summary, British Troops in Egypt and Libya – January to June 1942'. Each weekly summary includes a separate section on the AIF.

—— AWM 55, Current Translations, ATIS 12/29, 1084, 1123, 1181, 1218, 1222, 1230, 1297.

—— AWM 55, File 1/6, ATIS Bulletins Nos 431, 440.

—— AWM 55, File 2/1, ATIS SWPA Spot Reports Nos 28, 36, 44, 77.

IWM AL866/6, Panzerarmee Afrika, Tagesmeldungen.

MS9553, 17 Infantry Brigade Report on Campaign in Greece and Crete. Prepared by Brigadier S.G. Savige, with supporting documents, including reports by 2/6 and 2/7 Battalions.

2/8 Infantry Battalion Reports on Campaign on Crete. Donor: C. Crouch.

UNPUBLISHED POSTWAR REMINISCENCES

Only writings referred to in the Notes are listed.

Boas, H.J., 'Memoir, 1942–43'. Donor: Mrs J.A. Boas.

Bosgard, P.W., 'The Benghasi Handicap', n.d. AWM PR82/174.

Chislett, L.T., 'Advance in the South Pacific', n.d., MS10178.

Combe, G.D., 'My Three-Score Years and Ten', Part I, 1987. Donor: G.D. Combe, CMG, MC.

Crawford, J.A., 'Forward from El Alamein', n.d. AWM 3 DRL 368.

Hole, F., 'Record of Events, East Coast, Johore, December 1941/January 1942 as Remembered by a Private Soldier in a Rifle Company of an Infantry Battalion', n.d. AWM 3DRL 6922.

Jones, A.A., 'A Volunteer's Story', 1988. Donor: A.A. Jones.

Joyce, Ken, 'As I Saw It … From Tobruk to Tarakan 1940–1945', 1995. Donor: Pat Share.

Kennedy, C., 'World War 2: Campaigning in Papua', n.d. AWM PR85/305.

Martin, Cyril A., 'My Adventures as a Prisoner of War', 1942. Donor: Cyril A. Martin.

O'Brien, M., 'A Rat of Tobruk', n.d. Donor: M. O'Malley.

Randolph, Edgar, 'An Unexpected Odyssey: The Chronicle of a Field Ambulance Private 1940–1945', 1981. IWM 85/6/1.

Stokes, Joseph Placid, 'Taradale to Tarakan', n.d. AWM MSS 1120.

PUBLISHED WORKS

Only items mentioned in the Notes are included.

Ackland, John & Richard (eds), *Word from John: An Australian Soldier's Letters to his Friends*, Cassell, Sydney, 1944.

Allchin, Frank, *Purple and Blue: The History of the 2/10th Battalion, A.I.F.*, Griffin Press, Adelaide, 1958.

Austin, Victor, *To Kokoda and Beyond: The Story of the 39th Battalion 1941–1943*, Melbourne University Press, Melbourne, 1988.

Baillieu, Everard, *Both Sides of the Hill: The Capture of Company 621*, 2/24 Battalion Association, Melbourne, 1985.

Baker, Clive & Knight, Greg, *Milne Bay 1942*, Baker-Knight Publications, Loftus (NSW), 1991.

Baker, Sidney J., *The Australian Language*, Currawong Publishing, Sydney, 1966.

Barker, A.J., *Japanese Army Handbook 1939–1945*, Hippocrene Books, New York, 1979.

Barrett, John, *We Were There: Australian Soldiers of World War II Tell Their Stories*, Viking, Melbourne, 1987.

Barter, Margaret, *Far Above Battle: The Experience and Memory of Australian Soldiers in War 1939–1945*, Allen & Unwin, Sydney, 1994.

Bennett, Cam, *Rough Infantry: Tales of World War II*, Warrnambool Institute Press, Melbourne, 1985.

Bentley, A., *The Second Eighth*, 2/8 Battalion Association, Melbourne, 1984.

Bergerud, Eric, *Touched with Fire: The Land War in the South Pacific*, Penguin, New York, 1997.

Bolger, W.P. & Littlewood, J.G., *The Fiery Phoenix: The Story of the 2/7 Australian Infantry Battalion 1939–1946*, 2/7 Battalion Association, Parkdale (Vic.), 1983.

Bourke, Joanna, *An Intimate History of Killing: Face-to-Face Killing in Twentieth-Century Warfare*, Granta, London, 1999.

Brigg, Stan & Brigg, Les, *The 36th Australian Infantry Battalion*, 36th Battalion, Sydney, 1967.

Brown, James Ambrose, *Retreat to Victory: A Springbok's Diary in North Africa*, Ashanti Publishing, Johannesburg, 1991.

Brune, Peter, *The Spell Broken: Exploding the Myth of Japanese Invincibility*, Allen & Unwin, Sydney, 1997.

Budden, F.M., *That Mob: The Story of the 55/53rd Australian Infantry Battalion, A.I.F.*, F.M. Budden, Ashfield (NSW), 1973.

Caccia-Dominioni, Paolo, *Alamein 1933–1962: An Italian Story*, George Allen & Unwin, London, 1966.

Camarsh, F., *Diaries 1941–44*, reprinted in 2/17 Bn AIF Newsletter, April 1983–December 1987.

Carell, Paul, *Foxes of the Desert*, Schiffer, Atglen, 1994.

Chapman, Ivan D., *Iven G. Mackay: Citizen and Soldier*, Melway Publishing, Melbourne, 1975.

Charlott, R. (ed.), *Unofficial History of the 29/46th Australian Infantry Battalion (AIF)*, Halstead Press, Melbourne, 1952.

Charlton, Peter, *The Thirty-Niners*, Macmillan, Melbourne, 1981.

—— *War Against Japan 1941–1942*, Time-Life Books, Sydney, 1988.

Christie, R.W. & Christie, R. (eds), *A History of the 2/29 Battalion: 8th Australian Division AIF*, Enterprise Press, Sale (Vic.), 1983.

Clark, Alan, *The Fall of Crete*, Four Square, London, 1962.

Clift, Ken, *The Saga of a Sig*, KCD Publications, Randwick, 1972.

Combe, Gordon, Ligertwood, Frank & Gilchrist, Tom, *The Second 43rd*, Second 43rd Battalion AIF Club, Adelaide, 1972.

Cook, Haruko Taya & Cook, Theodore F., *Japan at War: An Oral History*, New Press, New York, 1992.

Coulston, S.J.M., 'A Regimental Aid Post in Tobruk', *Medical Journal of Australia*, 25 April 1942, pp. 494–6.

Crooks, William, *The Footsoldiers: The Story of the 2/33rd Australian Infantry Battalion, AIF in the War of 1939–45*, Printcraft Press, Brookvale (NSW), 1971.

Cumpston, J.S., *The Rats Remain: The Siege of Tobruk, 1941*, Grayflower Productions, Melbourne, 1966.

Dawes, Allan, *'Soldier Superb': The Australian Fights in New Guinea*, F.H. Johnston Publishing, Sydney, 1944.

Dear, I.C.B. & Foot, M.R.D. (eds), *The Oxford Companion to the Second World War*, Oxford University Press, Oxford, 1995.

Dennis, Peter, Grey, Jeffrey, Morris, Ewan & Prior, Robin (eds), *The Oxford Companion to Australian Military History*, Oxford University Press, Oxford, 1995.

Department of Information (Aust.), *Jungle Trail*, Sydney, 1944.

—— *The Battle of Wau*, Brochure No 1, n.d.

Dexter, David, *The New Guinea Offensives*, Australian War Memorial, Canberra, 1961.

Dower, John W., *War without Mercy: Race and Power in the Pacific War*, Faber & Faber, London, 1986.

Dunlop, E.E., *The War Diaries of Weary Dunlop*, Nelson, Melbourne, 1987.

Ellis, John, *The Sharp End of War: The Fighting Man in World War II*, David & Charles, Newton Abbot, 1980.

Elphick, Peter, *Singapore: The Pregnable Fortress*, Hodder & Stoughton, London, 1995.

Fancke, Dick (ed.), *Mud and Blood in the Field*, John Sissons, Hughesdale (Vic.), 1984.

Farquhar, Murray, *Derrick V.C.*, Rigby, Adelaide, 1982.

Fearnside, G.H., *Half to Remember: The Reminiscences of an Australian Infantry Soldier in World War II*, Haldane Publishing, Sydney, 1975.

—— (ed.), *Bayonets Abroad: A History of the 2/13th Battalion AIF in the Second World War*, Waite & Bull, Sydney, 1953.

Fry, Gavin, *Ivor Hele: The Soldiers' Artist*, Australian War Memorial, Canberra, 1984.

Fussell, Paul, *Wartime: Understanding and Behavior in the Second World War*, Oxford University Press, New York, 1989.

Gammage, Bill, *The Broken Years: Australian Soldiers in the Great War*, Penguin, Harmondsworth, 1975.

Gilbert, Adrian (ed.), *The Imperial War Museum Book of the Desert War*, Sidgwick & Jackson, London, 1992.

Gilbert, Adrian, *Sniper: One on One*, Pan Books, London, 1995.

Gillan, H. (ed.), *We Had Some Bother: 'Tales from the Infantry'*, Hale & Iremonger, Sydney, 1985.

Gilmore, Alison B., *You Can't Fight Tanks with Bayonets: Psychological Warfare against the Japanese Army in the Southwest Pacific*, University of Nebraska Press, Lincoln, 1998.

Givney, E.C. (ed.), *The First at War: The Story of the 2/1st Australian Infantry Battalion 1939–45*, Association of 1st Infantry Battalions, Earlwood (NSW), 1987.

Glenn, John G., *Tobruk to Tarakan: The Story of the 2/48th Battalion A.I.F.*, Rigby, Adelaide, 1960.

Goodhart, David, *We of the Turning Tide*, F.W. Preece, Adelaide, 1947.

Graeme-Evans, A.L., *Of Storms and Rainbows: The Story of the Men of the 2/12th Battalion*, vol. 1, Southern Holdings, Hobart, 1989.

Gray, J. Glenn, *The Warriors: Reflections on Men in Battle*, Harper Torchbook, New York, 1967.

Greene, Jack & Massignani, Alessandro, *Rommel's North African Campaign*, Combined Publishing, Conshohocken, PA, 1999.

Griffiths-Marsh, Roland, *The Sixpenny Soldier*, Angus & Robertson, Sydney, 1990.

Grossman, Lt-Col Dave, *On Killing: The Psychological Cost of Learning to Kill in War and Society*, Little, Brown, Boston, 1995.

Gullett, Henry ('Jo'), *Not as a Duty Only: An Infantryman's War*, Melbourne University Press, Melbourne, 1984.

Harries, Meirion & Harries, Susie, *Soldiers of the Sun: The Rise and Fall of the Imperial Japanese Army*, Random House, New York, 1991.

Harrison, Courtney T., *Ambon: Island of Mist*, T.W. & C.T. Harrison, North Geelong (Vic.), 1988.

Harrison, Kenneth, *The Brave Japanese*, Rigby, Adelaide, 1966.

Hartley, F.J., *Sanananda Interlude*, Book Depot, Melbourne, 1949.

Hay, David, *Nothing Over Us: The Story of the 2/6th Australian Infantry Battalion*, Australian War Memorial, Canberra, 1984.

Hayashi, Saburo, *Kogun: The Japanese Army in the Pacific War*, Marine Corps Association, Quantico (VA), 1959.

Haywood, E.V., *Six Years in Support: Official History of the 2/1st Australian Field Regiment*, Angus & Robertson, Sydney, 1959.

Heckmann, Wolf, *Rommel's War in Africa*, Smithmark, New York, 1995.

Hetherington, John, *The Australian Soldier: A Portrait*, F.H. Johnston, Sydney, 1943.

Holmes, Richard, *Firing Line*, Penguin, Harmondsworth, 1987.

Holt, Bob, *From Ingleburn to Aitape*, R. Holt, Brookvale (NSW), 1981.

Horne, Alistair, *To Lose a Battle: France 1940*, Penguin, Harmondsworth, 1979.

Irving, David, *The Trail of the Fox: The Life of Field-Marshal Erwin Rommel*, Futura, London, 1978.

Jewell, Derek (ed.), *Alamein and the Desert War*, Sphere, London, 1967.

Johnston, George, *The Toughest Fighting in the World*, Duell, Sloan & Pearce, New York, 1943.

—— *War Diary 1942*, Collins, Sydney, 1984.

Johnston, Mark, *At the Front Line: Experiences of Australian Soldiers in World War II*, Cambridge University Press, Melbourne, 1996.

—— 'The Civilians who Joined Up, 1939–1945', *Journal of the Australian War Memorial*, 29, November 1996.

Kennett, Lee, *G.I.: The American Soldier in World War II*, Charles Scribner's Sons, New York, 1987.

Knox, MacGregor, *Mussolini Unleashed, 1939–41*, Cambridge University Press, Cambridge, 1982.

—— 'The Italian Armed Forces', in Millett, Allan R. & Murray, Williamson (eds), *Military Effectiveness: vol. III. The Second World War*, Allen & Unwin, Boston, 1988.

Kyle, E.W., 'The Treatment of Wounded in Forward Areas', *Medical Journal of Australia*, 21 November 1942, pp. 459–63.

Laffin, John, *Forever Forward: The Story of the 2/31st Infantry Battalion*, 2/31st Australian Infantry Battalion Association, Newport (NSW), 1994.

Legg, Frank, *War Correspondent*, Rigby, Adelaide, 1964.

Lemaire, Charlie, 'A Boy from Balmain', *2/17 Battalion AIF Newsletter*, 248, June 1997, pp. 23–8.

Lewin, Ronald, *The Life and Death of the Afrika Korps*, Corgi, London, 1979.

Liddell Hart, B.H. (ed.), *The Rommel Papers*, Hamlyn, London, 1984.

Lloyd, Clem & Hall, Richard (eds), *Backroom Briefings: John Curtin's War*, National Library of Australia, Canberra, 1997.

Long, Gavin, *The Final Campaigns*, Australian War Memorial, Canberra, 1963.

—— *The Six Years War*, Australian War Memorial, Canberra, 1973.

—— *Greece, Crete and Syria*, Collins/Australian War Memorial, Sydney, 1986.

—— *To Benghazi*, Collins/Australian War Memorial, Sydney, 1986.

Lucas, James, *War in the Desert*, Beaufort, New York, 1982.

Lucas Phillips, C.E., *Alamein*, White Lion, London, 1973.

Macfarlan, Graeme, *Etched in Green: The History of the 22nd Australian Infantry Battalion 1939–1946*, 22nd Australian Infantry Battalion Association, Melbourne, 1961.

Macintyre, Stuart, *The Oxford History of Australia*, vol. 4, Oxford University Press, Melbourne, 1986.

Macksey, Kenneth, *Beda Fomm*, Pan/Ballantine, London, 1972.

Markus, Andrew, 'Racism', *Australians: A Historical Dictionary*, Fairfax, Syme & Weldon, Sydney, 1987.

Marshall, S.L.A., *Men Against Fire*, William Morrow, New York, 1947.

Masel, Philip, *The Second 28th*, 2/28th Battalion/24th Anti-Tank Company, Perth, 1961.

Mathews, Russell, *Militia Battalion at War: The History of the 58/59th Australian Infantry Battalion in the Second World War*, 58/59th Battalion Association, Sydney, 1961.

Maughan, Barton, *Tobruk and El Alamein*, Australian War Memorial, Canberra, 1966.

Mayo, Linda, *Bloody Buna*, New English Library, London, 1975.

McAllester, J.C., *Men of the 2/14 Battalion*, 2/14 Battalion Association, Melbourne, 1990.

McAllester, Jim & Trigellis-Smith, Syd, *Largely a Gamble: Australians in Syria June–July 1941*, Headquarters Training Command, Sydney, 1995.

McCarthy, Dudley, *South-West Pacific Area: First Year: Kokoda to Wau*, Australian War Memorial, Canberra, 1959.

McGuirk, Dal, *Afrikakorps: Self Portrait*, Motorbooks International, Osceola, 1992.

McKernan, Michael, *All In! Australia during the Second World War*, Nelson, Melbourne, 1983.

McLeod, John, *Myth and Reality: The New Zealand Soldier in World War II*, Reed Methuen, Auckland, 1986.

Medcalf, Peter, *War in the Shadows: Bougainville 1944–45*, Australian War Memorial, Canberra, 1986.

Miller, John Jr, *Guadalcanal: The First Offensive*, BDD Special Editions, New York, n.d.

Mollo, Andrew, *The Armed Forces of World War II*, Black Cat, London, 1987.

Moorehead, Alan, *African Trilogy*, Hamish Hamilton, London, 1965.

Nalty, Bernard C. (ed.), *Pearl Harbor and the War in the Pacific*, Smithmark, New York, 1991.

Nish, Ian, 'Japan at the Peace Conference', *History of the First World War*, vol. 8, Purnell, London.

Oakes, Bill, *Muzzle Blast: Six Years of War with the 2/2 Australian Machine Gun Battalion, AIF*, 2/2 Machine Gun Battalion War History Committee, Sydney, 1980.

O'Brien, John W., *Guns and Gunners: The Story of the 2/5th Australian Field Regiment*, Angus & Robertson, Sydney, 1950.

Parker, R.A.C., *Struggle for Survival: The History of the Second World War*, Oxford University Press, Oxford, 1989.

Paull, Raymond, *Retreat from Kokoda*, Heinemann, Melbourne, 1958.

Pike, P. et al., *'What We Have ... We Hold!': A History of the 2/17 Australian Infantry Battalion*, 2/17 Battalion History Committee, Balgowlah (NSW), 1990.

Porch, Douglas, *The French Foreign Legion*, Harper Perennial, New York, 1991.

Reid, Maj. Pat, *Prisoner of War*, Hamlyn, London, 1984.

Robertson, John, *Australia Goes to War*, Doubleday, Sydney, 1984.

Robinson, Bruce, *Record of Service: An Australian Medical Officer in the New Guinea Campaign*, Macmillan, Melbourne, 1944.

Rolleston, Frank, *Not a Conquering Hero*, Frank Rolleston, Eton, 1984.

Russell, W.B., *The Second Fourteenth Battalion*, Angus & Robertson, Sydney, 1949.

Schmidt, Heinz Werner, *With Rommel in the Desert*, George G. Harrap, London, 1953.

Serle, R.P. (ed.), *The Second Twenty-Fourth*, Jacaranda Press, Brisbane, 1963.

Share, Pat (ed.), *Mud and Blood: 'Albury's Own' Second Twenty-third Australian Infantry Battalion*, Heritage Book Publications, Frankston (Vic.), 1978.

Shaw, Patricia, *Brother Digger*, Greenhouse Publications, Melbourne, 1984.

Shelton Smith, Adele (ed.), *The Boys Write Home*, Consolidated Press, Sydney, 1944.

Spector, Ronald H., *Eagle Against the Sun*, Penguin, Harmondsworth, 1987.

Stanley, Peter, *Tarakan: An Australian Tragedy*, Allen & Unwin, Sydney, 1997.

Steward, H.D., *Recollections of a Regimental Medical Officer*, Melbourne University Press, Melbourne, 1983.

Stouffer, S.A. et al., *The American Soldier: Combat and its Aftermath*, Princeton University Press, Princeton, 1949.

Sullivan, Brian R., 'The Italian Soldier in Combat, June 1940–September 1943: Myths, Realities and Explanations', in Addison, Paul & Calder, Angus (eds), *Time to Kill: The Soldier's Experience of War in the West 1939–1945*, Pimlico, London, 1997.

Sweeting, A.J., 'Prisoner of the Japanese', in Wigmore, Lionel, *The Japanese Thrust*, Australian War Memorial, Canberra, 1957.

Trigellis-Smith, S., *Britain to Borneo: A History of 2/32 Australian Infantry Battalion*, 2/32 Australian Infantry Battalion Association, Sydney, 1993.

Uren, Malcolm, *1,000 Men at War: The Story of the 2/16th Battalion, AIF*, John Burridge, Swanbourne, 1988.

US War Department, *Handbook on Japanese Military Forces*, Greenhill Books, London, 1991.

Various, *Active Service*, Australian War Memorial, Canberra, 1941.

——, *Jungle Warfare: With the Australian Army In the South-West Pacific*, Australian War Memorial, Canberra, 1944.

von Mellenthin, F.W., *Panzer Battles*, Futura, London, 1977.

Walker, Allan S., *Middle East and Far East*, Australian War Memorial, Canberra, 1956.

Walker, Ronald, *Alam Halfa and El Alamein*, Department of Internal Affairs, Wellington (NZ), 1967.

Wall, Don, *Singapore and Beyond: The Story of the Men of the 2/20 Battalion*, 2/20 Battalion Association, Netley (SA), 1985.

Walshe, J.P., *Splinter's Story: '... and We were Young'*, Literary Productions, Sydney, 1989.

Watson, Peter, *War on the Mind: The Military Uses and Abuses of Psychology*, Penguin, Harmondsworth, 1980.

Wells, H.D., *'B' Company Second Seventeenth Infantry*, H.D. Wells, Toowoon Bay (NSW), 1984.

Wetherell, D. (ed.), *The New Guinea Diaries of Philip Strong 1936–1945*, Macmillan, Melbourne, 1981.

White, Osmar, *Green Armour: The Story of Fighting Men in New Guinea*, Wren Publishing, Melbourne, 1972.

Wigmore, Lionel, *The Japanese Thrust*, Australian War Memorial, Canberra, 1957.

Wilmot, Chester, *Tobruk 1941*, Angus & Robertson, Sydney, 1945.

Yarwood, A.T. & Knowling, M.J., *Race Relations in Australia: A History*, Methuen, Sydney, 1982.

Yeates, J.D. & Loh, W.G. (eds), *Red Platypus: A Record of the Achievements of the 24th Australian Infantry Brigade Ninth Australian Division 1940–45*, Imperial Printing, Perth, 1946.

Young, Desmond, *Rommel: The Desert Fox*, William Morrow, New York, 1978.

Index

Crawford, J.A. 39–40, 42, 46–7, 55, 133
Cremor, W. 35
Crete 27, 28, 29, 30, 31, 33, 34, 35, 38,
    39, 47, 48, 53, 55, 114, 130, 131,
    145, 156n82, 161n103, *see also*
    Heraklion, Retimo
Crooks, William 61
Curtin, J. 85
Cutler, A.R. 63

Damascus 60
Damour 66
Damour River 60, 69
Danmap River 109, 118
Dawes, Allan 114
Dawson, B.G. 142
dead, treatment of enemy 42, 50, 81–3,
    133
defeat, Australian responses to 34–5,
    105–6, 113, 115–16, 130–1, 141–2,
    155n62
defences, enemy 14, 66
de Gaulle, Charles 58–9
dehumanising enemies 2, 5
Department of Information 79, 113
Derna 137
Derrick, T.C. 33, 51, 108, 109
Dexter, David 107
Dove, R.R. 109, 118
drugs 31
drunkenness 23, 31, 130
dum dum bullets 95–6, 170n88
Dumpu 75
Dunkley, H.L.E. 92, 103

Ed Duda 27, 49, 161n103
Edwards, C.E. 77, 108, 117
empathy 4, 5
Eora 99
Er Regima 26, 31, 40
evil, enemies as 6

Fairbrother, W.T. 29
Fascism 15
fear 12
Fearnside, G.H. 44, 46, 49, 90, 120
Field, J. 95
fifth columnists 136–43
    Middle East 136–40
    Pacific 141–3
Finisterre Range 75

Finschhafen 75, 78, 80, 93, 104, 114,
    128
French, Free 58, 59, 68, 163n68
French, Vichy 58–70
    Algerian troops 58, 62, 145
    arrogance 63
    artillery 64, 66
    attitudes to Australians 69–70
    campaign against Australians,
        narrative of 58–60
    chivalry 63–4
    conversations with Australians 59, 61
    courage 65, 67
    determined or without heart 61, 65,
        67
    disliked 68
    disparaged as fighters 66–7
    enemy, status as 61
    fellow-feeling 68
    fifth columnists and 138–9
    Foreign Legion troops 62, 63, 68,
        69–70, 133–4, 145, 163n68
    Japanese, compared to 68
    Moroccan troops 58, 145
    nicknames for 58
    persuasion-before-force policy 58–60
    prisoners of Australians 63
    prisoners, treatment of Australian 68,
        163n64
    respect for Australians 69–70
    respected 64–5, 132
    Senegalese troops 58, 62, 67, 145
    Spahis 59, 65
    treacherous or dirty fighters 61–3,
        67, 162n26
    Tunisian troops 58, 145
    units that fought Australians, list of
        145
Fussell, Paul, 136

Gallipoli 66, 77, 136
Gazelle Peninsula 76
Gemas 73, 116
Gemencheh 110
Geneva Convention 41, 43, 63, 83,
    166n61
German army (Afrika Korps) 53, 54,
    133, 153n11, (8th Machine-Gun
    Battalion) 35
    units that fought Australians, list of
        145